Social Capital, Lifelong Learning and the Management of Place

An international perspective

Edited by
Michael Osborne, Kate Sankey
and Bruce Wilson

Routledge
Taylor & Francis Group

LONDON AND NEW YORK

First published 2007
by Routledge
2 Park Square, Milton Park, Abingdon, Oxon, OX14 4RN

Simultaneously published in the USA and Canada
by Routledge
270 Madison Ave, New York, NY 10016

Routledge is an imprint of the Taylor & Francis Group, an informa business

© 2007 selection and editorial matter, Michael Osborne, Kate Sankey
and Bruce Wilson; individual contributions, the contributors

Typeset in Times New Roman by
Keystroke, 28 High Street, Tettenhall, Wolverhampton
Printed and bound in Great Britain by
TJ International Ltd, Padstow, Cornwall

British Library Cataloguing in Publication Data
A catalogue record for this book is available from the British Library

Library of Congress Cataloging in Publication Data
A catalog record has been requested for this book

ISBN10: 0–415–42795–9 (hbk)
ISBN10: 0–415–42796–7 (pbk)
ISBN10: 0–203–94553–0 (ebk)

ISBN13: 978–0–415–42795–1 (hbk)
ISBN13: 978–0–415–42796–8 (pbk)
ISBN13: 978–0–203–94553–7 (ebk)

Contents

Figures

Tables

Contributors

Associate Professor Joan Abbott-Chapman is Associate Professor and Honorary Fellow in the University Department of Rural Health, University of Tasmania. She was formerly Associate Professor in the Faculty of Education before she retired in 2003. By training as a social anthropologist, Joan has researched and published extensively in education and youth studies with a focus on social justice and equity issues, youth efficacy and well-being. She gained international fieldwork experience in community development during her time as Sociologist with the British Ministry of Overseas Development and has continued this interest in joint research and publications on community efficacy and social capital with her co-author Sue Kilpatrick, with whom she has collaborated for a number of years.

Professor David Adams is a graduate of the Universities of Tasmania, Sheffield and Melbourne. He has previously been a Departmental Deputy Secretary in Tasmania (Health) and Victoria (Premier and Cabinet and the Department for Victorian Communities). He has been instrumental in Victorian policy initiatives captured in the *Growing Victoria Together* and the *Fairer Victoria* programmes. His major fields of research are around the locality drivers of innovation. He has published extensively in public policy and management focusing on local governance and its links to innovation and well-being. In the AIRC, his work focuses on the Tasmanian Community Assets survey and is based in the North and North-West of the State. David is a Director of Northern Tasmania Development and a Director of the OECD linked PASCAL Observatory on social capital, place management and learning regions and a Professor in the Australian Innovation Research Centre, University of Tasmania.

Corinne van Beilen works for the Central Administration of the University of Groningen's Department of Communication. Her principal research interest is sustainable development.

Dr Ralph Catts is the Senior Research Fellow for the Schools and Social Capital Network of the Scottish Applied Educational Research Scheme (AERS) at the

University of Stirling. His research interests include the role of social capital in access to and outcomes from education, and the development and evaluation of generic skills in higher education, with a particular interest in Information Literacy.

Dr Lesley Doyle is a Research Fellow with the Observatory Pascal. Her work includes promoting effective research development and dissemination in place management, social capital and learning regions, building national and international research links and developing collaborative research proposals. She was a theme leader (cultural impact) and steering group member in the ESRC seminar series *Higher Education's Effects on Disadvantaged Groups and Communities* (Report of an ESRC Network on cross-regional perspectives on the transformative impact of higher education on disadvantaged groups and communities 2006). For the EU-funded LILARA project (Learning in Local and Regional Authorities), she creates, tests and applies learning needs audits for Learning Regions. Her research interests include international perspectives on lifelong learning and learning regions, and education transitions.

Professor Ian Falk holds the Chair of Rural and Remote Education in the Faculty of Education, Health and Science (EHS) at Charles Darwin University, Darwin, NT. From 1997–2001 he was Director of a national Key Centre for Research and Learning in Regional Australia (CRLRA) at the University of Tasmania, and held various roles before that including Sub-Dean of Adult and Vocational Education. Ian spent two years at Griffith University (Queensland) as lecturer in charge of developing and delivering the communication, workplace literacy and learning courses, a job which followed two years as the Queensland State Government policy officer for adult language, literacy and numeracy. Before this time, Ian was Founder and Principal of a group of schools in North Queensland, including an Indigenous school, a manager in the vocational education and training sector, and a secondary school teacher. Ian is also an author of a range of literacy texts and novels for children of all ages. Professor Falk's research is in issues related to education, formal and informal learning, policy engagement, community development and well-being, social capital, learning communities, regions and cities, leadership and adult literacy.

Dr Tony Hall is Lecturer in Educational Technology in the Department of Education, National University of Ireland, Galway. He previously worked as a secondary school teacher (Physical Education, English and ICT) and school ICT administrator, before completing a PhD in computer science in 2004 at the University of Limerick, Ireland. His research focuses on the design of technology to enhance learning across the lifespan, and in different educational contexts, formal and elective; and he is a member of the EU Kaleidoscope Network of Excellence in Technology Enhanced Learning. Tony was formerly a research fellow in Learning Sciences at the Learning Sciences Research Institute (LSRI), University of Nottingham, UK, and a visiting researcher at the

Center for Informal Learning and Schools (CILS), the Exploratorium, San Francisco.

Professor Michael Hess is a graduate of the ANU (BA), the Melbourne College of Divinity (BD), the University of Papua New Guinea (MA) and the University of New South Wales (PhD). He has taught at the Australian National University, the University of New South Wales, the University of Western Australia and the University of Papua New Guinea. He came to the University of Tasmania in 2004 from the position of Director, Graduate Studies in Development Administration, Asia Pacific School of Economics and Management, Australian National University. His international research has focused on the role of labour in economic development and he edits the *Labour and Management in Development* journal. His Australian-based research is on the interface between government, business and communities. His work with David Adams articulates the intellectual underpinnings of the Victorian government's strategy of social innovation. A congruent current research interest is in the locality drivers of economic growth and social well-being. The later forms the intellectual core of the Tasmanian Community Assets Survey. He is currently Professor of Management located in the Australian Innovation Research Centre at the University of Tasmania.

Deirdre Hogan is Project Co-ordinator of the Ubuntu Network: teacher education for sustainable development, integrating development education into post-primary initial teacher education. Formerly Project Manager of the Programme for University Industry Interface, Deirdre has research interests in development education, lifelong learning, technology enhanced learning and science pedagogy.

Dr Ingrid Hunt is a Senior Researcher at the University of Limerick, where she is actively involved in the Programme for University Industry Interface. She has previously managed many European Union-funded projects and Enterprise Ireland projects. Areas of research include eBusiness, supply chain management and education in manufacturing. She also works closely with international universities and industries in designing global master degree programmes in manufacturing.

Kornelia Eftimova Ilieva is a full-time PhD student (2004–2007) at the Institute of Sociology, Bulgarian Academy of Science, Sofia. She has an MSc in Journalism and Mass Communications (1998) and an MSc in Sociology (2003) from the University of Sofia. She is researching lifelong learning concepts in Bulgaria within her doctoral thesis, 'Lifelong learning – institutionalisation and regulatory mechanisms'. She was an OSI/FCO Chevening Scholar at the University of Oxford (2005–2006). Her academic interests are in social network analysis, the historical pathway approach and, in general, the sociology of knowledge. She also works as an expert in adult education, policy analysis and consulting, and is a project manager of the Balkan Association for Lifelong Learning.

Dr Patricia Inman is a literacy specialist whose research interests focus on workplace literacy and regional policy development. She received her doctorate in Adult Education from Northern Illinois University. Her work on innovative programme development is strongly influenced by her study with Ivan Illich. Most recently she has provided consultation for the Gates Foundation Grant in Milwaukee, Wisconsin established to recreate secondary education as small learning communities. She currently serves as a lecturer for Aurora University in Williams Bay, Wisconsin and is co-editor of *Vitae Scolastica*, a journal of life narrative.

Professor Wolfgang Jütte is Professor for Continuing Education Research in the Department of Continuing Education Research and Educational Management at Danube University, Krems, Austria. He holds a doctoral degree in Adult Education from the University of Münster. His main research is focused on university continuing education, international and comparative adult education and co-operation and network research. He is a member of the Steering Committee of the European Society for the Research of Adults (ESREA).

Professor Max van der Kamp is Professor in Adult Education at the University of Groningen, and is a member of the Dutch National UNESCO Commission.

Associate Professor Sue Kilpatrick is Director, University Department of Rural Health, University of Tasmania. Her research focuses on rural issues, including health, workforce issues, social capital, community capacity and learning. She has published extensively in these areas, besides working as a consultant and researcher with rural communities at the local level.

Professor Eamonn McQuade is Professor of Computer Engineering at the University of Limerick and Chairman of the Programme for University Industry Interface (PUII). His research interests include adaptive and learning algorithms, eLearning in engineering education and educational development. He was formerly Dean of Engineering and Science and Dean of Engineering at the University of Limerick.

Professor Eamonn Murphy is Boart Longyear Professor of Quality and Applied Statistics at the Department of Mathematics and Statistics, University of Limerick. He holds a PhD from University College, Dublin and an MSc from the University of Limerick. Professor Murphy is a member of the Executive Board of the Programme for University Industry Interface (PUII). He has consulted on over 60 manufacturing projects in 40 companies in Ireland, the UK and Hungary. He is Director of the Enterprise Research Centre and is founder of both the National Centre for Quality Management, and the interdisciplinary group formed to strengthen industry–university linkages and the Small Firms Research Unit at the University of Limerick. He is involved with two EU 6th Framework Projects and one Leonardo Project and has participated in several EU projects in the past.

Dr Emma O'Brien is a postdoctoral researcher for the PUII in the University of Limerick. She has previously worked on several European projects under the Leonardo da Vinci and eLearning themes. Her research interests are Technology Enhanced Learning (TEL), barriers to training in SMEs and lifelong education for graduates.

Dr Fabio Sabatini has written numerous articles on social capital and is the author and editor of the *Social Capital Gateway* website providing resources for social sciences awarded by the *Journal of Economic Education* as an exemplary material for teaching and learning economics. He received a PhD in Economics at the University of Rome La Sapienza and is currently Senior Research Fellow at the University of Siena and Research Associate at the University of Rome La Sapienza.

Rhona Sherry is Project Manager of the PUII at the University of Limerick. She previously worked as project co-ordinator of the Transferable Skills Project, based in Trinity College Dublin, and also has a number of years' experience as a careers adviser and trainer in higher and vocational educational institutions both in Ireland and abroad. Her research interests include the integration of transferable skills into higher education programmes and the personal and professional development of graduates and students.

Dr Larry Swanson is Director of the Center for the Rocky Mountain West at University of Montana, and head of its Regional Economy programme. He previously was Director of Economic Analysis within the Bureau of Business and Economic Research at the University of Montana, and Associate Professor of Management. He was an economic consultant for over ten years, both independently from his office in Lincoln, Nebraska, and with a Washington, DC-based firm. He co-authored the Nebraska Groundwater Quality Protection Strategy, one of three EPA-designated model state studies in this area, and served on the US Office of Technology Assessment's panel on Groundwater Contamination in media, including the *Wall Street Journal*, *New York Times* and *Washington Post*.

Professor Duncan Timms has taught and researched at the Universities of Cambridge, Queensland, Auckland, Stockholm and Stirling. His most recent posts have been as Dean of the Faculty of Human Sciences and Director of the Centre for eLearning Development in the University of Stirling. He is currently an Honorary Professor in the Department of Applied Social Science at Stirling. His research interests span two areas: the role of early family experiences in later mental health and the social implications of information and communications technologies, especially the relationship between the internet, local communities and social capital.

Dr Erik Wallin had a background as a scientist and civil engineer before he entered the social sciences as a research associate in the research group on Process and

Systems Analysis in Human Geography at Lund University. His PhD dissertation in 1980 was on 'The Generative Grammar of Everyday Life', where he identified three basic generative grammars for everyday life production and reproduction. These grammars have later been transformed into a general model called the *Conversity* model for collaborative learning and co-construction of future relevant knowledge in the regional context. Currently Erik Wallin is an Associate Professor at the School of Economics and Management at Lund University, with responsibility for the PhD study programme in Informatics. He has co-ordinated a number of EU projects related to eLearning, eBusiness and eGovernance such as the *CoLabs.eu* project within the R3L initiative on learning regions. Erik Wallin is also the founder and CEO of a small authoring company called CITY Conversity AB, where he acts as a service provider and consultant to regional authorities, companies and other organisations in need of higher future readiness and new strategies to adapt to the third industrial epoch and the conditions for long-term sustainability.

Theresia Williams is currently a Sessional Instructor with the Department of Educational Policy Studies at the University of Alberta in Edmonton, Alberta and an Individualized Study Tutor in Education at Athabasca University in Alberta, Canada. Theresia has published and consulted extensively in areas of transformative learning, children and place attachment, place connection and community learning, workplace learning and ethics, social learning and community sustainability. She is currently working on the completion of her PhD in Adult Education.

Jacques Zeelen is an Associate Professor at the University of Groningen. His principal research interests are developmental co-operation and lifelong learning.

Jethro Zuwarimwe is a PhD candidate who has just submitted his thesis for examination at the University of Pretoria. His primary area of interest is rural development, specifically entrepreneurship development as an alternative source of livelihood. He also has extensive working experience with rural communities and seeks to contribute to entrepreneurship policy development through engaging in social capital and social learning forums. He is equally passionate about social capital as a conduit for social learning.

Chapter 1

Introduction

Mike Osborne, Kate Sankey
and Bruce Wilson

In the face of an increasingly globalised world, in which sudden shifts in investment can cause the loss of hundreds of jobs from a community, it is widely accepted that the quality of social relationships and social cohesion, described as social capital, can be an important resource for sustaining communities' resilience in difficult times. Both journalists and academics recount case studies of how social linkages have been the key resource as communities take stock of their situation and rebuild local economies, perhaps becoming more prosperous than they were before. Frequently, the case studies focus on how the social linkages have facilitated community learning, and on the significance of place in focusing both efforts to build anew, and to influence the policies of local and regional governments.

These stories have pushed the concept of social capital, made popular by Robert Putnam (2000), into the realms of being an important dimension of local and regional policy development. It has coincided with the strong interest, since the work of the OECD in the mid-1990s, in investment in learning as a critical contribution to local and regional economic development.

How does it work? Can the claims made for social capital and learning regions be empirically described and demonstrated? Are these concepts interdependent, really different sides of the same coin? What is the significance, conceptually and empirically, of the focus on place, on a particular community, neighbourhood, city or regional policy development *and* implementation?

This is an important question for the PASCAL Observatory, an international organisation concerned with matters of place management, social capital and learning regions that was established by three regional governments and two universities in 2003.[1] Efforts to address this question have been explored at four PASCAL conferences, at which there have been efforts both to promote and to analyse how the concepts of social capital and learning regions can be applied through coherent, 'place-based' policy development and implementation. The various contributions at these conferences, as well as other forums, have demonstrated widespread interest in these issues in all parts of the world.

Yet the research evidence remains relatively undeveloped and fragmentary, and reflects a variety of theoretical and methodological approaches. A review of papers presented in the PASCAL conferences reveals a number of dimensions to the discussion:

- uncertainty about the meanings, and the linkages between, the three key concepts of social capital, learning regions and place management,
- issues of methodology,
- challenges in linking research evidence and policy formation,
- linking research evidence and programmatic action,
- questions about the transferability of ideas and concepts from one region to another.

This book aims to contribute to clarifying these issues through bringing together inter-related research literature from three fields: social capital, learning cities/ regions and place management. It builds on two previous volumes in this series (Osborne et al. 2004; Edwards et al. 2006), and a third volume being published in parallel with this (Osborne et al. 2007). Each of these volumes relates to current themes of research within the domain of lifelong learning. In the case of this collection, we link lifelong learning to social capital, the development of regions and the management of place. Specifically, it draws upon and develops presentations made at the third international PASCAL Observatory conference in October 2005, and presents research on the development and implementation of policies and practices that improve the quality of living and working circumstances at local and regional levels, recognising the importance of social capital and the necessity of partnership for the successful implementation of policy. The book focuses on regional initiatives, particularly those which explicitly embrace lifelong learning, as a framework for developing a systematic planning framework that may encompass administrative, cultural, geographical, physical and/or political perspectives. Like the work of the PASCAL Observatory itself, this involves looking at life from the perspective of people and places, rather than separate programmes delivered for them.

The book begins with this introduction and is followed by chapters (Catts, Falk, Hess and Adams and Kilpatrick and Abbott) that focus on approaches to research, their merits and limitations, and connections with policy making. Timms reminds us that in discussions about social relationships and communities, new information and communications already influence patterns of relationships, and that online communities will affect our understandings of social capital. Sabatini follows this with a detailed review of the literature and research on social capital, particularly as it relates to economic development, and has a number of proposals about future research in this area. The next chapters (Jütte, Hall et al. and Zuwarimwe, Wallin, Ilieva, Inman and Swanson, and Williams) focus on specific pieces of empirical research related to social capital and learning regions, working with different examples of place. We conclude with three chapters, two of which (Doyle and Van Beilen et al.) consider specific themes important both in the context of the development of social capital and place: the role of universities, and sustainable development. There follows a concluding chapter. Throughout these chapters permeate three concepts integral to the concerns of PASCAL: social capital, place management and learning cities/regions.

The concept of social capital has become a popular conceptual vehicle that is used extensively throughout the social science community (see Putnam 1993, 2000; Baron et al. 2001; Field 2005) and refers broadly to three forms of connections and ties:

- bonding connections, which bring together people from a very similar background in close ties, such as family and close friends,
- bridging ties, which bring together people from rather similar backgrounds but more loosely, such as people with a shared interest (a hobby, a job, or living in the same neighbourhood),
- linking ties, which bring together people from dissimilar backgrounds.

Social capital has multiple attractions for different communities. For people working in business growth agencies, the idea of social capital is highly congruent with policies designed to promote innovation and dynamism, for example through business clusters and sectoral networks, where entrepreneurs and managers share ideas. Similarly, people working in regional government agencies often find the idea of social capital sits comfortably alongside policies designed to promote local economic regeneration and social development, where partnership working and community engagement are seen as central.

The second broad concept that we use is that of a learning city/region and this links closely to ideas within the realm of social capital, especially those related to trust and the role played by co-operative and collective learning (Sankey and Osborne 2006). The term 'learning region' has been used throughout the world to express the idea that multiple players have a role in promoting and facilitating learning that develops the economic and social well-being of their locality (Florida 1995). In recent documents produced by the European Commission amongst others, the concept refers to a region, city, urban or rural area, regardless of whether its identity is defined in administrative, cultural, geographical, physical or political terms (Longworth 2001). Following the impetus of work sponsored by the Organisation for Economic Co-operation and Development (OECD 1973, 2001) and others, there exist around the world numerous entities that describe themselves as 'learning cities' or 'learning regions', and in many countries well-developed networks of such cities and regions are working together in collaborative fashion. More recently in Europe, following the R3L initiative of the European Commission (2002), the appendage of 'lifelong' has frequently appeared along-side 'learning region', enhanced recently by a project that seeks to develop a sustainable network of lifelong learning regions.[2]

The third concept of place, or place-based, management has become particularly influential amongst government agencies (in Australia, especially, see Stewart-Weeks 2002), responsible for providing services to the same or overlapping groups of citizens and communities. A clearer focus on economic and social outcomes has meant that achieving greater focus on a local or regional framework for service delivery has been seen as an increasingly valuable policy lever for programme implementation. Place management uses the geographic dimension of data analysis (from census data, for example) to highlight the locational distribution of client groups, and the particular characteristics of needs for services. It assumes that, once patterns of needs are identified service providers can collaborate on developing appropriate programmes, which integrate the delivery of services. This kind of collaboration might involve both different levels of government (national, regional and local) as well as different agencies and types of agencies from the same level of government. A broad range of non-governmental service providers also have significant interests in this approach. A critical element of this approach involves community engagement in identifying the specific patterns of needs. Thus in the case of the UK, and Scotland in particular, it has resonance with the concept and process of community planning. This is a policy approach introduced through the Local Government Act Scotland 2003 (Scottish Executive). There is strong similarity with the Victorian government in approach, as the government seeks to bring governance closer to people and place. This raises questions about the nature of the relationship between place management and community engagement, and how this might strengthen social capital and in consequence the efficacy of social and sustainable development policies.

Overview of the contributions

In this collection we have brought together research that focuses upon the three concepts, drawing upon work within an international domain. The contributors come from various backgrounds, and varying perspectives on, and approaches to, the issues under review. We focus on that work within the domain of social capital that has closest links to the development of lifelong learning in a regional context. In turn, we look to research within the field of place management that offers a quite specific framework, essentially geographic, for programme measurement. This includes the various sets of indicators that can be used within a regional or local frame to evaluate the impact of policy measures.

Catts begins by pointing out that the conditions under which we learn to co-operate matter a great deal to the outcomes. Co-operation, trust and reciprocity depend on norms built over time, and on a network of interdependent co-operative arrangements that makes it costly for a person to exploit the reciprocity principle, by taking but not returning. However, Putnam also identifies another form of social capital that is hierarchical and in which people are coerced into co-operating. In this form the oppressed are left with little hope or opportunity. He suggests that the implications of these theories can be explored through efforts to quantify the nature of social capital. His chapter demonstrates how this might be done through defining categories of social capital, discussing criteria for selecting indicators of social capital at national and community level and in research, and identifying limitations and critiques of such indicators. The potential of quantitative indicators of social capital for national policy evaluation, and for policy implementation are assessed. Conclusions are illustrated in the context of schooling.

Ian Falk addresses directly some of the issues which arise from the apparent separation of quantitative and qualitative work. He focuses on the role and nature of evidence in policy formation and evaluation processes, arguing strongly for the importance of an approach which focuses on interactivity, the situational dimension of policy formation and implementation. Falk draws on some research with policy makers to draw out their understandings of what counts as evidence, and how it influences the advice which they develop. Two broad conclusions emerged: firstly, the focus on evidence applies typically only to promoting the *need for* policy, rather than to the nature of the evidence required to *develop, implement* and *evaluate* policy. His research identified also three levels of difference in understandings about what might count as an evidence base, with the overall conclusion that there is considerable divergence in the ways in which policy makers understand evidence and its role in the policy process.

Falk concludes by suggesting that one way of resolving uncertainty about the value of quantitative and qualitative research is to recognise that the most important question is the question about policy effectiveness to which an answer is being sought. Different kinds of evidence will be relevant to different kinds of questions. The connectedness of social capital, learning and place, with its implications for identity, means that a focus on interactivity and communication will help to sharpen the focus on evidence that gets at the heart of policy implementation and evaluation processes. In other words, evidence on the quality and quantity of interactions in each of the four stages of the situated policy intervention process could not only provide important insights, but also contribute to enhancing learning and social outcomes.

The next two chapters, by Hess and Adams and by Kilpatrick and Abbott, focus on questions related to the consequences of social capital, and how it can be demonstrated that policy or programme interventions can lead to positive outcomes for communities. Hess and Adams draw on international evidence and experience to show that community-based approaches to policymaking and implementation can be used to address deficits in traditional centralist and programmatic approaches to public administration. Initially this was most evident in social policy areas. Increasingly, practitioners and commentators are identifying community engagement as a factor in improved economic performance and social well-being. In Victoria in Australia, there is six years' experience in implementing a community-based approach to government. This chapter suggests a set of theoretical conclusions to be drawn from this which capture the lessons for both communities and governments. It focuses particularly on how the governance of the community/government interface impacts on the likelihood of successful implementation of community strengthening policies. A key research issue concerns the importance of research which can support thoughtful measurement of 'community engagement' (rather than social capital) and provide a more effective bridge between government action and community imperatives.

Kilpatrick and Abbott, from Tasmania in Australia, introduce a new way of thinking about the social capital of a community, linked to the community's capacity to deliver favourable outcomes for its members. This capacity is termed community efficacy. The chapter reports on the initial stages of a project that is building the knowledge base and developing a framework for measurement of outcomes that accrue to rural communities, drawing on two case study communities in Tasmania, Australia.

Their model of community efficacy illustrates the link between community activity infrastructure and community efficacy and between the structural and dynamic elements of community transactions which go to make up the concept of social capital. This paves the way for a measurement framework against which a community's efficacy and the well-being outcomes of its members may be rated within any nominated social domain, and the robustness of its social capital may be assessed. The framework recognises that social capital resources are used at the point of interaction between community members; hence, at a practical level opportunities for interaction are important.

Their work began with the recognition that social capital remains notoriously difficult to measure, despite many attempts to do so. There is consensus that social capital is the 'property' of a community or collective, yet in measurement frameworks social capital is normally aggregated across individuals and different levels. They argue that, as communities are not socio-economically homogenous, the differential capacity of various groups within the community to participate, and their differential access to decision-making structures, should be included. Further, social capital must be set in context – social capital resources that are effective in one context are not necessarily effective in another.

By way of contrast with Kilpatrick and Abbott's strong emphasis on place, Timms focuses on virtual communities, and on the ways in which the internet can foster online social capital. He proposes that the internet provides new bases for the enhancement of social capital in local communities. Online relationships provide the foundation for the development of virtual communities. Where these are harnessed to local interests they enable an enhancement of local social capital. The development of community, online as well as offline, requires ongoing patterns of interaction, common identity and the evolution of group norms. Community building requires an effective focus: eLearning provides one way in which this may be attempted. As part of an EC project investigating the use of the internet for collaboration online, an eLearning module has been developed which attempts to build community through the presentation of community portraits. Initial runs of the module in geographically marginal areas have suggested that the approach possesses considerable promise. Developments in information and communications technologies are leading to a further diminution of the power of geography in the determination of community, and the latest incarnation of 'Community Portraits' largely eschews geography in favour of a socio-cultural basis of identity. In the future, Timms believes, community may have more to do with cyberspace than with geography.

The preceding chapters all point to some of the problems with the use of the concept of social capital as a focus of research activity. Sabatini emphasises a stronger conceptual framing of social capital, and carries out a critical review of the empirical literature on social capital and economic development. He points to six main weaknesses affecting the empirics of social capital. Identified weaknesses are then used to analyse, in a critical perspective, some prominent empirical studies and new interesting researches published in the last two years. He emphasises the need which emerges to acknowledge, also within the empirical research, the multidimensional, context-dependent and dynamic nature of social capital. Furthermore, he notes that, although it has gained a certain popularity in the empirical research, the use of 'indirect' indicators of social capital may be misleading. Such measures do not represent social capital's key components identified by the theoretical literature, and their use causes a considerable confusion about what social capital *is*, as distinct from its *outcomes*, and what the relationship between social capital and its outcomes *may be*. Research reliant upon an outcome of social capital as an indicator of it will necessarily find social capital to be related to that outcome. This chapter suggests focusing the empirical research firstly on the 'structural' aspects of the concept, therefore excluding by the measurement toolbox all indicators referring to social capital's supposed outcomes.

A quite different methodological approach emerges in the next chapter, in which Wolfgang Jutte shows how network analytical concepts can serve as a framework of reference and analysis for an investigation. His study is of the local institutional landscape of continuing education in a medium-sized Austrian town. He takes the view that the ensemble of interacting actors as a whole and their inter-relations form a local–regional functional system. This includes the fact that those acting there – as is the case in every system – are dependent on interaction, communication and co-operation. In short, they form a social network. Through using various quantitative and qualitative research strategies, and a technique of data visualisation, relations, which would otherwise remain hidden or not be immediately apparent, are made visible. In addition, the visualisation of complex structures of relations makes it easier to relate the actors' patterns of interpretation and action to structures. Looking at the actors' structural embeddedness provides a keener understanding for their subjective interpretations and choices.

The next three chapters concern issues of social relationships and learning in two countries, which might be regarded in the context of these debates as regions: Ireland, the 'Celtic Tiger' of the European, so-called because of its economic successes in the late twentieth century; Zimbabwe, a post-colonial country struggling with the challenges of development within the contending forces of African political economy; and Bulgaria, currently shaping-up to join the European Union in 2007. Tony Hall and colleagues contextualise their chapter within the need to ensure Ireland's competitiveness in the emerging global knowledge economy, within which it is argued that it is crucial for enterprises to identify and address their future training and competency development needs. This is particularly resonant for companies in the Irish manufacturing sector, where the priority is to move towards the creation and deployment of high-value products and services. While lifelong learning will provide part of the solution to Ireland's continued economic success in manufacturing, important and complex questions remain: what is the future landscape of Irish manufacturing likely to look like? And, what specific types of skills will enterprises require to remain competitive in that environment? The chapter presents the results of the analysis of a pioneering innovation: the Programme for University Industry Interface (PUII), which is concerned with creating more responsive forms of partnership between academia and industry, using the Community of Practice (COP) model most closely associated with Lave and Wenger (1991). This consultative approach is growing in popularity in the education and training fields; it is increasingly being employed in domains such as Information Technology (IT) design for business settings and instructional design of educational applications and systems. The chapter exemplifies how COP, as a collaborative methodology, can help to create productive, sustainable partnerships between industry and tertiary level education. Furthermore, the story of PUII may serve as an exemplar for those interested in enhancing lifelong learning and social capital, especially in the further education and professional development of graduates in industry.

Zuwarimwe, presents a much more empirically-based study of how social relationships, as understood through the idea of social capital, can be studied through a focus on social networks and intra-enterprise processes in an African context, in Zimbabwe. He draws attention to the differences between entrepreneurs and explores their different approaches to the use of social relationships in the business activities. From this analysis, he highlights a number of policy implications, especially in terms of recognition of the complexities in the application of the concept of social capital in the economic sphere.

There is a tendency in many countries to put under the umbrella of lifelong learning and learning regions a number of the disparate initiatives that have been introduced in different parts of their education and training systems, loosely rationalising them as responding to the objectives of modern education systems. Papadopoulos (2002) puts forward this point in the context of lifelong learning, and the prevalence of the learning region concept as an all-embracing envelope is very evident in Germany.[3] Using Bulgaria as a case of a country-region, Kornelia Illieva considers the way in which a country-specific national 'package' of institutions (for example, its education and employment systems and welfare state regime) and its own historical development shape the opportunities for lifelong learning. At a theoretical level, her approach uses new institutional theory to test its descriptive efficiency in relation to lifelong learning institutionalisation. She considers the dialectical relationship between identity and institution. Her focus lies within three sub-themes: current reforms and new community priorities in the public, local and regional sectors of Bulgaria; creating and managing linkages across levels, portfolios and sectors; and links between social capital and lifelong learning.

Much of the research on learning and learning regions has been drawn from the experiences of small communities, especially in a number of European states. Erik

Wallin presents and discusses some of the lessons learnt from the completed *CoLabs.eu* project within the R3L initiative on *European Networks of Lifelong Learning Regions*. In the project, the author led a team which carried out some concrete social experiments in order to 'make the village a virtual campus'. He starts this chapter by making a general introduction to the research area and introduces the reasoning behind the project. He describes the objectives of the project as it relates to learning regions and the 'third mission'[4] for universities and how the project was carried out in each regional case, the regions being located in Denmark, Finland, Germany, Italy, Sweden and the UK. Wallin presents and discusses the outcomes of the experiments with regional collaborators and the general results achieved within the lifetime of the project. In the last section of the chapter he discusses the results in more general terms and makes some recommendations on how to make villages not only learning-oriented, but also innovative and creative, which indicates his perception of the need for a new framework for knowledge creation where *place and people* really matter.

The next chapter looks at the relationship between quality of life, economic prosperity and social capital and examines a Regional Economies Assessment Database (READ) tool in supporting regional centres as the engines of growth. Inman and Swanson describe a situation where the interaction of people with a powerful history of agricultural production complement a thriving arena of commerce. But due to much perturbation in the social and economic world, the situation is best tackled through an integrated regional approach, thus cutting across physical, social and economic space.

Inman and Swanson bring a case study of rural/urban divide to the table, where with public/private leadership, an economic development partnership has been created to find the value of the regional approach. The research methodology was to examine all the regional initiatives to look for commonalities in thinking and regional development and so understand how the economy is organised in space. This is based on a data system, READ, which enables regional planning and which benefits the individual by identifying workplace needs, career and educational guidance. It also enables social programmes which co-ordinate resources and transportation opportunities which reflect regional needs. Thus thoughtful economic development would take place in the context of informed regional analysis. While cities and rural areas often face different social issues, the fabric of a local economy ties them together.

A further advantage of the regional profile approach presented by regional data analysis is suggested by a new urban–rural integration for cluster-based enterprise. This connection of small to medium-sized enterprise allows for flexible adaptation to changing local needs. The face of the new economy that emerges from such a creative data analysis reflects the continuing developments in information technology, growing internationalisation, massive restructuring within traditional industries and changing patterns of population growth and migration. By focusing on the specifically regional character of these and other issues, Inman and Swanson assert that we embrace a broader set of solutions.

Williams draws her experience from questioning the impact of commodification (privatisation) of social space in provincial government in Canada. She addresses one of the important issues of changed economics and politics and globalisation. The chapter has a particularly important place in this book as it exposes the fragility of the link between social capital and place management The policy framework of Public–Private Partnerships (PPPs) is heralded as giving local communities economic and social ownership of their public spaces and services but, according to Williams, may actually undermine the very framework on which social connectiveness depends, representing merely a cost-cutting measure and a 'provincial downloading of responsibilities without providing sufficient resources' (Grant 2003: 9). This is sold to the local communities as a way to build better lives for themselves and their families. The provincial government sees it as a way of investing in Alberta's future. But Williams believes that 'the communal commons of public place becomes altered when we commodify it'. One problem comes from employing a rational choice approach of cost–benefit analyses where economic considerations are the prime and sometimes only consideration. This is a serious concern for those who do not have the economic means to access private services and resources that were previously accessible to all sectors of the population. Williams advocates for a 'sincere democracy' – one which requires a commitment to meaningful empowerment and participation of all members of a society in decision making. The role of democratic government is to consider seriously the challenges of globalisation and an advanced state of capitalism. Williams contrasts rational choice policy with democratic policy analysis which invites a postmodernist perspective of civic mindedness, active listening, active promotion of community discourse, inclusive participation and empowerment and education (Friere 1970; Clemons and McBeth 2001). This approach is comprehensive and embraces the principles of sustainable development focusing on long-term impacts and employing the precautionary principle.

We have seen that learning regions, social capital and place management, the fundamental elements of the agenda for PASCAL, are intimately linked. The chapters so far reveal the intimate connections and the implications for adopting such an holistic and interactive policy approach. Like life itself, the fundamental systems are diverse and linked. This is what gives strength, robustness and sustainability to the whole system. This diversity can be analysed at a variety of levels and scales. However there are certain policy imperatives that run through and across the chapters and deserve consideration as contemporary key themes. These will help to throw light on matters of scale and influence. Two such themes are addressed in the final chapters: by Doyle on the cultural presence of higher education institutions, and issues of researching and analysing soft data; and by Corinne van Beilen et al., on sustainable development.

Doyle, like Wallin, also looks at the so-called and much trumpeted 'third mission' of universities, and explores the mutual influence ('cultural presence') that higher education institutions (HEIs) have on the cultural life of their local and regional communities. In particular, she focuses on the added value which flows to the disadvantaged in the region since it is here that the university should be able to make a positive contribution. She interrogates the literature and the theoretical underpinning for this relationship. Her chapter seeks out the evidence to support and understand the nature of the received wisdom, 'that HEIs across the board make a huge contribution to the "buzz" of a place – both in what they do in the way of public access and also in the role their staff and students play in the cultural life of a place' (Hamilton and Sneddon 2004). However, Hamilton and Sneddon, who were commissioned by the Scottish Higher Education Funding Council's newly established Knowledge Transfer Taskforce, found that there is little if any data or analysis on the types of activity or interaction (outputs) nor of any transformative impact (outcomes) on disadvantaged groups and communities.

Doyle reports on a piece of scoping research carried out through telephone interviewing with a group of stakeholders in the community. The findings are disappointing and question the reality in 'outcome' terms of HEI's contribution to strengthening of social capital and enhancing the engagement with the local community and region. She is critical of the actual role which the HEI plays within the socio-economic region. Certainly, the scoping study could not be specific because the type of qualitative data necessary to reveal transformative impact was not easily available and indeed is not part of the quantitative management information collected by HEIs.

Throughout there is an assumption that HEIs have an enriching effect on communities but this does not take into account the well-documented, if little researched, so-called 'town–gown divide'. It is suggested here that the concept of social capital would be a useful aid to unpicking the drivers and barriers to both HEIs' contribution to cultural lifelong learning in disadvantaged communities, and the level of engagement to and from those communities.

The second theme is that of sustainable development. Corinne van Beilen et al. examine what lifelong learning contributes to sustainable development. The chapter describes research carried out in the Netherlands, with a specific focus on reaching 'groups-at-risk' which have a tendency to be disengaged with lifelong learning across the board. This of course raises a further challenge – that of identifying innovative practices which will excite and stimulate learning for sustainable development. Sustainable development is commonly defined by three interconnected systems or pillars: Society, Environment and Economy. With Doyle's chapter in mind, it is interesting to see that van Beilen et al. suggest that the role of culture might be underestimated within this scheme. In some cases culture is intimately tied to the pillar 'society' (social-cultural dimension), although it is better seen as a cross-cutting element – an 'inter-connector' or interlink' between the three areas. UNESCO's Draft International Implementation Scheme for the UN Decade of Education for Sustainable Development provides helpful clarification regarding the role of a cultural context across the three systems:

The values, diversity, knowledge, languages and worldviews associated with culture predetermine the way issues of sustainable development are dealt with in a specific context; culture in this sense is a way of being, relating, behaving, believing, and acting and which is in constant process of change and exchange of other cultures.

Corinne van Beilen et al. describe the characteristics of lifelong learning policies and practice spanning the three systems and developing active citizens with increased social capital and political participation. She stresses the importance of this learning agenda for engaging with learners in solving complex problems of the future. This is a huge agenda and one which will call upon global commitments and political priorities.

The chapter is important as it documents a series of case studies in lifelong learning for sustainable development. These are set in the context of the Dutch national framework, 'Learning for Sustainable Development (LvDO) 2004–2007'. Some of the key challenges are highlighted which are important for consideration in this book. A recurring theme is that of joined-up policies – in many cases, sustainable development policies are not central but add-on or at worst peripheral. For example, case studies in the schools system indicate that there has been very little integration with the regular curriculum. The case studies deal in different ways with all the three main systems but in all cases the cultural context is particularly significant. The success in engaging people in the learning process has depended on dealing with the immediate and the local (the 'here and now'). This is relevant to people's well-being; however, it is the future and the global which need to be addressed for sustainable development policies to be effective. A final lesson which the research demonstrates is the importance of networks, partnerships and alliances.

Why the focus on research?

A persistent challenge for social researchers is to be able to demonstrate that the claims that they wish to make about particular policy or theoretical questions and issues are legitimate and warrant serious attention. This can be very difficult, particularly where there are:

- issues of methodology,
- challenges in linking research evidence and policy formation,
- linking research evidence and programmatic action,
- questions about the transferability of ideas and concepts from one region to another.

The chapters in this collection all demonstrate these challenges, and offer a range of options. At the most specific, some researchers rely on the empirical data, assuming that the 'facts' will speak for themselves. Others recognise the theoretical and conceptual difficulties, and acknowledge the need for sophisticated methodologies which try and provide assurance about the value of the insights which are offered.

Each of our chapters offers some insights into these questions, but a range of issues remain unresolved. These issues are addressed in our concluding chapter.

Notes

1 See http://www.obs-pascal.com.
2 The PASCAL European Network of Lifelong Learning Regions (PENR3L) seeks to 'establish a dynamic and growing working network of expertise centres and forward-looking local and regional authorities that will work together to accelerate the growth throughout Europe of learning cities and regions' (see http://www.obs-pascal.com).
3 See, for example, the proceedings of the BMBF/EU Conference 'Regionale Netzwerke für Lebenslanges Lernen – Strukturelle Innovationen für Bildung und Ausbildung' [Regional Partnerships for Lifelong Learning – Structural Innovations in Education and Training], Berlin, 8 September 2004, at: http://www.lernende-regionen.info/dlr/index.php.
4 Edquist and Flodström (1997) describe this mission in Swedish universities During 1998 a parliamentary committee undertook preparatory work for establishing government policy in university research (*Forskning 2000*) and proposed that the 'third mission' for the universities, *co-operation with society*, should not be regarded as equal to that of education and research. However, the response to the committee's work and the actual proposition from the government took an opposite view, declaring that the co-operative mission for universities still is one of their major three imperatives (Department of Education 1999). Doyle's later chapter returns to this theme.

References

Baron, S., Field, J. and Schuller, T. (eds) (2001) *Social Capital: Critical Perspectives*, Oxford: Oxford University Press.

Clemons, R. and McBeth, M. (2001) *Public Policy Praxis: Theory and Pragmatism, A Case Approach*, Upper Saddle River, NJ: Prentice Hall.

Department of Education (1999) *Certain Research Questions – A Summary of the Governmental Proposition 1998/99:94*, Stockholm: Governmental Office, Letter of Fact, U 99.007, April.

Edquist, C. and Flodström, A. (1997) *Den tredje uppgiften: universitet och samhälle i samverkan. [University and Society in Cooperation]*, Stockholm: SACO.

Edwards, R., Gallacher, J. and Whittaker, S. (2006) *Researching Experiential and Community-based Learning*, London: Routledge.

European Commission (2002) *Call for Proposals (EAC/41/02): European Networks to Promote the Local and Regional Dimension of Lifelong Learning (the 'R3L' Initiative)*, Brussels: Commission of the European Communities.

Field, J. (2005) *Social Capital and Lifelong Learning*, Bristol: Policy Press.

Florida, R. (1995) 'Towards the learning region', *Futures*, 27(5): 527–536.

Friere, P. (1970) *Pedagogy of the Oppressed*, New York: Continuum Publishing.

Grant, J. (2003) 'Planning responses to gated communities in Canada', conference proceedings from Gated Communities: Building Social Division or Safer Communities?, September, at: www.bris.ac.uk/sps/cnrpapersword.

Hamilton, C. and Sneddon, N. (2004) *Scoping Study on Cultural Engagement and Knowledge Transfer in Scottish Universities*, Glasgow: Centre for Cultural Policy Research.

Lave, J. and Wenger, E. (1991) *Situated Learning: Legitimate Peripheral Participation*, New York: Cambridge University Press.

Longworth, N. (2001) *The Local and Regional Dimension of Lifelong Learning: Creating Lifelong Learning Cities, Towns and Regions – A European Policy Paper*, Brussels: Commission of the European Communities.

Organisation for Economic Co-operation and Development (OECD) (1973) *Recurrent Education: A Strategy for Lifelong Learning*, Paris: OECD/CERI.

OECD (2001) *Cities and Regions in the New Learning Economy*, Paris: OECD.

Osborne, M. Gallacher, J. and Crossan, B. (eds) (2004) *Researching Widening Access*, London: Routledge.

Osborne, M., Houston, M. and Toman, N. (eds) (2007) *The Pedagogy of Lifelong Learning: Understanding Effective Teaching and Learning in Diverse Contexts*, London: Routledge.

Papadopoulos, G. (2002) 'Lifelong learning and the changing policy environment', in D. Istance, H. Schuetze and T. Schuller, *International Perspectives on Lifelong Learning: From Recurrent Education to the Knowledge Society*, Buckingham: Society for Research into Higher Education and Open University Press, pp. 39–46.

Putnam, R.D. (1993) *Making Democracy Work*, Cambridge, MA: Harvard University Press.

Putnam, R.D. (2000) *Bowling Alone: The Collapse and Revival of American Community*, New York: Simon and Schuster.

Sankey, K. and Osborne, M. (2006) 'Lifelong learning reaching regions where other learning doesn't reach', in R. Edwards et al. (eds) *Researching Learning Outside the Academy*, London: Routledge.

Stewart-Weeks, M. (2002) 'Assessment of evaluation strategies and tools for place management and community renewal projects', paper presented at Australasian Evaluation Society International Conference, Woolongong.

Chapter 2

Quantitative indicators of social capital

Measurement in a complex social context

Ralph Catts

Introduction

Social capital has been identified as a construct that may be related to desired outcomes in a range of policy areas including social, educational, and community development. In the forms considered by Putnam and others to be beneficial, social capital requires cooperation, trust, reciprocity, civic engagement and collective well-being (Putnam 1993: 177–181). These conditions are said to foster individuals, and to support growth and development for society as a whole. The conditions under which we learn to co-operate matter a great deal to the outcomes. Cooperation, trust and reciprocity depend on norms built over time, and on a network of interdependent cooperative arrangements that makes it costly for a person to exploit the reciprocity principle, by taking but not returning (Putnam, 1993: 169). However Putnam also identifies another form of social capital that is hierarchical and in which people are coerced into cooperating. In this form the oppressed are left with little hope or opportunity.

One way to explore the implications of these theories is to define and to quantify the nature of social capital. In this chapter, categories of social capital are defined, criteria for selecting indicators of social capital at national and community level and in research are discussed, and limitations and critiques of such indicators are identified. The potential of quantitative indicators of social capital for national policy evaluation, and for policy implementation are assessed. The complexities of measurement are illustrated in the context of education.

Over the past two decades surveys that employ indicators of social capital have been conducted in most developed countries, both by national statistical offices and by various social scientists (for example, Coleman 1988; ABS 2004). The social capital possessed in various communities has been estimated and shown to be correlated with many desirable aspects of human existence, including quality of health and housing, longevity, educational qualifications, levels of employment, assets and salaries. These findings have attracted the interest of social scientists. To the extent that these relationships have implications for policy, the findings are of interest also to governments. Some social scientists and most notably Putnam and his associates have made strong claims for the benefits of enhanced social capital. For example, Putnam and Feldstein (2000: 4) make the following claims for the effects of social capital:

> Economic studies demonstrate that social capital makes workers more pro-ductive, firms more competitive, and nations more prosperous. Psychological research indicates that abundant social capital makes individuals less prone to depression and more inclined to help others. Epidemiological reports show that social capital decreases the rate of suicide, colds, heart attacks, strokes, and cancer, and improves individuals' ability to fight or recover from illnesses once they have struck. Sociology experiments suggest that social capital reduces crime, juvenile delinquency, teenage pregnancy, child abuse, welfare dependency, and drug abuse, and increases student test scores and graduation rates.

Interestingly, other writers have argued for causality to be attributed to other factors that lead to an improvement in social capital. For instance, Feinstein and Hammond (2004) have shown improvements in well-being and social capital engagement after adults participated in adult education programmes, with the effects occurring after completion of one or two courses.

What is social capital?

Like many terms that have been accepted in political and policy debates as well as the academic research community, there are many views about what constitutes social capital, and just as many critiques of the construct. The concept has been popularised in terms advanced by Putnam (1993: 167) as 'features of social organisation, such as trust, norms, and networks, that can improve the efficiency of society by coordinated actions'. According to Putnam (1993: 177), stocks of social capital are 'self-reinforcing and cumulative'. Coleman (1990) argued that economic prosperity could be enhanced through human capital, and that the correlation between indicators of social capital and levels of school qualification justify addressing social capital as part of schooling policy. In contrast, critics argue that problems of social exclusion stem from the inequitable distribution of economic capital in society. This critical strand is reflected in the work of Pierre Bourdieu, who claimed that economic capital underpins social capital and interacts with wider structures to reproduce social inequalities. Social capital, he said, is found in social networks and connections, and in contacts and group memberships that potentially support access to valued resources (Bourdieu 1993: 68). These resources are connected to class advantage, and are reinforced by the link between culture and social networks (for example, bingo or bridge groups) which connect to and reinforce class inequalities. Thus critics argue that social capital may be misused to conceal the effects of economic capital and power, and may reinforce a culture of 'blame' on those who fail to observe middle-class norms.

Several authors have expressed reservations about the use of social capital as a tool for reform (e.g. Allard 2003) and about the appropriateness of using quantitative methods to measure social capital (e.g. Horvat et al. 2003). Hence we need to interrogate the validity of the construct in various contexts and acknowledge alternative views. The following questions can inform a quantitative approach to researching social capital:

- Do operational definitions of social capital promote a particular moral agenda that suggests that middle-class norms are intrinsically good and that deviation from those norms is undesirable or blameworthy?
- Is it possible to identify and agree on norms that are acceptable to all, including parents, young people, community workers and policy makers? If so, what are included in these norms? For example, is engagement with lifelong learning, active citizenship, well-being and access to employment acceptable? If so, do these terms have common meanings to all?
- Can social capital help explain or change outcomes at individual, community, institutional or system level? If so, how can this knowledge be utilised?
- Might social capital inform the assessment and allocation of inputs, both material, including financial resources, as well as intangible, such as skills of community members?

Issues of measurement

As noted earlier, at the level of national policy, social capital has been defined in terms of a range of indicators that have been reported to correlate with desired outcomes of social policy, including improvements in health, employment and well-being.

These reported correlations do not provide a causal explanation for why measures of social capital are correlated with desired outcomes. There are several alternative hypotheses that can explain the observed relationships, and these need to be explored. One explanation is that the way these variables are measured involves a degree of circularity, so that measures of social capital contain either elements of the variables with which they are correlated. A second is that both social capital and other outcomes are all indicators of an underlying variable, such as economic power. It is necessary therefore to be cautious about bold claims for the benefits of social capital such as those made by Putnam.

An analysis of the types of questions used in these surveys suggest that at least some items privilege white middle-class values, and hence describe the advantages held by the middle class in economic and social well-being. Scales have been proposed by national agencies for statistical data (ONS 2001; ABS 2004) and by prominent researchers such as Coleman and Putnam. Most national agencies urge caution in defining indicators of social capital (e.g. ONS 2001), but this advice has not always been heeded either by politicians or some advocates of the utility of social capital as in the example cited above from Putnam and Feldstein. A fundamental issue is ensuring that indicators are valid in the context of interest. For example, the scale for measuring community involvement proposed in the US context by Putnam and Feldstein (2000) includes the following items:

- Signed a petition in past 12 months (26A).
- Number of times attended public meeting discussing school or town affairs in past 12 months (56L).
- Volunteered for needy, volunteered for school or youth programmes (59C).
- Number of categories of formal secular group involvement [33B-R].

An example from the Australian context is the indicators of social capital adopted by Onyx and Bullen (2000) who, for community involvement used items including:

- Are you on a management committee or organising committee for any local group or organisation?
- Have you been part of a project to organise a new service in your area (e.g. youth club, scout hall, child care, recreation for disabled)?

These examples of community involvement depend to an extent upon literacy and also on the type of agency that is acceptable, such as school or youth agency. Such items are targeting parents and its is known that middle-class parents are more likely to be involved in such agencies, if only to ensure the well-being of their own children (Bagnell et al. 2003).

A further Australian example comes from the list of indicators proposed by the Australian Bureau of Statistics. They suggest as an indicator of general trust (ABS 2004: 30), the respondent's perception of safety on public transport at night. This example illustrates another issue in interpreting some indicators.

One can ask whether many middle class people use public transport at night. The responses of those who do not use the services are likely to be from a position of ignorance, whereas people who rely upon buses or trains at night on a frequent basis will have first hand knowledge of the situation. Their responses would thus be informed and of a different order to the fears or prejudices of people with no direct experience of night-time use of public transport.

In using quantitative indicators of social capital one must first define the construct and then the purpose for which measurement is to occur. Once these issues are established, one needs to consider the characteristics of the measurement instrument, and then the manner in which the results are utilised. This means, in other words, that first the content validity needs to be established, then the construct validity and reliability, and finally the predictive validity of the instrument. These basic concepts of measurement have been ignored by some in their haste to generate answers for government. Especially when the answers are those that are desired, namely that improving social capital relates to improvements in other indicators of well-being, the rush to use quantitative indicators of social capital is understandable, but not acceptable.

Coleman (1988), for instance, measures the social capital of pupils in terms of a variety of indicators derived from their parents. He considered how many parents were living in the home, and also the number of siblings. From this, he postulated that single-parent families and large families provide less social capital for each child, and showed that his parent to child ratios were correlated with their attainment in school. This type of analysis has been drawn upon by politicians to justify the assumption that the nuclear family unit should be preserved. There are three types of problem with such broad conclusions. First, the analysis fails to explore adequately the possibility of underlying causes, including poverty. Second, it discounts the many exceptions, such as the two-parent family in which abuse occurs, and finally it can lead to policies that actually aggravate the underlying economic causes of the disadvantage. In other words, policy decisions are based on a misreading of the causality and result in blaming the victim.

There are many contexts in which indicators of social capital are of interest. One is the use of social capital indicators at a national level to inform policy makers, especially in relation to community development. Another is the measurement of community social capital. A third is the measurement of community and individual social capital to inform policy implementation and research within a community. At all these levels, proponents assume that social capital can make a difference.

Measuring social capital at national level

At a national level, the focus is normally on the well-being of the nation as a whole and attempts to estimate social capital are considered to be important as a means of describing the social condition of society. The question therefore is how best to make national and regional assessments. Putnam (2000) has proposed three criteria to address in selecting national indicators, namely comparability, continuity and comprehensiveness. A core principle that Putnam (ibid.) advocates is that 'no single source of data is flawless'. Hence he advocates what amounts to triangulation of data sources around any significant component of social capital. Multiple sources allow a search for congruity among outcomes across components of social capital to secure evidence of current status and, more importantly, of change over time. If various indicators provide seemingly conflicting data, post hoc explanations of difference require judgement which should be documented to guard against rationalisation or wishful thinking.

Continuity of populations

Data collected at one point in time cannot inform about the changes occurring in a particular community. The temptation to use differences between generations in a cross-cohort assessment should be avoided because there are normally several communities within a geographical area and there may be little interaction among them. These age cohorts often represent waves of migration into the community and hence there may be little continuity or inheritance of the norms, values and perceptions of one generation by the different people who make up the next generation. This same flow of population also makes it difficult to conduct longitudinal studies. Basing these on a geographical region makes it likely that over time the people who remain in an area will not be representative of the population that moves. This is a particular problem when tracking the effects of regeneration. The people who relocate and do not return are likely to be different or have changed their norms and values, in comparison to those who either stay or return to new housing. To the extent that private housing is available in the mix of new housing, people who can afford to purchase may be different from those they displace. Hence longitudinal studies of a geographic region are prone to confuse changes in social capital with changes in populations of people from whom the data is collected.

Comparability of data

Issues in considering the comparability of data include the continuity of the respondents as described above. Other factors are the consistency of the survey form, the consistency of administration, and the consistency of the construct on which data is collected. Technical and social changes can prompt a change in survey questions. For example, people now use mobile phones to communicate by text, and the fax is less frequently employed. A survey designed 15 years ago could not have anticipated these technological changes that affect ways of networking and hence questions might need to be adjusted to include current methods. Changes in the order as well as changes in the questions in a survey form can influence responses to items that have remained stable. For instance, in asking about feelings of trust and security, Onyx and Bullen (2000: 40) asked in order if people went outside their local community to visit their family, and then if they know where to find information. The first question might prompt people to think about asking family members for information. If it were deleted, then the response to the second question might be changed by the loss of the unintended prompt. Next, it is necessary to consider changes in the administration of a survey, such as when a new manager takes over the training of data collectors. Therefore, before longitudinal data can be compared, it is necessary to identify all survey changes and consider them as potential competing explanations for changes in outcomes.

Changes in the economic structure of society over many years can result in a need for changes in survey questions designed to measure community social capital. For instance, Putnam's approach is criticised because the surveys place an emphasis on membership of formal institutions such as Parent Teacher Associations (PTA) and political parties. Membership of such bodies has been reported by Putnam to have declined and he concludes that there is therefore a decline in community social capital. However, other less formal community networks may have replaced these formal community organisations. More flexible networks may be a response to a more flexible labour market. The changes in work conditions mean that many people of all ages can no longer take part in formal activities that occur at a regular time in the week or month. For instance, many people work in casual jobs in the service industry where their shifts change from week to week, making it difficult for them to take part in functions scheduled at a regular time. However, by sending text messages such people can organise and communicate more easily than was the case when such mobile technology was not available. Hence, survey questions may be missing new informal forms of social capital that have to some extent have replaced formal community organisations.

The role of formal organisations in access to social capital is also problematic. In a UK context, Bagnall et al. (2003) looked at PTA membership to examine how social diversities frame narratives of involvement amongst parents in the North West of England. The middle classes, who are also more mobile, tend to use the PTA as a means of getting involved, gaining a sense of belonging and getting ahead. This is described by Putnam as weak ties and bridging social capital around diffuse networks. Working-class parents generally do not use school-based organ-isations and often reject them. They are also less mobile, so have tighter kin and residence networks. This corresponds with Putnam's bonding social capital with strong ties by which people 'get by'. It can also be questioned how far involvement in the PTA represents an accurate indicator of parents' desire to 'put something back' into the education system. The primary reasons for involvement cited by middle-class parents in the above study stemmed from self-interest (competitive social capital), rather than concern for the quality of educational experiences for all young people (co-operative social capital).

Comprehensiveness and timeframes

Putnam (2000: 417) argues that social capital does not change quickly, and that it is best measured over decades in order to be assured that changes have occurred and are substantial. This claim needs to be considered from a range of perspec-tives. For instance, does a traumatic effect such as a flood or war, have a short-term or long-term effect on sense of security in a community or a nation? Is it possible that a deliberate intervention to change the quality of social capital and possibly access to existing social capital, leads to measurable change within the normal policy cycle of about five years? Putnam (2000: 417) advocates many data collection points over time to confirm trends, and claims that real change takes decades. To test this we need surveys that have been administered regularly and over a long period of time.

The timeframe of relevance to funding and policy-making bodies is political watersheds. Politicians would most likely be interested in whether the change in government policy has had an effect before the next election. Therefore, surveys that provide time-sequenced data prior to and since a government formed will be sought. There are likely to be significant dates in policy making that will be important. Critical elements of policy change need to be identified. For instance, in the field of education in Britain these might include the ending of the selective eleven plus examination in England at the end of primary schooling and the introduction of integrated community schools in Scotland. Other policy initiatives would include changes in labour market policies.

Over time, respondents will change in two ways. First people who we follow longitudinally will change as they age, especially when there are life transitions such as children leaving school. Second, we may get responses from different people in the same community on different occasions. These types of change are normally managed by using stratified random sampling. However, it is not possible to anticipate or measure all possible changes in community characteristics. For instance, members of one ethnic group may tend to relocate to live with children as they age, and members of another ethnic group may tend to live at home alone.

Comparisons over time within a community may be possible, and comparisons of trends between communities are likely to be informative. Putnam also raises the question of whether absolute or relative changes are important. We need to be careful about how we interpret our data. Putnam (2000: 418) points out that the reliance on proportions (relative) rather than absolutes is particularly an issue when levels of education have changed across a community over time. If we try to control for the effects of educational level on social capital variables, we may have two problems. First, the proportion that complete twelve years of schooling has increased in most developed countries. This may reduce the value of a high school diploma in the labour market, but does it follow that the value of schooling is reduced in terms of social capital outcomes? Secondly, if a broadening of the curriculum has been employed, does this enhance sorting and streaming for post-school destinations, and consequently reduce the benefits of completing secondary schooling for those in some of the so called non-academic streams?

Measuring community social capital

At the level of a community, there is interest in the way in which support can be provided for the well-being of citizens. Both in Australia and in Britain there have been government initiatives that have sought to improve economic and social opportunities for deprived local communities. It is generally assumed that such initiatives are likely to be more successful than overall national approaches, both because they can achieve a whole government approach to complex prob-lems, and because if they achieve local commitment the initiatives may be more sustainable. These initiatives have inevitably included an evaluation but these tend to be by people commissioned by those responsible for the funding of the project who might have an interest in securing a favourable outcome (Johnson et al. 2003).

One approach to measuring community social capital is to utilise national indicators by analysing at the level of census collection districts. One concern has been that such use of national indicators may mask variation within a community. In a study of social well-being, Johnston et al. (2004) have compared the factor loadings on social indicator sub-scales at various collection area aggregations from areas of about 500 people to 3,000. They conclude that for many indicators factor loadings increase with size, some remain static and very few decline. In the former group they include indicators such as long-term sickness and sole-parent families, while an exception was outright home ownership. This supports concerns about blurring of variability, since the smaller aggregations make it possible for differences to be more easily detected.

An attempt to measure social capital constructs at the community level, described by Onyx and Bullen (2000), concluded that there were significant differences in the structure of five sub-scales derived from a 34-item scale when applied separately in five rural Australian communities. This suggests that at least in terms of their indicators, social capital was not a stable construct across different communities. If the forms of social capital are different in communities with different average economic circumstances, then this instability in factor structure for components of social capital would be a predictable outcome. It might be explained, for instance, if poorer families relied more on bonding (we look after our own) while more affluent families are more independent of their immediate neighbours and use linking social capital to facilitate their access to materials and opportunities. However, Onyx and Bullen (ibid.) also reported a single general underlying factor that explained half the variance. It was in the sub-scales that the variability was observed.

The Victorian Government in Australia has invested considerable effort in enhancing and in monitoring what it calls community strength, and justifies this by pointing to the relationships between various indicators and outcomes in education, public health and economic performance (Broad 2003). A framework of three levels of indicators has been described (Pope 2006) for monitoring community strength. The first level is described as personal networks. This broadly equates to the concept of bonded social capital and is operationalised by evidence of getting help from family or neighbours. The second level is described as associational or community networks and broadly equates to the concept of linking social capital. It is operationalised by participating in community events, volunteering and being members of clubs or other community organisations. The third level is termed government networks which is described as access to power, institutional resources and information and includes holding office in community bodies. Although this does not equate precisely with the notion of bridging social capital, a connection can be drawn in the sense that access to governmental networks might include access to people who can make decisions of benefit to an individual and the community in which they live.

A different approach to measuring community social capital that is more comprehensive than the national approach outlined above has been described by Cock et al. (2006). What they term as 'community capacity' is an audit procedure for use by community planners to identify the strengths and areas of need in a community. The tool is meant as a procedure for capacity building and as such is not designed for comparative research. The five components are community involvement (strength); shared attitudes; resources and infrastructure; social networks; and social co-operation (termed social capital). Interestingly, they recommend that in gathering data informants be asked to identify the importance of each element, and their confidence in their assessment. These qualifications on estimations may prove useful in making effective use of indicators of social capital for policy development and implementation.

Measuring individual social capital

Within any social context different individuals make different use of community agencies. Individual social capital can be defined as the capacity of an individual to access and to generate social capital. This may be a different construct from community social capital, but it is a valuable notion, especially if individuals can learn this capacity. In considering the issue of deprivation in Scotland, Bailey et al (2003: 39) recommended that a measure of individual deprivation be developed as a priority. They point out that individual measures need to be based on surveys of individuals, rather than area statistics. They concluded that relating individual and area measures may provide useful insights into deprivation (Bailey et al., 2003: ii). It follows that similar insights could be gained by relating area and individual measures of social capital.

Social capitals in education research

One field of public policy where social capital could be expected to have a significant effect is in education. For example, in research into the provision of adult education it is recorded that middle-class people avail themselves of learning opportunities more frequently than do disadvantaged people, including opportunities that are targeted at people in need.[1] In addition, in research into school industry links, writers have identified that success depends on a champion in the community and another in the school, who form a link and lead their respective communities in engagement (Purnell and Catts 2000).

In school-based research it may be useful to consider multiple categories of social capital, and to refer to social capitals. The first category is the family unit which is one part of what Pope describes as close personal networks. Within the context of schooling, it is a problematic construct, both because a family unit can fracture, and because the scope of a family unit may differ in systematic ways across ethnic or social class. For instance, if people from three generations live in the same accommodation, people who otherwise would be classed as relatives might better be included in the family unit. Nonetheless, it seems useful to identify the family 'unit' as a category of social capital. In extreme cases, some people belong to no family unit, or have at best tenuous access.

A second category of social capital is the neighbourhood. I define neighbourhood social capital as the connections with the people in the physical area where the person lives. If one lives in a block of flats with a single entrance, or in a particular street, there are people one cannot avoid. This may be a positive or a negative characteristic and so neighbourhood social capital could be a positive or negative value. This form of social capital is also defined by Pope as part of close personnel networks. However the distinction is necessary because the family unit may hold different norms and values to those of others in the immediate neighbourhood.

A third category of social capital relevant to the school is community social capital, defined by the organisations that one volunteers to join. This category is defined by Pope as part of associational and community networks. These groups could include choirs, sporting teams and gangs. Some might have a formal constitution and others might be informal but coherent groups. These groups can contribute both positive and negative social capital, if one defines this concept in terms of enhancing or restricting access to opportunities to achieve socially and politically acceptable outcomes from schooling. People have a capacity to belong to more than one community group, and the number of voluntary community memberships may be correlated with social class (Horvat et al. 2003). It is possible to have separate community social capital elements with different values and directions of social capital. There are other community organisations to which one does not necessarily belong by choice. For instance, young people may be obliged by their family to attend a particular church, or be expected to support a particular sporting club. Again, one could be a member of one or more such groups, and each might offer hierarchical or distributed forms of social capital.

Another category of social capital is institutional social capital. This is another form of what Pope described as associational and community networks. It might include the place where one works or goes to school. For unemployed people, it is the Government Offices where one is obliged to register to claim and maintain benefit payments. There is a degree of obligation to be part of institutional social capital and there are limited choices. Most people work where they can get a job, and many young people and especially those from poor families, have little choice about where they go to school. In this regard it is possible that the quality of institutional social capital is related to affluence. The poor often have just one option, the benefits office, a limited range of marginalised jobs, or the local government school. This lack of choice in schooling may influence the way a young person approaches education. In addition, the access to advantageous social networks will be related to the nature of the school, and the networks available to others attending the school. This can in turn affect access to work, both while at school, and as a destination after leaving school.

These categories of social capital that impact in the school context illustrate the complexity of the measurement tasks required to undertake quantitative research to inform public policy. To address the complexity outlined above, a multivariate and multi-level research model is required to explore both the relative contributions of various forms of social capital and to seek for interaction effects among various forms of social capital. If economic capital and forms of cultural capital are included in the model, as well they may need to be, then large scale longitudinal or cross-cohort studies are necessary to make effective use of quantitative methods.

The point of exploring the influences of social capital in a schooling context would be to establish the relationship with outcomes of schooling, and there are multiple outcomes of which attainment is but the most publicised. Other outcomes include a commitment to lifelong learning and the skills to do so, citizenship, and acceptance of social norms and values. In the area of attainment, it is known from a wide range of research evidence that instructional interventions normally produce small effects (Hattie 1992). The reason for such small effects is the cumulative nature of school-based learning over many years, and the complexity of the other variables that impinge on outcomes. If, as Putnam argues, changes in social capital also take long periods of time, then interventions in the quantity or quality of available social capital, or changes in the capacity of individuals to access available social capital, may result in similar small effects. Therefore the tools used to measure social capital will have to be sensitive to changes in social capital that may be small relative to the full range of social capital across the broad community. If the distribution of scores on social capital indices is relatively small, the restricted nature of the variance will impinge on the capacity to detect changes for people in the most disadvantaged groups.

The approach of considering multiple forms of social capital extends the method adopted by Coleman who underlined the significance of parental social capital for outcomes of schooling. He argued that social capital develops when families are linked to each other in networks including school networks, which share and reinforce common values. 'Intergenerational closure' results when parents get to know the parents of their children's friends and the result of this is 'a set of effective sanctions that can monitor and guide behaviour, and a set of rules and expectations for the child in and out of the home' (Coleman 1988: 107). He argued for instance that parents show high levels of trust and shared responsibility when taking and collecting their own and others' children from school and looking after them as appropriate. The message is that the community as a whole is important in creating social capital, and Coleman contends that the wealth of community social capital has an impact on educational outcomes.

Conclusion

In summary, and drawing on the views of Stone (2001), the requirements for using quantitative indicators of social capital succinctly are as follows:

- Recognition that social capital is a multidimensional concept comprising networks of social relations characterised either by coercion or by norms of trust and reciprocity.
- An understanding that each of these dimensions must be measured in a comprehensive and valid investigation of social capital.
- A conceptual and empirical distinction between social capital and its outcomes, facilitating unambiguous research design which may properly inform upon the relationship between social capital and other factors.
- Avoidance of mistaking a range of factors/outcomes that may be related to social capital for measures of social capital itself.

- Research which is able to explain how the forms of social capital relate to one another, as well to how these relate to competing explanations of outcomes.

Social capital is a term that embraces a set of constructs about networks of norms and values that impact upon the effectiveness of economic performance and on the ways in which social institutions operate, normally to transmit economic advantage, and exclusive forms of cultural capital. Hence it is important to understand the complexity of how social capitals operate in order to appreciate the ways in which effective community development can lead to economic opportunities.

To make effective use of quantitative methods to help understand social capital, we need a comprehensive elucidation of the nature of social capitals and we then need the development of measurement models that accommodate multi-factor latent variables that provide indicators of the complex nature of social capitals. These measurement tools might then be applied using multi-level multivariate statistics to better inform both research and especially policy formation and administration.

Note

1   This has prompted some to urge saturation supply as the most effective way to meet the needs of disadvantaged people. The argument is that once the middle-class needs are satiated, opportunities will be accessible to those who would otherwise be excluded (Paterson 2003).

References

ABS (2004) *Measuring Social Capital: An Australian Framework and Indicators*, Information Paper 1378.0, Canberra: Australian Bureau of Statistics.

Allard, A. (2003) 'Capitalizing on Bourdieu: how useful are concepts of social capital and social field for researching marginalized young women?', *Theory and Research in Education*, 3(1): 63–79.

Bagnall, G., Longhurst, B. and Savage, M. (2003) 'Children, belonging and social capital: the PTA and middle class narratives of social involvement in the North-West of England', *Sociological Research Online*, 8(4); located March 2007 at: http://www.socres online.org.uk/8/4/bagnall.html.

Bailey, N., John Flint, J., Goodlad, R., Shucksmith, M., Fitzpatrick, S. and Pryce, G. (2003) *Measuring Deprivation in Scotland: Developing a Long-term Strategy Final Report*, Scottish Centre for Research on Social Justice, Universities of Glasgow and Aberdeen.

Bourdieu, P. (1993) *The Field of Cultural Production*, Oxford: Polity Press.

Broad, C (2003) 'The Victoria Government agenda for building stronger communities', paper presented to The Centre for Public Policy, Melbourne University, 9 Sept., at: http://www.neighbourhoodrenewal.vic.gov.au (see related papers).

Bryk, A.S. and Schneider, B. (2002) *Trust in Schools: A Core Resource for Improvement*, New York: Russell Sage Foundation.

Cock, G., Keele, L., Cheers, B., Kruger, M. and Trigg, H. (2006) 'Measuring community capacity: an electronic audit template', Beechworth, Australia, proceedings of APEN

International Conference, March, at: http://www.regional.org.au/au/apen/2006/refereed/1/2896_cockgj.htm.

Coleman, J.S. (1988) 'Social capital in the creation of human-capital', *American Journal of Sociology*, 94: 95–120.

Coleman, J.S. (1990) *Foundations of Social Theory*, London: Belknap Press of Harvard University Press.

Feinstein, L. and Hammond, C. (2004) 'The contribution of adult learning to health and social capital', *Oxford Review of Education*, 30(2): 199–221.

Gamarnikow, E. and Green, A.G. (1999) 'The Third Way and social capital: Education Action Zones and a new agenda for education, parents and community?', *International Studies in Sociology of Education*, 9(1): 3–22.

Hattie, J. (1992) 'Measuring the effects of schooling', *Australian Journal of Education*, 36: 5–13.

Horvat, E., Weininger, E.B. and Lareau, A. (2003) 'From social ties to social capital: class differences in the relations between schools and parent networks', *American Educational Research Journal*, 40(2): 319–351.

Johnson, D., Headey, B. and Jensen, B. (2003) *Communities, Social Capital and Public Policy: Literature Review*, Melbourne Institute Working Paper No. 26/03, Melbourne: University of Melbourne.

Johnston, R., Jones, K., Burgess, S., Propper, C., Sarker, R. and Bolster, A. (2004) 'Scale, factor analysis and neighbourhood effects', *Geographical Analysis*, 36(4): 350–368.

ONS (2001) *Social Capital: A Review of the Literature*, London: UK Office of National Statistics, at: http://www.statistics.gov.uk/socialcapital/down loads/soccaplitreview.pdf.

Onyx, J. and Bullen, P. (2000) 'Measuring social capital in five communities', *Journal of Applied Behavioral Science*, 36(1): 23–42.

Paterson, L. (2003) *Scottish Education in the Twentieth Century*, Edinburgh: Edinburgh University Press.

Pope, J. (2006) *Indicators of Community Strength: A Framework and Evidence*, Melbourne: Department for Victorian Communities.

Purnell, K. and Catts, R. (2000) *Implementing VET in Remote Schools*, Brisbane: Education Queensland.

Putnam, R.D. (1993) *Making Democracy Work: Civic Traditions in Modern Italy*, Princeton, NJ: Princeton University Press.

Putnam R.D. (2000) *Bowling Alone: The Collapse and Revival of American Community*, New York: Simon and Schuster.

Putnam, R.D. and Feldstein, L. (2000) 'Better together', Seminar on Civic Engagement in America, at: http://www.bettertogether.org/pdfs/ FullReportText.pdf.

Scottish Executive (2004) *A Curriculum for Excellence*, Edinburgh: Scottish Executive, at: http://www.scotland.gov.uk/Resource/Doc/26800/0023690.pdf.

Stone, W. (2001) *Measuring Social Capital: Towards a Theoretically Informed Measurement Framework for Researching Social Capital in Family and Community Life*, Research Paper 24, February, Adelaide: Institute of Family Studies.

Chapter 3

What *should* count as 'evidence' for effective 'situated policy'?

Ian Falk[1]

> To have a policy is to have rational reasons or arguments which contain both a claim to an understanding of a problem and a solution. It puts forward what is and what ought to be done.
>
> (Parsons 1995: 15)

Parsons's quote above points a finger at the real problem with policy and its implementation in Western polities today. The problem is that we have been, and remain, focused on the nature of the policy itself, and the evidence for justifying its existence. Yes, this is important, but it is only part of the story. The bigger part of the story, which remains largely ignored, is about 'rational reasons' and 'arguments' as to how the policy is (a) actually developed, (b) framed in the policy documents and structures so as to maximise its impact and sustainability, (c) implemented, and (d) concurrently evaluated along a number of 'measures' of effectiveness. Such a narrow focus on 'having a policy' as opposed to the remainder of the policy process does, however, explain why we have to date been more preoccupied with evidence for justification as opposed to evidence for the larger, and arguably, most important part of policy – its enactment.

The theoretical and conceptual framework underpinning this chapter is based on ethnomethodology's (Sacks 1963; Garfinkel 1967; Heritage 1984, for example) requirement for the unit of analysis as interactivity, as opposed to individual activity, and on the requirement for empirical accountability in interactivity between people, objects and places where interactivity occurs. In this normatively and empirically based theory of social action, structures such as a bonding tie are constructed in the process of interactivity, and structure and process are mutually constituted. Falk and Kilpatrick (2000) built on this to form a new theory showing *how* the ways the mutual constitution of structure and process through interactivity could be seen as *learning* interactions, since it is through interactions that knowledge and identity resources are drawn on, and through this process social capital is built and used. This latter strand of research shows how learning can involve a process of building social capital, which links to this book's wider purpose of demonstrating the connectedness between social capital, learning and place management.

This chapter focuses on the role and nature of evidence in policy formation and evaluation processes. Experience over the last 20 years with policy-related research in Australia has shown that policy personnel draw on a mixture of qualitative and quantitative research in about equal proportions. Moreover, it has been shown that, even when a research funding body has rhetoric that explicitly values quantitative over qualitative research, it nevertheless has a publicly demonstrable track record of being influenced strongly by qualitative (including case study) research outcomes, often over and above the influence of quantitative evidence (Falk and Guenther 2006: 1). The exploration of this point raises the issue of the legitimacy of qualitative research as being able to provide governments and the public (as partners in policy) with a strong evidence base that supplements or indeed replaces quantitative evidence through its variety of rich data. While quantitative data is often useful in providing part of the necessary background to a policy case, it does not provide vital information concerning the ways in which policy effectively reaches its target groups.

Policy is developed by people, for people, and for people who live in a particular place at a particular time. *Effective* policy is always and irretrievably *situated* socio-culturally and historically and is the product not of individual effort (as sometimes seen), but rather of the interactivity between those individuals at various levels in the bureaucratic hierarchy, and between these personnel as well as more (and less) implicated stakeholders of that policy. That is, policy is the product of interactivity between people, places and things, and effective policy is the product of particular kinds of interactivity that, in other research, we define using social capital elements (Wallace and Falk 2006). Agency for effective policy development, implementation and evaluation lies in the interactions between people and their places. People are the targets of effective policy, yet the 'people' and 'place' element is often ignored – not intentionally, but nevertheless to the detriment of the policy's effectiveness. Strong empirical qualitative methodology that takes seriously the interactive element of effective policy (that which accounts for social capital) can provide strong evidence for effective policy (Knight and Falk 2005). This points also to the crucial, practical and strategic role of categories of experience in identity formation (individual, group and place) via interactivity, in all aspects of the policy process.

The adoption of the unit and focus of analysis as interactivity as opposed to individual action alleviates the need to reconcile issues of macro versus micro social order (since the micro interactivity constructs and re-constructs the macro), and the measurement issue. Regarding the latter, it seems that existing measurement attempts are restricted to social capital at a macro level and disregard local level data on interactivity. This chapter supports the view that, if the qualities and profile of local interactivity are able to be gauged in the first instance, we are in fact (a) measuring genuine *social* capital formation (as opposed to only the individual capacity portions that are assumed to result from those events), and (b) assuring that the processes will indeed achieve the hoped-for outcomes, since the outcomes are observable in the process of their production. This component of the research also adds to the attention on the building of social capital and what is required/involved for its effectiveness (sought by Cox 2006; Woolcock 2006), as well as critiques of unsuccessful policies from the impact of lack of interactivity, or their 'top-down' nature (Hugonnier 1999, for example).

Coherent connections between policy, 'evidence', social capital, learning and place

Whilst Keynesian advocacy for government intervention in the economy during periods of economic slumps has been diminished, the argument that government interventions should be based on rational decision-making process, knowledge and reasoned experiment (Parsons 1995: 170), providing an evidence base, remains prominent in the contemporary practice of government. What is an 'evidence base' and how is it applied in the public policy context? Which aspects of the policy process should evidence be used to guide? That is, given the often political imperative for statistical or quantitative rhetoric to justify political actions, what, in fact, *does* contribute to policy effectiveness, and what evidence *should* be used to support policy action in its various stages of intervening in the lives of people? The three sections that follow – evidence base, social capital and policy – form an argument about the necessary nature of evidence-based research.

'Evidence-based' research

Evidence-based research has emerged as an essential ingredient in the public policy process of Australian and other governments across the breadth of portfolio areas. Evidence-based research has its foundation in the healthcare work of Cochrane. His argument was that healthcare resources would always be limited and properly designed evaluations are required to discriminate between them (Cochrane Collaboration 2005). Historically, the drafting and enacting of government legislation, through a government's policy intent, did not necessarily reflect the 'evidence', particularly with regards to the alignment of policy, programme and adequate fiscal appropriation for underpinning a policy's effectiveness (Simon 1970: 195). In the current period, the notion of evidence-based research is proving attractive to policy makers, including both executive government and bureaucracies, in policy justification, formation and accountability processes within the limited resource context of contemporary governments. Questions remain around two main points: the selectivity of evidence for specific and politically motivated policy decisions, and the degree to which the notion of 'evidence base' is used rhetorically to convince audiences about a policy's integrity compared with the actual use to which evidence has been put in such cases.

However, as Wallace and Falk's (2006) research shows, evidence is required for each and every stage of the policy intervention cycle if that policy is to be effective. As can be seen from the above overview, however, most evidence bases gain their credibility and use to support the *need* for a particular policy *rhetoric*, and have so far not paid attention to the nature of the evidence required to *develop, implement* and *evaluate* policy. It is important, even vital, to pay attention to the full policy intervention cycle for two reasons: (a) because policy is the whole of the policy intervention cycle, not just the justification at its inception, and (b) to ensure its effectiveness and sustainability once implemented.

The reality is, however, that the use of evidence-based research is still fraught, given various complexities that arise in government decision making, and a simple reliance on numbers. A basic survey (Knight and Falk 2005) about the uses of evidence in a government department found that three levels of commentary are distinguishable about understandings of the term 'evidence-based research'. At the lower level of workplace classification, quantitative research data is reported as comprising 'evidence' as opposed to qualitative research. It appears that the lower level personnel of the government bureaucracy who responded possess a generalised understanding of 'evidence-based research' as 'statistical rhetoric'. This understanding is confirmed by statements such as 'evidence-based research within a government department is based on validation or evidence'; and by their reference to it being a 'hypothesis', backed up by 'evidence of statistics'.

Middle management showed a more descriptive understanding of the term, using terms such as: 'measurable', 'quantifiable', 'real data', 'statistical data', 'measurable evidence', 'database extracts', and so on. Such views of what constitutes the 'evidence base' rhetoric within a bureaucracy may have their origins in the timelines imposed by senior executive and/or executive government, where the ready availability of a set of numbers obtainable on a website provides an immediate source of 'evidence' for justifying a policy's direction, and for the preparation of ministerial documents which are required within an urgent timeframe (perhaps in response to a 'hot' parliamentary debate or media issue).

At the senior executive level, the majority of the responses received were much more likely to demonstrate more than a simple statistical understanding of the term 'evidence-based research'. One person provided detailed understanding of evidence involving qualitative and quantitative components. This is the level of government where 'peak' advice is provided to executive government. It might be expected that there would be a common understanding on the part of all senior executives in regard to the application of evidence-based research. However, there was no clear single understanding of what evidence-based research is. One senior executive was non-committal in providing a written comment. Another response reconstructed the question into a statement, and provided no substantive definition of evidence-based research. Yet another response provided a more complex and analytical understanding of evidence-based research, recognising it as both quantitative and qualitative. The main conclusion drawn from the differences in responses of the three levels of the bureaucratic workforce was that the more engaged in policy and its development and implementation the workforce is, the greater is the diversity of understandings of the rhetorical term, 'evidence-based research'.

In most cases, reliance on (or rhetorical commitment to) 'quantitative' discourse stems from societal conceptions of 'real science' as somehow involving only numbers. The 'magic' of a number – a percentage or digit of some kind that is easy for the media to pick up and report – lies at the core of the acceptance of the elevated status of numbers. However, the impact on governments of 'people power' through elections in a climate where election results are becoming increasingly 'marginal', is causing a closer attention to the effectiveness with which policy impacts on the grassroots level.

Social capital and identity

From long experience, it seems that research on effective social action, from both 'ends' of the activity spectrum – policy and providers working at grassroots level – has been missing a serious focus on interactivity which is the genuinely *social* capital component – the 'people power' referred to in the above section – as opposed to the *individual* human capital element. Falk and Kilpatrick (2000) proposed that effective social action is the product of both individual capacity or resources (called, for the sake of comparison, human capital) and identity resources. While identity was established as being central to effective social action, additional research into its precise nature and impact was not conducted until the early 2000s.

In this context, 'place-identity' is a key dimension of the overall construct of 'identity', that is, essential to consider in relation to effective policy making: it is the interactivity between policy/people/places that is central for policy-personnel and those for whom policy is intended to provide outcomes. Place-identity is centrally relevant to effective social processes that we call learning and the outcomes that can be achieved through learning for individuals, communities and organisations. When people interact – learning occurs through interaction (Falk and Kilpatrick 2000) – they interact with both human and non-human elements of their entire environment. Place is the physical setting component of that environment and, as Korpela (1989: 246) explains, attachment to place or 'place-belongingness' is the basis for place-identity.

Evidence-based information or data sought by government for policy formation without consideration of qualitative research of place-identity may ignore the 'people' element of public policy and diminish the social capital fundamentals of such public policy, particularly within a regional identity context. 'Places', Sarbin (1983: 339) explains, serve as 'contextual markers for establishing one's social identity'. Proshansky et al. (1983: 74) conceive place-identity as:

> . . . clusters of positively and negatively valanced cognitions of physical settings. The substantive and evaluative natures of these cognitions help to define who and of what value the person is both to himself and in terms of how he thinks others view him.

Rather than place-identity being just one aspect of identity, Twigger-Ross and Uzzell (1996: 206) argue that 'all aspects of identity will, to a greater or lesser extent, have place-related expectations' and conclude that the 'environment becomes a salient part of identity as opposed to merely setting a context in which identity can be established and developed' (ibid.: 218).

In contrast to the focus on self taken by most theorists of place-identity, Dixon and Durrheim (2000) theorise place-identity using discursive approaches to social psychology. They state that places in environmental psychology and human geography are being 're-conceived as dynamic areas that are both socially constituted and constitutive of the social' (Dixon and Durrheim 2000). This approach views place-identity as a social construction 'that people create together through talk' rather than a personal construction of the individual.

As a result of the existing research on identity on which this chapter draws, Table 3.1 (Falk and Balatti 2003: 185) provides a schema that was developed to summarise the range of identity dimensions from the various strands of research noted above that are implicated in policy. According to Falk and Balatti (ibid.), the

Table 3.1 Dimensions of identity in social activity

Processes applied to experience	Categories of experience for identity (sources)		Identity	Resources produced from the processing of experience
Interacting and storying through	Individual	Group	Place	
Anticipating	Age	Class	Buildings	Behaviours
Choosing	Appearance	Communities	Built environment	
Creating	Education	Consumer		Beliefs
Evaluating	Health	Ethnicity	Climate	
Experiencing	Name	Family	Dwellings	Feelings
Feeling	Physicality	Gender	Geography	
Performing	Sexual orientation	Language	Institutions	Knowledges
Redefining		Occupation	Landscape	
Remembering	Spirituality	Profession	Natural environment	
Talking about	Time	Religion		
Thinking	Voice	Work	Neighbourhood	
			Workplaces	

Processes column describes the interactive or 'doing' dimension of identity formation, reformation and co-construction that occurs in learning. The list points to some of the more significant ways in which the two key processes of identity building – 'storying' and interacting in the present – take place. The next three columns – Individual, Group and Place – show the categories of experience from which identity resources are generated by the processes listed in column one. The last column identifies the different categories of identity resources that are called on and/or generated in learning through the processes of interacting and 'storying'.

Identity is conceived of in the research reported above both as a resource drawn on by public policy makers, and as an output of those policy processes. In other words, effective policy will engage various identity resources of people and their places, and provide mechanisms for identity to be built in positive ways through the policy, so enabling a longer-term, 'sustainability' component to the policy process. It is important therefore to relate the elements of identity to practical ways of identifying and analysing data where elements of the discourse of policies are identified as having components of identity involved in their enaction.

Policy

Public policy and political science literature over the past 50 years or more has been described as what governments do, why they do it and what difference it makes (Dye 1976: 1). Lasswell (Lester and Stewart 1996: 5) views policy as a projected programme of goals and values and practices of government, whilst Anderson views it as a 'purposive course of action followed by an actor or set of actors in dealing with a problem or matter of concern' (Stewart 1999: 52). Stewart adds policy as representative of government's political executive, where engaging in public policy is expected to ultimately achieve an outcome (Stewart 1999: 52). Dye refers to public policy as both an art and a craft, in that as an art, policy-makers require insight, creativity and imagination in identifying problems, describing them and thence devising and analysing public policies which might alleviate such problems. Dye further contends that policy is therefore a craft, as it requires tasks to be undertaken which require knowledge of economics, political science, public administration, sociology, law and statistics (Dye 1987: 8).

Whilst such scholarly definitions of public policy are rich in description, to the layperson policy is not necessarily viewed as an action at all or a form of complex activity that undergoes extensive political, community, bureaucratic or academic processes. For those to whom policy is targeted, the relationship between policy and outcome as a contemporary requirement of government does not necessarily come to mind. To the wider community, public policy is viewed merely as a label or term with no discriminating aspects and understandings of inputs, outputs and outcomes (Stewart 1999: 52).

Notwithstanding this gulf between the policy maker and the public's understanding and application of the policy cycle, public policy in a government context is a process of social influencing by government for targeted purposes which impact or influence people, with its formation originating from possible multiple sources. The sources may originate from an election commitment, a party platform position or reaction to a lobby group or the international influence of diplomatic or trade considerations. However, one point remains constant: with few exceptions, governments expect and plan for their policies to actually reach the target groups, although it is often difficult to tell this from the way they behave. By this, I mean that the way governments go about implementing their policies (which have often been developed rigorously) lacks attention to the profile of stakeholder groups, the places the stakeholders inhabit, and the most effective means of engaging the policy stakeholders in the implementation and, by extension, sustainability of the policy outcomes.[2]

Public policy is undoubtedly government action developed by people for people. In the main, public policy is fundamentally what governments choose to do or not to do. However, with regards to social capital, it is the people element that provides the agency for such public policy development, implementation and evaluation, and it is people who are its target. With the people element in mind, contemporary governments are 'outcomes focused' and require 'evidence' for policy formation and implementation. Governments require their bureaucracies to measure a policy's activity in the form of a reportable outcome, that is, evidence or validation of a policy's success or failure, for both internal and external audiences – the public. The challenge is how to understand policy effectiveness in a way that will enable policy to become more effective to more people. This requires a more comprehensive understanding of the whole policy process.

Situated policy: using the qualitative–quantitative divide to policy effectiveness

Taking the 'outcomes focus' seriously, Wallace and Falk (2006) explore the relationship between social capital and policy effectiveness. They find that the

> . . . social capital discourse provides a means of enabling policy effectiveness. It does this by providing an articulation of previously unrecognised or implicit enablers of policy effectiveness.
>
> (ibid.: 1)

Wallace and Falk base their research around the four main stages (Falk 2003) of a social intervention, namely: (1) Trigger Stage, (2) Initiating Stage, (3) Developmental Stage, and (4) Management and Sustainability Stage. These four stages can be used to explore how all policy stakeholders relate to the structures or networks involved. The whole of this dynamic is overviewed in Table 3.2. By making explicit the link between policy as a structure, and the processes required for its effective development, implementation and evaluation, the connections are therefore made between the 'rhetorical' significance of policy and its enactment in real life contexts in an effective and sustainable way.

Table 3.2 Synthesised principles and their criteria (Wallace and Falk 2006: 19)

Principle for policy effectiveness	Capacity building	Structures (networks)
Principle 1: *Effective policy depends on understanding the dynamics of at 'the local' level*	• Jointly develop project detail	• Scopes of Works for project documentation should detail project requirements intervention stage
Principle 2: *Gaining benefits from policy depends on engaging the intended recipients: inclusive and consultative processes are slow, but they pay off*	• Develop common understandings of jointly used terms • Nature, duration and frequency of interactions and with a spread of participants	• Nature of structures (for example, IDCs [*interdepartmental committees*], working parties, etc.) will emerge from process and embed a diversity of interactions from informal to formal
Principle 3: *Continuity of resources, including structure and personnel, provides short- and long-term sustainable success*	• Audit through meetings and consultations the human, economic and social resources available to the intervention	• Produce audit document (could be 'progress report', for example) from previous process • Personnel have time in field, work across layers horizontally and vertically where possible (or this is the criteria for hiring)
Principle 4: *Ensure 'market forces' are supplemented by resourced capacity-building*	• Policy personnel, project team and providers to work in to develop criteria to ensure policy will reach target group/s	• In tender processes (e.g.), ensure criteria are built in so that respondents can apply for resources to build capacity to put in full application down the track
Principle 5: *Policy cycle effectiveness requires availability and responsiveness of an evidenciary base. This includes continuous and iterative evaluation of individual projects*	• Review appropriate evidence base for all levels of project	• Establish appropriate evidence base for all levels of project

Conclusion: situated policy in (inter)action

The purpose of this book is to explore and demonstrate the connectedness of social capital, lifelong learning regions and place management, and to explore the implications for policy research. This chapter has been founded on the theoretical assumption that, ultimately and irretrievably, these items are connected through each and every interaction that occurs between people, their places and the technologies with which they interact, such as computers. In these interactions, people bring to bear their identity resources related to themselves as individuals, and to the groups and places to which they affiliate. Their identity resources are produced from four categories of experience, namely behaviours, beliefs, feelings and knowledges. They apply to their experiences, processes such as anticipating, choosing, talking, story-telling, debating, evaluating and so on. When people interact, whether the interactions are over the development of policy, or at the other end where people discuss the merits of a policy intervention that they become aware of, they simultaneously bring their identity resources to bear on the situation, while at the same time evaluating how the policy implications 'fit' with their identities. If policy processes explicitly account for identity formation and re-formation, they will both reach target stakeholders more effectively and be taken up 'on the ground' resulting in greater sustainability.

The practical means for developing policy that accounts for identity is to apply the five principles of effective policy by embedding opportunities for inter-action (communication) in the *structures* comprising the policy (such as the policy documents and role descriptions of personnel) and *capacity building* interactions (learning interactions between key personnel and stakeholders) at each of the four stages of a policy intervention, namely: (1) Trigger Stage, (2) Initiating Stage, (3) Developmental Stage, and (4) Management and Sustainability Stage. Evidence for the effectiveness or success of the policy will therefore be related to the outputs and outcomes of processes and structures at each of these four stages. Importantly, the nature of the 'evidence' required to demonstrate policy impact and effective-ness will depend entirely on the question to be answered. For example, this could be a question we need to answer: *What is it that contributes to this policy's effectiveness or otherwise?* To answer this question, we would ask what kinds of evidence might assist in doing so. Some of the evidence may indeed be quan-titative – for example, we may need to know how many people had been aware of a new policy at Stage 1 of the intervention, as an indication of the policy's market penetration. This information would be important also at Stage 4, as would evidence of a qualitative nature about *why* there were different levels of awareness at different stages. Additional qualitative evidence may help answer the question by informing us as to the nature and capacity of the different non-governmental organisations – information vital to any policy success yet neither quantitative nor usually made explicit in policy.

Interactivity can be seen as a 'flash' word for communication. It is through communication that the jobs of policy development, implementation and evalua-tion get done. The focus on interactivity (as opposed to individual action) has been surprisingly simple to apply in practical and complex policy situations (two of these are described in detail in Wallace and Falk (2006)). Conceptually, this focus on communicative opportunities (interaction) avoids the usual discussions about macro versus micro issues: for example, by focusing on communicative interactivity, where and how it happens and should happen according to each of the four stages of an interaction, we automatically encompass or account for research areas such as 'governance', 'sociology', 'psychology', 'management' or indeed 'anthropology'.

Interactivity *is* the social mechanism whereby identities are simultaneously brought to light, used and re-constructed/altered/confirmed. Macro structures are only relevant as they provide the opportunity for specific and specified interactions designed to facilitate communication between stakeholders about the policy. Interactions are where those macro structures are brought to life (for example, a policy Working Party is only a name unless it meets regularly and interacts meaningfully over policy issues). Positive interactions that bring about change (policy implementation, for example) are defined as learning (Falk and Kilpatrick 2000; Falk 2006). This kind of learning relies on both identity and knowledge resources appropriate to the purpose of the stage of the intervention. This learning process whereby social capital is simultaneously used and built links with the issue of measurement – in the broader sense – in social capital debates: measuring a refined and abstracted entity we choose to call 'social capital' has limited value in that it does not assist understanding of what makes effective policy work. By measuring (or *evaluating* using appropriately designed formative evaluative methodologies) the quality and quantity of interactions that best meet the purpose of each of the four stages of the situated policy intervention process, we provide an evidence base that is fit-for-purpose.

Notes

1 I would like to thank Scott Knight, a PhD candidate, for his considerable work on an earlier version of this paper. Some of the original material remains, and the Knight and Falk (2005) paper formed the basis for one of the forming ideas here, that of the role of evidence in policy-making spheres.
2 Exceptions to government desire for policies to reach stakeholders could cynically be assumed to fall into the category of 'the devil is in the detail': as an example, perhaps a government may wish to show the public that they *have* a policy which *sounds* good, but make the detail so difficult to comply with that the allocated funds can never be taken up.

References

Cochrane Collaboration (2005) *The Cochrane Collaboration: The Reliable Source of Evidence on Health Care*, at: http://www.cochrane.org/docs/archieco.htm.
Cox, E. (2006) 'The ethics of social capital', paper presented at Australian Social Sciences Academy forum, Social Capital and Social Justice: Critical Australian Perspectives, Brisbane, Australia at Queensland University of Technology (QUT), July.

Dixon, J. and Durrheim, K. (2000) 'Displacing place-identity: a discursive approach to locating self and other', *British Journal of Social Psychology*, 39(1): 27–44.

Dye, T.R. (1976) *What Governments Do, Why They Do it, What Difference it Makes*, Tuscaloosa: University of Alabama Press.

Dye, T.R. (1987) *Understanding Public Policy*, Englewood Cliffs, NJ: Prentice Hall.

Falk, I. (2006) 'Essence of engagement: social capital in workplace learning', in R. Gerber and G. Castelton (eds) *Improving Workplace Learning: Emerging International Perspective*, New York: Nova Science Publishers Inc.

Falk, I. and Balatti, J. (2003) 'Role of identity in VET learning', refereed paper in conference proceedings for Enriching Learning Cultures: 11th Annual International Conference on Post-compulsory Education and Training, Queensland, 1–3 December, Centre for Learning Research, Griffith University, pp. 179–186.

Falk, I. and Guenther, J. (2006) *Generalising from Qualitative Research: Case Studies from VET in Contexts*, at: http://www.voced.edu.au/docs/confs/ncver/vetconf15/tr15guenther.doc.

Falk, I. and Kilpatrick, S. (2000) 'What *is* social capital? A study of a rural community', *Sociologia Ruralis*, 1(40): 87–110.

Garfinkel, H. (1967) *Studies in Ethnomethodology*, Cambridge: Polity Press.

Heritage, J. (1984) *Garfinkel and Ethnomethodology*, Cambridge: Polity Press.

Hugonnier, B. (1999) 'Regional development tendencies in OECD countries', keynote address to Regional Australia Summit, Parliament House, Canberra, October.

Knight, S. and Falk, I. (2005) 'Qualitative research legitimacy: what counts as "evidence" for policy makers and researchers working together?', Making Knowledge Work, 3rd International PASCAL Conference, University of Stirling.

Korpela, K.M. (1989) 'Place-identity as a product of environmental self-regulation', *Journal of Environmental Psychology*, 9: 241–256.

Lester, J. and Stewart, J. (1996) *Public Policy: An Evolutionary Approach*, Minneapolis, MN: West Publishing Co.

Parsons, W. (1995) *Public Policy; An Introduction to the Theory and Practice of Policy Analysis*, Aldershot: Edward Elgar.

Proshansky, H., Fabian, A. and Kaminoff, R. (1983) 'Place-identity: physical world socialization of the self', *Journal of Environmental Psychology*, 3: 57–83.

Sacks, H. (1963) 'Sociological description', *Berkeley Journal of Sociology*, 8: 1–16.

Sarbin, T. (1983) 'Place-identity as a component of self: an addendum', *Journal of Environmental Psychology*, 3: 337–342.

Simon, H. (1970) *Administrative Behaviour: A Study of Decision-making Processes in Administrative Organisations*, London: Collier Macmillan.

Stewart, R. (1999) *Public Policy: Strategy and Accountability*, Melbourne: Macmillan.

Twigger-Ross, C. and Uzzell, D. (1996) 'Place and identity processes', *Journal of Environmental Psychology*, 16: 205–220.

Wallace, R. and Falk, I. (2006) 'Social capital, higher education and policy performance', paper presented at Australian Social Sciences Academy forum, Social Capital and Social Justice: Critical Australian Perspectives, Queensland University of Technology (QUT), Brisbane, July.

Woolcock, M. (2006) 'Reflections on proceedings', paper presented at Australian Social Sciences Academy forum, Social Capital and Social Justice: Critical Australian Perspectives, Queensland University of Technology (QUT), Brisbane, July.

Chapter 4

Governance and community strengthening
A case study from Victoria, Australia

Michael Hess and David Adams

Introduction

From the mid-1990s and building on experiences from the community development strategies of the 1960s and 1970s, community-based approaches to policy making and implementation have been adopted in many market-oriented democracies as governments have tried new ways of addressing the complexity of their tasks. The link between governance models and the likelihood of place-focused policies succeeding in particular areas was noted as a characteristic of this trend by European commentators (Geddes and Benington 2001). More recently, Considine's review of approaches over the last decade in European countries (2004a, 2004b) identified both the wide range of differences between the approaches used and the unevenness of their success. Despite this variety, his review finds that governance factors, that is to say the ways in which the links between people and institutions are established, are constantly crucial components of success. This is especially the case in respect of how local institutions and partnerships build networks which facilitate local level co-operation. This chapter explores the ways in which research can assist with the formation of government policies which facilitate the kinds of partnerships and networks which enable community strengthening.

For government, the changes required for a successful community strengthening policy can be divided into structural, instrumental and work culture/skills changes. Structural changes include: roles for the community sector; a role for local government as the steward of community strength; moves away from the programme format; and the organisation of democratic decision making within the policy function. The emerging problem here is that, in general, it is hard to see how departments based around centralised decision making and expert knowledge, with an institutional interest in defending 'their' territory, can succeed as *bona fide* partners in community strengthening. In terms of the instruments required to give community strengthening the greatest chance of success, we need to be thinking about the barriers presented by annual budgeting, fragmented grants, the planning fetish and the obsession with short-term monitoring and reporting. We also need to consider the opportunities we have at hand in instruments like output budgeting and community consultation. Challenges in the area of work culture and skills are more subtle. Here the entrenched orientation of many agencies towards public choice reasoning has had the effect of devaluing local knowledge and undermining the idea that public administration is about service. On one hand, in whatever form it takes, the cult of the expert undermines the possibility of effective community strengthening because it devalues knowledge from outside the circle of bureaucrats and consultants. On the other, market-oriented instruments, while strong on cost signals, are weak on community service.

For communities there are also serious challenges if community strengthening is to be made to work. One is the issue of sustainability. For any community the effort–reward balance of engagement with policy processes must be demonstrably positive if it is to be sustainable. So connections into local institutions which bring additional resources into the community are important. Another is the nature of leadership and involvement in the community. If there are too few activists in a community the work of engaging with policy processes and implementation will fall too heavily on too few people. Distributed leadership and broad engagement is necessary to spread the burden. Finally there needs to be tangible, and probably economic, benefit to the community to convince people that the cost of maintaining their involvement is worth their while.

At State level in Australia, all governments now have a department, unit or minister responsible for community development. Victoria was the first to embark on this process and has the most developed whole-of-government community-based approach. Two broad areas of interest have emerged from this experience. One is the actual experience of implementing community strengthening as a central policy in the State of Victoria. This has been evident in prominent policy documents (Victoria 2001), as well as in the establishment of and research undertaken by the Department for Victorian Communities (DVC) (Hess 2003; DVC 2004a, 2004b, 2005a, 2005b, 2006). The other is the need for some serious thinking about the coherence of the ideas underpinning the practices. Without a systematic thinking through of its fundamental principles and implications, community strengthening runs the danger of becoming no more than a passing policy fashion. If such coherence can be achieved, however, it may be possible to build the practices we are now observing into something genuinely new and valuable in addressing the increasingly complex problems of contemporary government in market-oriented democracies.

The practice: community strengthening in Victoria

In the Victorian government's policy approach of the last five years, the nexus between community strengthening and governance has increasingly emerged as a significant factor in the likelihood of policy success. Considerable experience and action research now make it possible to understand how governance contributes to making community strengthening effective and what this implies for the future shape of public administration. The key governance issues which have emerged from this practice are:

- the understanding that what makes a community strong is connectivity and it is networks which create the connections linking individuals and social institutions,
- the understanding that the relationship between such local level activity and central government processes needs to be based in partnership and co-operation.

DVC has sought to capture this in its definition of community strengthening as creating sustained networks through local-level partnerships involving key stakeholders and community representatives to achieve agreed policy and service delivery outcomes (Blacher 2005). At one simple functional level, then, community strengthening describes an approach to policy aimed at increasing the number of people who participate. The ideas which have underpinned this and the instruments which made it possible provide answers to the questions of 'why?' and 'how?' community strengthening has emerged as a whole government approach in Victoria.

In terms of ideas, Victoria's community-based policy approach began with the realisation that communities, be they of location or interest, are important for the simple reason that they are where people live their lives. This has a series of implications for government, not the least of which is that communities, of location and interest, shape both the perception and reality of government services. Mounting international evidence that strong communities are better able to look after their members and to access and use services has now been borne out in Australian research. For example, Vinson's Victorian study demonstrates that community strengthening interventions can drive a wedge in the cycle of disadvantage. This study found that children born into communities with low social cohesion (networks) had high school drop-out rates. Those born into disadvantaged communities with high social cohesion had much lower drop-out rates. The study also showed a link between communities with high levels of early school leaving, low social cohesion and imprisonment. Similar disadvantaged communities with high levels of early school leaving but with high social cohesion had low levels of imprisonment (Vinson 2004).

In terms of instruments, community strengthening describes an approach to policy aimed at increasing the number of people who participate. While participation is hardly a new phenomenon, its application in the processes of administration today is different in fundamental respects. The Victorian government, for instance, has a long history of working with communities, starting back as far as the 1970s with initiatives such as Neighbourhood Houses, Disadvantaged Sites, and AA Plans, while in the 1980s, Community Health, Landcare, the Rural Women's Network and the rural Employment Networks were important policy initiatives involving community-based participation. The differences in the contemporary policy settings are about both quantitative and qualitative factors. Not only are huge resources being put into the approach (the current *A Fairer Victoria* programme is costed at $780 million), but it is a thorough, whole government policy setting which makes it fundamentally different from the silo-based, project or programme delivery under which most public administration has operated for the last 100 years.

While a whole government level commitment is essential to providing policy coherence and mainstreaming, it is not the level at which the benefits of community strengthening as a strategy for delivering outcomes is clearest. Nor is it the level at which the connections between basic values, governance processes and the potential of community strengthening as a policy approach are most evident. The evidence to support the contention that local level co-operation builds stronger communities which in turn create the preconditions for effectively addressing complex policy problems comes, not unnaturally, from the locality level itself. In particular the relationship between building trust, the new governance models and the likelihood of successful community strengthening is reflected in the academic commentary (Alford 2004; Considine 2004c; Wiseman 2004) but is also evident in the published work of practitioners (ABS 2000; Klein 2004; Trewin 2004).

The evidence: measuring community strengthening

While measurement is hardly new to administrative science both the type of measure and the impact of measurement for community strengthening make it an especially crucial activity. The immediate context in which measurement of community strengthening has taken place has been the need to balance economic and social factors in public administration. Under new public management practices, policy makers and public managers became adept at measuring. This added vital hard data to the public administration knowledge base and made measurement instruments *de rigueur* for government at all levels. One practical problem has been the tendency for measurement to be based around *outputs* rather than *outcomes*. From the Key Performance Indicators (KPIs) of specific jobs to the project or contract completion criteria of particular work units, measures may focus on what is being done rather than on what impact this has had. Community-based knowledge has the potential to address this because it is in communities that we see the results of policies. Furthermore, in democratic systems based on residential electorates, it is in communities of location that votes get counted. Community-based measurement has clear potential for decision makers in terms of political sustainability because unlike the National Performance Measures (NPMs) it can tell us how particular communities are affected by and are reacting to policy outcomes.

Even where the importance of community-based impact measures are accepted, however, measuring or even defining what they are in respect of particular policy areas is not simple. The definitional difficulty of confusing outputs and outcomes has already been mentioned. A further need for definitional clarity is called for by the need to differentiate those social capital factors which lay the foundation for community capacity and the institutional arrangements which facilitate and/or hinder efforts to transform capacity into outcomes. So definitions need to take account of both the capacity factors and the means by which it can be turned into action which is effective in terms of policy.

Community strengthening and the future of public administration

DVC has defined strong communities as those endowed with social, economic and environmental assets and organisational structures that work towards their sustainable use and equitable distribution (DVC 2004b). In developing practical ways of bringing community into policy processes in Victoria, it has become evident that there is a causal connection between the strength of particular communities and the nature and extent of their members' engagement in community activities. Because of this, DVC has moved to measure the concrete activities of community engagement rather than the more abstract idea of community strength. Engagement activities have two advantages in terms of measurement. The simple one is that because these are activities which can be observed they are more easily measured than an abstraction like community strength. The subtle one is that the action of measurement itself adds status to engagement in general as well as to the particular activities which are being measured. It does this by focusing attention on the fact that the activities have significance beyond their immediate objectives and that this is of importance for the way in which contemporary public administration seeks to balance fiscal and social objectives. Beyond the actual impacts of measurement, engagement activities are significant in assessing the potential of community strength as part of policy processes because they create connectedness and build networks. These characteristics of connectedness and networks within communities are, as we will see in the next section, fundamental underpinnings of the governance of the community–government interface. So some of the DVC indicators of community strengthening describe the outcomes of connectedness such as community safety, feeling there are opportunities to have a say, tolerance of diversity and the ability to get help when needed. Others focus on the forms of participation that enhance social connectedness and lead to local network formation.

International and Australian research findings show that the benefits of participation extend to personal and collective well-being reflected in: better physical and mental health; higher educational achievement; better employment outcomes; lower crime rates; decreases in maltreatment of children; and an increased capacity for a community to respond to threats and interventions (Coleman 1988; Vinson et al. 1996; Porter 1998; Berkman and Glass 2000; Lin 2001; OECD 2001; Szreter and Woolcock 2004). Overall, this body of research claims that community engagement diminishes the impacts of social disadvantage. Specifically in Victoria, the 2003 *Community Adversity and Resilience Report* (Vinson 2004) showed that social cohesion, measured by participation in sport and ability to get help when needed, is associated with lower levels of negative social outcomes such as increased rates of imprisonment and early school leaving. The association between participation and physical well-being noted internationally (Young and Glasgow 1998; Berkman and Glass 2000) is also reflected in the DVC findings (DVC 2004b, 2005a). So participation also has an independent positive effect on health (Young and Glasgow 1998). Given the weight of research opinion, it is hardly surprising to find that governments are trying many practical ways to enhance citizen participation as a means of addressing the specific problems and priorities of local areas (Coleman and Gotze 2001; Gilchrist 2004).

A recent DVC research report, *Indicators of Community Strength at Local Government Area Level in Victoria* (DVC 2005a), builds on the previous work of the *Indicators of Community Strength in Victoria* report (DVC 2004b). The latter took time series data relating to 11 indicators of community strength from the Victorian Population Health Survey and applied it to four Local Government Areas (LGAs). The 2005 report adds to this by examining the indicators of community strength across all 79 LGAs in Victoria. It includes four new indicators not included in the first report: parental participation in schools; participation in organised sport; participation on decision-making boards and committees; and liking the community in which you live.

From the viewpoint of developing better public administration practices, the capacity to measure this engagement is a vital activity for two reasons. First, community engagement cannot be legitimised as part of the mainstream of policy making and implementation unless it is measurable. This is the case because measurement enables decision makers to see the impacts of policy and to feel confident that its outcomes translate into community support. Second, because this measurement makes the connection between policy objectives and outcomes explicit, it provides a bridge between government and community. The problem of communicating the objectives of policy and establishing that the policy works is thus brought into the lives of people in ways which enable them to see its efficacy from their direct experience. In this sense, measurement becomes a central issue by connecting the process (community engagement) to the outcomes (improvements in implementation in crucial policy areas). The actual connecting point is through indicators which can demonstrate both process (e.g. rates of participation) and outcomes (e.g. improvements in safety and well-being). The DVC experience of the communities agenda in government then points at the same time to the hard realities of measurement as a practical issue in policy, and to this particular subtlety the act of measurement can bring to the government community interface. The Victorian experience shows that the act of measuring community engagement adds value to the policy process. The subtle value in measurement in this case is that the indicators can also build a bridge between the theoretical abstractions (e.g. that community engagement is democratic) and the practical reality (that we really need to know what a particular community wants/needs). The desired result is a better understanding of the policy agency of community and the ways in which public administration might need to change to promote community-oriented policies.

The DVC research agenda around community engagement seeks to reveal the nature of the gap between what residents feel their communities need and how they feel government is responding to these needs. It is increasingly bringing together three themes. Firstly, the focus on indicators of community engagement is providing real knowledge upon which to base continued learning both for public administrators and community players. These indicators have been used in the published and internal documents upon which this chapter is based (DVC 2004b, 2005a, 2005b). Secondly, the indicators themselves are throwing new light on central problems of policy which have been overlooked in the recent past. These particularly include the risk and protective factors associated with social well-being and economic prosperity. The use of these indicators is providing us with an increased ability to compare the links between community and individual/family strength. Thirdly, evidence is emerging on how 'governance' factors intermediate both family and community level dynamics. While it is taken up in the following section, it is worth noting here that DVC research now uses local government area boundaries to organise data. This is because of the insight that the robustness and outlook of local institutions – and how they choose to organise – is a key determinant of community strength.

In the DVC experience, then, measurement of community engagement has been important in clarifying the nature of community as a part of policy. It has also played a significant role in helping develop understandings of the characteristics of particular communities. The fact that these characteristics vary greatly makes this local-level research important if policy impacts in particular locations are to be really effective. Measuring at a community level also has the potential to reveal actual outcomes in ways at which we've previously only been able to guess. This enables policy makers to have a degree of certainty about the impact of allocating resources and particularly about how to target those allocations to maximise their real impact in the lives of people.

While efforts to develop more effective measures and to use them as part of policy process can tell us a lot about what is happening and how it is happening, they do little to address the deeper questions of why new practices are gaining momentum. In the case of community strengthening, this is compounded by the fact that there is as yet no single catchy title under which the changes in public administration described above can be conveniently grouped. There is, however, an argument that they do represent a fundamental change in the way in which government does business. While many of the ideas behind the practice are old, the ways in which they are being brought together and their implications for the structures and skills demanded of public administration indicate that there is room for an argument that they represent fundamental change for two reasons. First, the underpinning concepts which are legitimising the changes are so different from those they are superseding and are establishing a new set of meanings in public sector activity and the way in which it fits into society. This is underpinning the ways in which the knowledge being used in public policy and management is altering (Hess and Adams 2002). In broad terms this may be seen as a shift in the approach to knowledge from positivism to constructivism. This change is significant for the way in which we go about the business of government in many of its aspects because under it the drivers of activity and the judgements about the efficacy of that activity shift from being located within the processes of government to being located in the relationships between government and communities of location and/or interest. The second element of paradigm shift in the contemporary public policy and management is that the new concepts are proving powerful in illuminating issues of public policy and management which have proven impervious to orthodox understandings and instruments. In particular, it may be seen as a response to deficits in NPM outcomes.

One implication is that rather than being a discourse resistant to external ideas, because they represent sectional interest, public administration increasingly becomes involved in an active search for new interpretive ideas and instruments because they reflect the experience of particular policy communities. So in episte-mological terms traditional positivist approaches describe problems and identify the knowledge required to address these. They then either develop that knowledge within the processes of training bureaucratic experts or import it in the form of hired expertise. In an alternative constructivist approach, policy work actually interprets and constructs the meanings of the ideas and what constitutes usable knowledge about the ideas in any given policy area. Rather than searching for the 'right' definition of such ideas and applying objective knowledge to the rational pursuit of ranked goals, the constructivist approach posits that policy networks and the discourse within the networks constitute policy and policy commences with struggles over the meaning of ideas. These include the basic constructs of what constitutes the 'objective' or the 'rational' knowledge in particular policy areas. A partial conceptualisation of the difference is that the fundamental questions of positivist public administration are about 'what': what is the problem? What is the relevant expertise? What is the cost? On the other hand, those under a constructivist approach are about 'how': how can the appropriate people be involved? How can new knowledge be created? How can this be used in the particular policy setting?

Conclusion

Community has come into public management in a relatively unsystematic way. Because it has lacked a single coherent body of theory to underpin it, there is a possibility that it will remain just a series of isolated instances of clever practitioners solving problems they encounter in their daily operations. The experience of the communities agenda in Victoria indicates that there is more potential in these changes than *ad hoc* problem solving and that adopting a constructivist approach to the knowledge base of the new practices provides both clues to understanding its significance and to systematising its practice. Among the practical implications are issues of how the skills and organisation of public administration work need to change to generate and make best use of this new knowledge. If government is to integrate community concerns into policy making, public servants will need the skills required to 'put oneself in another person's shoes and build trust' (Davis and Rhodes 2000: 96). Some work on linking the theory of what needs to be done with the practical issues of how to do it is already happening in Australia (Hess and Adams 2002; Reddel 2004), but more is required.

In summary, the move towards a community focus in public policy and management implies a straightforward logic of change. In order to address the non-linear complexities confronting policy makers in market-oriented democracies, we need non-linear structures, non-positivist knowledge and non-rational (not irrational!) ways of working. In the experience of community strengthening we are seeing the beginnings of what this might mean for the future of public administration.

References

ABS (Australian Bureau of Statistics) (2000) *Measuring Social Capital: Current Collections and Future Directions*, discussion paper, November, Canberra, at: http://www.abs.gov.au/websitedbs/D3110122.NSF/0/6CD8B1F3F270566ACA25699F0015A02A?Open.

Alford, J. (2004) 'Building trust in partnerships between community organisations and government', paper presented at the Conference on Changing the Way Government Works, new interests – new arrangements, Melbourne, 5 October.

Berkman, L.F. and Glass, T. (2000) 'Social integration, social networks, social support, and health', in L. F. Berkman and I. Kawachi (eds) *Social Epidemiology*, Oxford: Oxford University Press.

Blacher, Y. (2005) 'Changing the way government works', speech given to Engaging Communities 2005, United Nations Conference, Brisbane.

Coleman, J.S. (1988) 'Social capital in the creation of human capital', *American Journal of Sociology*, 94: S95–S121.

Coleman, S. and Gotze, J. (2001) *Bowling Together: Online Public Engagement in Policy Deliberation*, London: Hansard Society.

Considine, M. (2004a) *Building Connections: Community Strengthening and Local Government in Victoria*, Melbourne: Department for Victorian Communities.

Considine, M. (2004b) *Community Strengthening and the Role of Local Government*, Melbourne: Department for Victorian Communities.

Considine, M. (2004c) 'Stronger communities through improved local governance: an idea whose time has come?', paper presented at the Conference on Changing the Way Government Works, new interests – new arrangements, Melbourne, 5 October.

DVC (Department for Victorian Communities) (2004a) *Changing the Way Government Works: New Interests, New Arrangements*, Melbourne: DVC.

DVC (2004b) *Indicators of Community Strengthening in Victoria*, Melbourne: DVC.

DVC (2005a) *Indicators of Community Strength at Local Government Area Level in Victoria*, Melbourne: DVC.

DVC (2005b) *Indicators of Community Strength in Melton: A Discussion Paper for the Caroline Springs Partnership*, Melbourne: DVC.

Geddes, M. and Benington, J. (eds) (2001) *Local Partnership and Social Exclusion in the European Union – New Forms of Social Governance?*, London: Routledge.

Gilchrist, A. (2004) 'Developing the well-connected community', in H. McCarthy, P. Miller and P. Skidmore (eds) *Network Logic: Who Governs in an Interconnected World?*, London: DEMOS.

Hess, M. (2003) 'Governance and knowledge in the post-market state', *Canberra Bulletin of Public Administration*, 109: 33–36.

Hess, M. and Adams, D. (2002) 'Knowing and skilling in contemporary public administration', *Australian Journal of Public Administration*, 61(4): 68–79.

Klein, H. (2004) 'Neighbourhood renewal: revitalising disadvantaged communities in Victoria', *Public Administration Today*, September/October: 20–29.

Lin, N. (2001) *Social Capital: A Theory of Social Structure and Action*, Cambridge: Cambridge University Press.

OECD (Organisation for Economic Co-operation and Development) (2001) *The Well-being of Nations: The Role of Human and Social Capital*, Paris: OECD, at: http://www1.oecd. org/publications/e-book/9601011E.PDF.

Porter, M.E. (1998) 'Clusters and the new economics of competition', *Harvard Business Review*, 76 (6): 77–90.

Reddel, T. (2004) 'Exploring the institutional dimensions of local governance and community strengthening: linking empirical and theoretical debates', paper presented at the Conference on Changing the Way Government Works, new interests – new arrangements, Melbourne, 5 October.

Szreter, S. and Woolcock, M. (2004) 'Health by association? Social capital, social theory, and the political economy of public health', *International Journal of Epidemiology*, 33: 1–18.

Trewin, D. (2004) 'How do we measure community strength?', paper presented at the Conference on Changing the Way Government Works, new interests – new arrangements, Melbourne, 5 October.

Victoria (2001) *Growing Victoria Together. Innovative State. Caring Communities*, Melbourne: Department of Premier and Cabinet.

Vinson, T. (2004) *Community Adversity and Resilience: The Distribution of Social Disadvantage in Victoria and New South Wales and the Mediating Role of Social Cohesion*, Melbourne: Jesuit Social Services.

Vinson, T., Baldry, E. and Hargreaves, J. (1996) 'Neighbourhoods, networks and child abuse', *British Journal of Social Work*, 26(4): 523–543.

Wiseman, J. (2004) 'Community strengthening . . . opportunities, limitations, challenges', paper presented at the Conference on Changing the Way Government Works, New Interests – New Arrangements, Melbourne, 5 October.

Young, F. and Glasgow, N. (1998) 'Voluntary social participation and health', *Research on Aging*, 20(3): 339–362.

Chapter 5

Community efficacy and social capital

Modelling how communities deliver outcomes for members

Sue Kilpatrick and Joan Abbott-Chapman

Background to the research: difficulties in measuring the impact of community social capital on well-being outcomes

For over half a century, since the pioneering Peckham Experiment in central London (Pearse and Crocker 1943), there has been a growing body of evidence linking a community's social sufficiency, self-help and social cohesion with improved mental and physical health and general 'well-being' outcomes of its members (Eckersley 1998). However, despite countless studies over the years, establishing causal links between community social capital and community members' well-being outcomes has proved exceedingly difficult. For example, recent reports from the United Kingdom have shown the impact of positive social interactions and social support on young people's mental health and well-being (Edwards 2003), but, at the level of area level data, findings on the contribution of social capital indicators to defined health outcomes are inconclusive (Mohan et al. 2004). Social capital, what it is and what it does, is notoriously difficult to measure (National Statistics 2001; Productivity Commission 2003) but the policy imperatives for finding measured evidence of such a link, as the key to community capacity building, are increasing. The OECD (1999, 2001) and National Statistics (2001), all note the link between socio-economic outcomes and social capital. Policy makers are looking to research to establish 'what works' in terms of social policy interventions, and social, education and health service delivery; how to intervene in communities effectively and how to work with communities through community participation and community capacity building (Reddel 2002).

We contend that the way in which these elements interact within any community may be modelled within a multidimensional framework with standardised 'elements', in such a way that the 'strong' and 'weak' points in the structure may be identified. A 'diagnostic tool', which brings together research capacity and local knowledge of community residents, will assist community members and policy makers alike in identifying points at which timely intervention will achieve desired community goals (Kilpatrick et al. 2003; Kilpatrick and Abbott-Chapman 2005).

In this chapter we present work in progress on our model of community efficacy and associated measurement matrix as applied to health and well-being outcomes data in two small rural communities in Tasmania, Australia. In this context, community social capital represents processes of social interaction producing particular community outcomes, rather than as an outcome in itself, and hopefully clarifies some current confusion on this point (Fenton et al. 2000: 118). The development of our interactive model of community efficacy grew out of our attempts, through a series of Australian rural community studies, to address those problems or weaknesses that we see as inherent in much of the body of work on social capital over recent years. These are, in brief: variations in definition and application of the concept of social capital in different social contexts; difficulties in identifying and measuring community inputs and outputs along a range of well-being dimensions; inadequate attention to the contribution made by community institutions to community social capital; shortcomings in identifying the weak as well as strong points in the structure of social capital; under-estimation of the unequal distribution of access to community social capital and lack of attention to community inequalities and power structures; and inability to satisfactorily meld 'local knowledge' with 'research expertise'.

Just a few comments in elaboration will explain what we mean. In a World Bank publication (Woolcock and Narayan 2000), and the OECD's examination of the relationship between human and social capital (2001), social capital has been defined as the shared information, norms, values and social networks that enable people to work together to achieve beneficial outcomes for the collective. These and other international studies reveal that there are many different definitions of social capital which may vary across case studies, but that most recognise the importance of positive social networks, trust and mutual support (all in themselves however presenting problems of measurement and cultural variation).

Despite many attempts to do so, it is widely recognised that social capital is notoriously difficult to measure in relation to a range of economic, social and well-being dimensions (ABS 2001a, 2002). The Australian Bureau of Statistic's social capital framework (ABS 2004a) conceives social capital as the aggregation of individuals' outcomes and perceptions. This approach undervalues the contribution of community institutions to community social capital, and so to outcomes for individual members. The challenge is to unravel the impact of elements which make up the community infrastructure and those which make up community resilience, belonging and solidarity as they interact together to produce development or decline. In short, a dynamic element which takes account of a community's past, present and future is necessary.

The need to take account of shortcomings as well as strengths in community capacity to deliver outcomes for community members is also evident. The nature and quality of opportunities and access to resources, for example, are unequal since communities are not socially homogenous and some groups have manifestly more social and/or economic power than others. Community 'can look very different depending on where one is sitting' (Walter 1997: 72). Therefore, the differential capacity of various groups within the community to access opportunities, information and social networks and participate (Herbert-Cheshire 2003) must also be fully factored into the social capital equation. Models and measures of community social capital must take into account the diversity of the community, its sub-groups and sub-cultures and the potentially unequal access of groups and individuals to the community social capital.

Our own research suggests that it is highly possible that 'community' social capital may exclude some groups. This is the 'dark' side of social capital referred to by Putnam (2000). Groups excluded from aspects of community social capital are likely to be excluded from related social and economic well-being. In addition, research has shown that provision by government of facilities and services within a community, such as health services and educational institutions, will not ensure take up, effective utilisation and community benefit. Models need to be able to identify the degree of social and physical access to facilities and resources as integral components, and usually cannot. The quality of local leadership, and patterns of governance, also have a large impact on each community's capacity to take up social and economic opportunities and to manage change (Gittell and Vidal 1998; Falk and Kilpatrick 2000; National Statistics 2001). Taking into account all of the above factors, it is clear that the degree of social impact and community outcomes will vary from community to community, even with similar infrastructure, and any model of community capacity or efficacy needs to recognise this. Our model has been designed to incorporate all of these features in a multidimensional and dynamic approach which allows for community comparisons.

Developing the model of community efficacy

The concept of 'community activity infrastructure' is a novel addition to thinking about community social capital. This includes the framework of institutional facilities, services and socio-economic resources as applied to specific behaviour settings (Wicker 1991). These are available at different levels in each community, and facilitate and help to shape the social capital interactions and relationships of community members. This concept embeds Giddens' theory of 'structuration'; of structure as 'both enabling and constraining'; and the 'mutual dependence of structure and agency' (Giddens 1990: 69) in seeking to explain the relationships between systems, structures and the interactions of individual actors, in particular communities. Recent research on capacity building for rural health has revealed the important role that is played by 'boundary crossers' in facilitating and enabling the community to maximise political, financial and physical resources (Kilpatrick et al. 2006). The community activity infrastructure acts to enable the development of community capacity, well-being and social capital, through what we have called community efficacy. This concept modifies and applies Bandura's famous concept of individual agency or efficacy (Bandura 1977, 1982) at the level of community. Our model of community efficacy enables the efficacy of institutions (formal and informal) to be assessed as part of the whole. Community efficacy is built through participation in common activities, shared understandings and values, extensive networks (internal and external), previous successful experience of working together where perseverance has been exercised, internal and external partnerships between government and non-government organisations and long-term aims that overlap the goals of the diverse groups involved. Failures, on the other hand, undermine efficacy. Community efficacy reflects levels of social trust in civic institutions (Misztal 1996). Our model allows us to discover community members' own sense of what is good about their own community and what shapes their aspirations for themselves and their children (Abbott-Chapman and Kilpatrick 2001; Kilpatrick and Abbott-Chapman 2002). The views of representative community members as well as panels of experts are thus included in the assessment of dimensions of community activity infrastructure and social capital. The model of community efficacy is best applied in operation as a measurement matrix. We know of only one other recent approach to the measurement of social capital which has similar features to ours in its use of an interactive model, but the elements and inter-relationships are quite different as are the modes of measurement (Cheers et al. 2005).

Applying the community efficacy measurement matrix

The community efficacy measurement matrix relates the structural aspects of community activity infrastructure along one axis and the quantifiable and qualitative elements of social capital along the other. The first dimension encompasses the facilities, services and resources which are available, or the structure of opportunities. It includes the government, community and commercial institutions in the community, the physical and socio-economic resources which provide opportunities for activity choice, interaction and the framing of life chances. The second dimension covers participation, access, diversity, leadership and internal/external orientation as the elements which make up community social capital. Community efficacy is the product of each element along one dimension interacting with each element on the other dimension. 'Raw' data in each matrix 'cell' can be scored so that the level of community efficacy overall may be quantified. The measurement matrix is shown in Figure 5.1.

Indicators are being developed for each cell of the quality of social capital columns in the measurement matrix. These will be drawn from suites of quality performance and benchmarking measures wherever possible. In the health section, for example, the Tasmanian government, through the Tasmania Together initiative, has identified the need for a range of health and well-being benchmarks.[1] The Quality Improvement Council's suite of quality performance indicators for health institutions includes areas such as community participation.[2] The combination of qualitative and quantitative measures and judgements is an integral part of this model, and distinguishes it from purely or mainly statistical approaches.

Community activity infrastructure – Structure of opportunities		Structure access and change		Quality of community social capital					
		Physical and economic access	Indicators of activity growth or decline	Participation, including by sub-groups	Community knowledge, trust, valuing and support	Partnerships and linkages (intrinsic to community)	Partnerships and linkages (extrinsic inc government)	Local leadership, governance and advocacy	Orientation local, national, global
Education and training opportunities	Schools								
	Post-school education and training								
	Structured and informal learning opportunities outside the formal education and training sector								
Commercial activity and employment opportunities	Employers (businesses, government and community services and industries)								
	Job agencies and employment services (government and NGOs)								
	Commercial community services, e.g. banks, post office, shops retail and wholesale, cafes, tourist enterprises								
Health and welfare services and institutions	Medical health services (physical and mental)								
	Community health, welfare and support services and programmes, govt and not-for-profit (including aged care)								
	Allied health services								
Voluntary social groups	Social, arts, cultural and sports clubs								
	Civic, political, business associations								
	Religious/spiritual groups, churches								

Figure 5.1 Measuring community efficacy – structure and agency.

The first stage of the research for the measurement matrix is the gathering of evidence in the form of raw data for each of the elements in the matrix. This evidence is then submitted to independent panels of community members and experts (Edwards et al. 2000), who are asked to evaluate the standing of the community on each of those elements. Once the primary and secondary data for each element have been evaluated they are given a weighted score. The final score in each cell in the matrix summates the community activity infrastructure score multiplied by the quality of social capital score. This is a complex process which we are working to refine. A pilot programme of primary and secondary data collection has been completed in two Tasmanian communities with the aim of identifying, and measuring, elements in the matrix which are most closely associated with health and well-being outcomes. The first stage in the process was the identification of measured health and well-being outcomes which might be expected to be affected by the relative strength of a community's 'efficacy'. Key indicators or outcomes of health and well-being within Tasmania were identified using the national health data library (Department of Health and Ageing 2004). After examination of the literature, nine key indices, which have recognised social correlates, were selected and the rates of incidence were plotted for every statistical area in the whole of Tasmania (population 484,000). These indices are: injuries, poisonings and violent deaths; accidents, excluding motor vehicle traffic hospital separations; accidents, motor vehicle traffic hospital separations; motor vehicle transport accident deaths; attempted suicide or self-inflicted injuries and poisoning hospital separations; intentional self-harm deaths; diabetes mellitus deaths; ischaemic heart disease deaths; cerebrovascular disease – stroke deaths. The rates for each of these indices were then scored 1 to 8 where 1 is 'low' and 8 is 'high' (where low represents a relatively good outcome for community members and high represents a relatively poor outcome for community members). These became the indicative health and well-being outcomes we are seeking to relate to community efficacy.

We hypothesised that if two geographically bounded rural communities of similar size, socio-economic status and access to the nearest regional centre could be found which have widely different health outcomes against these measured indices, then by applying our measurement matrix we would be able to investigate any differences in activity infrastructure and social capital which might help to explain these differences. This chapter shows how we went about this.

Health and welfare data in the case study towns

Tasmania has been chosen as the starting point for our investigations for two main reasons. Firstly, Tasmania has some of the worst socio-economic, education and health indices of the nation (Glover et al. 1999; ABS 2004b), so that finding social 'triggers' for health and well-being is an urgent practical necessity. Secondly, Tasmania has a very active University Department of Rural Health, which is building partnerships in local communities and has set up Rural Health Teaching sites, whose key result areas include development of innovative health service delivery and rural community engagement at many levels (Auckland 2005). Local community collaborations and partnerships are likely to ensure the success of 'bottom up' community consultations. What we discover in the rural communities of Tasmania will form useful models for similar communities throughout Australia, and hopefully in other parts of the world.

The 26 Tasmanian statistical local areas were ranked in terms of their overall scores on all our health indices. A number of possible case study communities were selected which ranked low or high on the indices. These possible choices were then compared for size, access and socio-demographic characteristics, using a modified version of the model of educational handicap (Abbott-Chapman et al. 1991). The two communities chosen, called A (better health outcomes) and B (poorer health outcomes) to preserve anonymity, are of similar size (around 6,000 inhabitants), and are local government area bounded communities about an hour's drive from the nearest regional centre. Despite differences in dominant industry, with Community A's economy largely based on agricultural and pastoral activities and Community B relying heavily on industrial activities, they are closely comparable on a range of socio-demographic indices (ABS 2001b). These include median age (p. 61), median personal weekly income (p. 59), age pensions per thousand (p. 60), youth allowance per thousand (p. 61), unemployment allowance per thousand (p. 61), number of car licences (p. 109) and home ownership (p. 120). Having matched the two communities on key indicators, we feel confident to look for evidence of community efficacy differences which might explain the differences in specified community health outcomes. Community A ranked 1 or 2 on five of the nine indices, and 7 or 8 on none, while Community B ranked 7 or 8 on six indices, and 1 or 2 on only one (injuries, poisonings and violent deaths).

In the first stages of 'raw' data gathering (prior to scoring and scaling), we have focused on the matrix 'health and welfare' sections, and intend to cover all other sections as the research progresses. Firstly, programmes and institutions were identified in the two communities from the internet and publicly available documents. We then examined evidence available from secondary sources that related to the elements in the quality of social capital columns of the matrix which might produce positive health and well-being outcomes for community members. This evidence included detailed local government documents. We found evidence not only about physical and economic access, but also evidence of growth, partnerships between services and institutions within and outside the communities and local leadership, governance and advocacy. It was inevitable that a number of institutions or services would also be represented in other sectors of community activity infrastructure, such as church welfare groups. We noted that multi-dimensional representation of particular institutions or programmes is an expected feature of the matrix and is consistent with the flexible nature of the model.

Discussion of findings and issues to be addressed

A number of similarities between the communities have emerged with regard to the 'community activity infrastructure' of health and welfare services. Both communities have access to a range of medical, allied health and community health and welfare services. Both have developed linkages and partnerships between local organisations and with external organisations. Links with the nearest major population centre are another key feature of both communities, particularly in providing allied health services on a visiting basis and by subsidised transport for access to health services not available locally. Community A has a community care centre that provides residential care, community care, primary health services, community housing and transport. Community B has a well-developed health care infrastructure, including a hospital, council-run community services and an aged care facility.

There are however some key differences between Communities A and B in terms of local leadership and governance. These seem to underline the importance of proactive local leadership and public participation in identifying and meeting local needs, rather than a more compliant community response to services provided by government. Community B relies heavily on state and local government funded community services, which are largely organised by the local council or through the state government hospital. Community A, in contrast, has shown remarkable local leadership and advocacy through forming a group of concerned health professionals and local community members to address previous significant gaps in the provision of health services in the community. This group lobbied the Australian Government Department of Health and Ageing to provide funding to support a new range of services in the community. Despite initial scepticism from the local community, the group developed a significant partnership with a local aged care facility, which has resulted in the establishment of a community health centre providing over 14 new medical, allied health and community services to the region. This leadership and advocacy inspired the local community and many of these services are now provided by local private practitioners. The community health committee considered local needs and worked to meet them, in spite of a lack of leadership from local government. For example, it identified a need for mental health services, a need common to most Tasmanian rural communities. It arranged a link to an interstate 24-hour support service, resulting in a service that is more extensive than that available in other Tasmanian communities, including Community B. An extension of the work would be to interview leaders in both communities and to conduct surveys to evaluate local responses to changes taking place, and then to submit this evidence to community and expert panels.

Published documentary and data analysis so far suggest a difference in social capital between these two communities, and in 'use' of activity infrastructure, which qualitative surveys will need to investigate. While Community B is well organised and has an established health infrastructure, the local community seem mainly consumers of services without being instrumental in identifying and meeting needs in the community. Conversely, Community A has responded to a perceived lack of leadership in the local council by rallying the local community and the Australian government to effect considerable change in their community. The outcome is health and welfare services that appear to have become more closely aligned with identified community needs over time. It is too early to say how this will translate into the measurements within our matrix but findings are suggestive.

Conclusion

We acknowledge the difficulty in proving causal links between community efficacy and health and well-being outcomes, and the demonstration of such links may be a long way ahead. There is also the question of the direction of causation: does Community A have better health outcomes *because* it has a higher quality of social capital? Is the more established health infrastructure in Community B there *because* Community B has poor health outcomes that need to be addressed? However, this raises the question of why Community B continues to have poorer health outcomes, despite its long-established services. Data gathering processes which include established quality performance measures, and perception tools as well community and expert panel evaluations will help us to answer such questions. The conclusions we reach here are suggestive rather than definitive. The purpose of this chapter is to demonstrate the way in which our matrix can be used and developed as a 'diagnostic' tool in examination of complex data to highlight some of these possible connections. Our matrix will help to identify specific elements within communities which strengthen or weaken community efficacy in influencing particular outcomes for their members.

Notes

1 See the Tasmania Together 2020 website, at: http://www.tasmaniatogether.tas.gov.au.
2 See the Quality Improvement Council website, at: http://www.qic.org.au.

References

Abbott-Chapman, J. and Kilpatrick, S. (2001) 'Improving post-school outcomes for rural school leavers', *Australian Journal of Education*, 45(1): 35–47.

Abbott-Chapman, J., Hughes, P. and Wyld, C. (1991) *Improving Access of Disadvantaged Youth to Higher Education*, Evaluations and Investigations Program, Higher Education Division, Commonwealth Department of Employment, Education and Training, Canberra: Australian Government Printing Service.

ABS (2001a) *Measuring Wellbeing: Framework for Australian Social Statistics*, Canberra: Australian Bureau of Statistics.

ABS (2001b) *Regional Statistics: Tasmania*, Catalogue no. 1362.6, Canberra: Australian Bureau of Statistics.

ABS (2002) *Measuring a Knowledge-based Economy and Society: An Australian Framework*, Canberra: Australian Bureau of Statistics.

ABS (2004a) *Measuring Social Capital: An Australian Framework and Indicators*, Canberra: Australian Bureau of Statistics.

ABS (2004b) *Australian Social Trends*, Canberra: Australian Bureau of Statistics.

Auckland, S.R.J. (2005) 'Rural health teaching sites: foundations for innovative rural community partnerships', AUCEA National Conference 2005, Melbourne, pp. 1–20.

Bandura, A. (1977) 'Self-efficacy: toward a unifying theory of behavioural change', *Psychological Review*, 84: 191–215.

Bandara, A. (1982) 'Self-efficacy mechanism in human agency', *American Psychologist*, 37: 122–149.

Cheers, B., Cock, G., Kruger, M., McClure, L. and Trigg, H. (2005) 'Measuring community capacity: an electronic audit template', *Proceedings 2nd National Conference on the Future of Australia's Country Towns*, 11–13 July, Bendigo, Victoria: La Trobe University.

Department of Health and Ageing (2004) *HealthWiz*, Canberra: Department of Health and Ageing.

Eckersley, R. (1998) *Measuring Progress: Is Life Getting Better?*, Collingwood, Victoria: CSIRO Publishing.

Edwards, L. (2003) *Promoting Young People's Wellbeing: A Review of Research on Emotional Health*, Research Report 115, Glasgow: S.C.R.E. Centre, University of Glasgow.

Edwards, R.W., Jumper-Thurman. P., Plested, B.A., Oetting, E.R. and Swanson, L. (2000) 'Community readiness: research to practice', *Journal of Community Psychology*, 28(3): 291–307.

Falk, I. and Kilpatrick, S. (2000) 'What is social capital? A study of interaction in a rural community', *Sociologia Ruralis*, 40(1): 87–110.

Fenton, C., MacGregor, C. and Cary, J. (2000) *Framework and Review Capacity and Motivation for Change to Sustainable Management Practices, Final Report Theme 6*, National Land and Water Resources Audit, Canberra: Bureau of Rural Sciences.

Giddens, A. (1990) *Central Problems in Social Theory; Action, Structure and Contradiction in Social Analysis*, Berkeley: University of California Press.

Gittell, R. and Vidal, A. (1998) *Community Organizing: Building Social Capital as a Development Strategy*, London: Sage.

Glover, J., Harris, K. and Tennant, S. (1999) *A Social Health Atlas*, 2nd edition, Adelaide: Public Health Information Development Unit.

Herbert-Cheshire, L. (2003) 'Translating policy: power and action in Australia's country towns', *Sociologia Ruralis*, 42(4): 454–473.

Kilpatrick, S. and Abbott-Chapman, J. (2002) 'Rural young people's work/study priorities and aspirations: the influence of family social capital', *Australian Educational Researcher*, 29(1): 43–68.

Kilpatrick, S. and Abbott-Chapman, J. (2005) 'Community efficacy and social capital', *Proceedings 2nd National Conference on the Future of Australia's Country Towns*, 11–13 July, Bendigo, Victoria: La Trobe University.

Kilpatrick, S., Abbott-Chapman, J., Williamson, J. and Bound, H. (2003) 'Identifying the characteristics of rural learning communities: implications for rural development', SPERA 19th International Conference, Conference Proceedings, Society for the Provision of Education in Rural Australia, 29 September–1 October, pp. 83–92.

Kilpatrick, S., Auckland, S., Johns, S. and Whelan, J. (2006) 'Building capacity for rural health: the role of boundary crossers in coalition maturity for partnerships with external agents', PASCAL International Observatory Fourth International Conference, Building Stronger Communities – New Learnings, Better Governance, Future Directions, Melbourne, 14 July.

Mistzal B. (1996) *Trust in Modern Societies*, Oxford: Polity Press.

Mohan, J., Bernard, S., Jones, K. and Twigg, L. (2004) *Social Capital, Place and Health: Creating Validity and Applying Small Area Indicators in the Modelling of Health Outcomes*, London: NHS Health Development Agency, at: http://www.hda-online.org.uk/Documents/socialcapital_place_health.pdf.

National Statistics (2001) *Social Capital: A Review of the Literature*, London: Office for National Statistics.

Organisation for Economic Co-operation and Development (OECD) (1999) *Social Indicators: A Proposed Framework and Structure*, Paris: OECD.

OECD (2001) *The Well-being of Nations: The Role of Human and Social Capital*, Paris: OECD.

Pearse, I. and Crocker, L. (1943) *The Peckham Experiment: A Study of the Living Structure of Society*, London: George Allen & Unwin.

Productivity Commission (2003) *Social Capital: Reviewing the Concept and its Policy Implications*, research paper, Canberra: Ausinfo.

Putnam, R. (2000) *Bowling Alone: The Collapse and Revival of American Community*, New York: Simon & Schuster.

Reddel, T. (2002) 'Beyond participation, hierarchies, management and markers: 'new' governance and place policies', *Australian Journal of Public Administration*, 61(1): 50–63.

Walter, C. (1997) 'Community building practice: a conceptual framework', in M. Minkler (ed.) *Community Organizing and Community Building for Health*, New Brunswick, NJ: Rutgers University Press.

Wicker, A.W. (1991) 'Behaviour settings reconsidered: temporal stages, resources, internal dynamics, context', in D. Stokols and I. Altman (eds) *Handbook of Environmental Psychology*, Malabar, FLA: Krieger Publishing Company, pp. 613–653.

Woolcock, M and Narayan, D. (2000) 'Social capital: implications for development theory, research and policy', *World Bank Research Observer*, 15(2): 225–249.

Chapter 6

Identity, local community and the internet

Duncan Timms

Introduction

The relationship between information and communications technologies, especially the internet, and social capital has recently become a topic of considerable salience. Putnam (2000: 180) adopts a neutral position:

> The Internet will not automatically offset the decline in more conventional forms of social capital, but it has that potential. In fact it is hard to imagine solving our contemporary civic dilemmas without computer-mediated communication.

A few writers, in the early days of the internet, suggested that the growth of computer-mediated communications might be at the expense of community involvement (e.g. Kraut et al. 1998). The more general consensus is that the internet augments other means for developing and maintaining social relations. The Pew Internet and American Life Project (2005), reporting on the use of the internet at the end of 2004, concludes:

> The internet enhances social interaction. People use email to deepen their connection to the people they like and love and increase the volume of communication they have with them. . . . The internet is more than a bonding agent, it is also a bridging agent for creating and sustaining community.

Summarising a number of empirical studies, Wellman et al. (2002: 151) report 'that rather than weakening community, the internet adds to existing face-to-face and telephone contact'. Arnold (2003: 83) states that 'for the ordinary citizen, social interaction is the "killer application" of the Internet'. Boase et al. (2006: 43) conclude that, 'the Internet has become part of everyday life – and has broadened our social networks in the process'. This has wide implications, affecting not just social capital, but the very bases of community and identity.

Community and identity

It is part of the symbolic interactionist *credo* that a person's identity is derived from his or her relations with others and from the imagination of the others' perceptions and evaluations. As put by Charles Cooley (1902: 179–185) a century ago:

A social self of this sort might be called the reflected or looking-glass self:

'Each to each a looking-glass
Reflects the other that doth pass.'

As we see our face, figure, and dress in the glass, and are interested in them because they are ours, and pleased or otherwise with them according as they do or do not answer to what we should like them to be; so in imagination we perceive in another's mind some thought of our appearance, manners, aims, deeds, character, friends, and so on, and are variously affected by it. A self-idea of this sort seems to have three principal elements: the imagination of our appearance to the other person; the imagination of his judgment of that appearance, and some sort of self-feeling, such as pride or mortification.

There is a close relationship between personal identity and community identity, encapsulated in the definition of communities as 'networks of inter-personal ties that provide sociability, support, information, a sense of belonging and social identity' (Wellman 2001: 18). Individual identity includes a notion of belonging to a community of people who are similar to the self. The answer to the question, 'Where are you from?' – or, in the Scottish vernacular, 'Where do you stay' – has provided a base for group identification and a label for distinguishing members of one's own group from others. Historically, the friction associated with communicating across time and space has been high and the negotiation of identity has involved interaction with others physically sharing time and space. Propinquity and physical community have been defining elements in the creation and maintenance of identity. The development of electronic means of communication, especially the internet and the mobile phone, has the potential to dramatically weaken the constraints of time and space.

Suttles (1972) has pointed out that the process by which communities come to be identified is essentially the same as that involved in the negotiation of personal identity, involving distinctions from those who are perceived to be different. Suttles pays particular attention to 'defended communities', individuals and groups living in stigmatised urban neighbourhoods who may come together in defensive alliance in order to deal with perceived external threats, emphasising the positive features which set them apart from others.

By the last quarter of the twentieth century it was apparent that developments in communications technology were rendering obsolete the concept of the community as a physically bounded place, characterised by the sort of relationships which early social scientists treated as primary groups. The 'urban mosaic', envisaged by Wirth (1938) and the other Chicago human ecologists, composed of distinct physical neighbourhoods providing a backdrop for differentiated ways of life, has been replaced by a system which owes more to social space than to physical geography. The evolution of new forms of communication that allow time and space constraints to be overcome, notably the internet, has broken the link between interaction and propinquity and provided a new basis for both community and identity. Castells (1996, 2001) outlines the way in which a society based on local communities and other closed groups is being replaced by new social structures which form the 'Network Society'. Wellman points out that in Western society at the beginning of the twenty-first century,

> Communities are far-flung, loosely bounded, sparsely knit, and fragmentary. Most people operate in multiple, thinly connected, partial communities as they deal with networks of kin, neighbours, friends, workmates and organ-isational ties. Rather than fitting into the same group as those around them, each person has his or her own 'personal community'.
>
> (Wellman 2001: 17)

The internet provides a new basis for community, which Wellman terms 'networked individualism'.

> Rather than relying on a single community for social capital, individuals often must actively seek out a variety of appropriate people and resources for different situations.
>
> (Boase et al. 2006: ii)

Trust and online relationships

The development of the internet has greatly increased the possibility for creating and maintaining multiple relationships and their associated identities, some of which may only exist in cyberspace. The growth of computer-mediated communi-cations has accompanied and supported the development of what Anthony Giddens (1991) describes as a more reflexive, individualistic society. To inhabitants of cyberspace, new forms of community based on shared cyberplaces become pos-sible, augmenting or supplanting those based on physical geography. To those who are connected, computer-mediated communications offer the opportunity to search for information, support and affirmation of identity regardless of the constraints of time and space. Much of the information searched for may be trivial, say relating to the time and cost of travel, but other forms of information may relate literally to matters of life and death. Browsing the internet to search for medical information is apparently the second most frequent form of surfing (after searching for pornography and other sex-related activities). Sufferers from rare – or indeed common – medical conditions can check the diagnosis and treatment being suggested by their own physician, seek alternative remedies or seek support from others sharing their experience through joining an online support group.

The ability of users to control what aspects of themselves to reveal makes the internet particularly appealing to those suffering – or believing that they suffer – from potentially embarrassing or stigmatising conditions. As the *New Yorker* cartoon put it: 'On the Web, nobody knows you're a dog.' Equally, nobody need know that you live in a stigmatised area, are a member of a stigmatised racial group, are disfigured, a spotty adolescent – or any other devalued status. Reid (1998: 35) points out:

> The freedom to obscure or re-create aspects of the self on-line allows the exploration and expression of multiple aspects of human existence. The research on virtual communities is filled with tales of masks for age and race, gender and class; masks for almost every aspect of identity.

The freedom of the internet enables people to experiment with self-presentation, but along with the freedom come several dangers. Reid (1998: 35) comments:

> The projection of the self into the virtual has been talked about as freeing the self from the confines of the actual – as opening up possibilities for exploration – as something to be celebrated and embraced. However, these tales do not always have happy endings.

A number of dangers have been identified, ranging from age and gender misrepresentation to instances of 'virtual rape' (e.g. Dibbel 1999). The ability of presenters to control what aspects of themselves to make available on the internet is by no means absolute, but does open up possibilities for deliberate deception or accidental misinterpretation.

Trust on the internet is a fragile commodity. Even when there is no deliberate attempt to mislead, the relative paucity of contextual cues generally available online provides opportunities for the recipients of messages to read in more – or less – than was intended. A related phenomenon is the tendency for participants in online relationships to indulge in behaviours which appear relatively disinhibited when compared with the norms of face-to-face interaction. Disinhibition in emails and other forms of computer-mediated communication may lead to 'flaming' – the expression of extreme views on such matters as gender, race or politics – and is also implicated in the burgeoning field of cyber-pornography. The effects of disinhibition may not always be negative: a positive effect is associated with the success of online self-help groups. There are innumerable self-help groups on the internet, each composed of individuals who share experiences which they might otherwise be loathe to admit and who engage in high levels of self-disclosure. At a lower level of emotional intensity, a similar effect appears in online tutorials, where students who may remain silent in face-to-face classrooms readily participate in discussions in bulletin boards.

Networked individualism allows the individual to maintain and present many disparate images. When the 'looking glass' was comprised of a closely-bound set of others it was difficult to dissemble, when the looking glass is fragmented it may be easy to maintain a number of disparate identities.

Virtual communities

Social relations, whether on- or offline, do not occur randomly. As in 'real' life, interaction online is channelled into more-or-less structured forms, with persistent sets of relations providing the basis for the development of community. In these circumstances, Rheingold (1993: 5) has popularised the use of the term 'virtual community':

> Virtual communities are social aggregations that emerge from the Net when enough people carry on . . . public discussion long enough, with sufficient human feeling, to form webs of personal relationships in cyberspace.

Describing the experience of participating in one of the earliest online communities, the WELL, a text-based bulletin board system run in California, Rheingold (1993: 3) provides a colourful description of life in a virtual community:

> People in virtual communities . . . exchange pleasantries and argue, engage in intellectual discourse, conduct commerce, exchange knowledge, share emotional support, make plans, brainstorm, gossip, feud, fall in love, find friends and lose them, play games, flirt, create a little high art and a lot of idle talk. People in virtual communities do just about everything people do in real life, but we leave our bodies behind. You can't kiss anybody and nobody can punch you on the nose, but a lot can happen within those boundaries.

The essence of community membership is the sharing of a common identity and the development of trust. Membership in one virtual community does not preclude membership in others, or, indeed, in a variety of 'real' communities. The early concerns that people who spend a considerable amount of time on the 'Net may withdraw from other forms of interpersonal contact have found little support in empirical surveys (Fallows 2004; Boase et al. 2006) – apart from a small number of addicted gamers. Membership of virtual communities may be at the expense of watching television and/or sleeping, but does not result in a withdrawal from personal relationships.

> People routinely integrate the internet into the ways in which they communicate with each other, moving easily between phone, computer and in-person encounters.
>
> (Boase et al. 2006: 43)

The internet increases the range of possible social networks that a person can connect to and adds elements of diversity:

Computer supported social networks are not destroying community, but are responding to, resonating with, and extending the types of community that have already become prevalent in the developed Western world.

(Wellman 1997: 185–186)

By providing new avenues for social interaction, the internet has the potential for enhancing social capital amongst the connected (and, conversely, for further impoverishing the non-connected).

Virtual community and local community

Electronic communications may have greatly attenuated the impact of geography on people's experiences, but where someone lives in geographical space still has an effect. Virtual presence has not usurped physical presence for all activities. To let it be known that one lives in one part of a city rather than another, let alone in one country than another, still possesses social relevance. The nature of the relationship between virtual community and local community remains a significant question.

Early writers on the potential impact of the internet on local communities (e.g. Doheny-Farina 1996) believed that the spread of the internet was incompatible with the preservation of strong geographical communities; most later writers have seen electronic communication as being another means for (re-)creating community. Internet users maintain more relationships at both local and distant locations than non-users and have access to more resources for information and assistance (Boase et al. 2006).

The belief that the internet can provide a foundation for strengthening local community provides the mainspring for what has been termed the *Community Networking* movement, devoted to the use of local computer-based networks (or *local nets*) as means of enhancing local identities. It is the emphasis on the local that distinguishes local nets from other forms of online community:

Unlike the similarly named 'on-line communities' or 'virtual communities', community networks are based on a physical place – what participants have in common are their cities and neighbourhoods.

(Beamish 1995)

The coincidence of online and offline relationships characteristic of a local net provides a potent force for the reinforcement of solidarity and community feeling. According to Blanchard and Horan (1998: 293):

social capital and civic engagement will increase when virtual communities develop around physically based communities and when these virtual communities foster additional communities of interest.

The construction of local identity on the 'net

At its simplest, the establishment of a local net may provide a means for (re-)-creating the 'shared ways of thinking, believing, perceiving, and evaluating' that are among the defining characteristics of an integrated community (Broom and Selznick 1977: 56). Etzioni (1998: xiii) defines communities as 'webs of social relations that encompass shared meanings and above all shared values'. The development of such shared meanings demands communication among those who share membership in the community: sets of people who fail to communicate cannot compose a common culture and cannot, therefore, constitute a community. Through ensuring that access to a two-way communication is open to all who acknowledge residence in a defined place, local nets help to provide an infrastructure on which a sense of community can be built. They may also provide a means by which stigmatised communities can attempt to defend themselves, emphasising the positive characteristics which set them apart from others.

The formation and maintenance of a sense of community demands that members share feelings of togetherness and connectedness that confer the sense of belonging. Such feelings do not just happen. In a speech given as part of the *BBC Online Community Day* (17 June 1999), Rheingold pointed out:

> In order to succeed, a virtual community has to have an affinity – the answer to the question 'what would draw these people together?'

In order to form a community, 'virtual' or 'real', participants need to share a common purpose. Common residence and a concern for local issues may provide just such a rationale, providing a basis for claiming distinction from those in other areas. For this to happen locality must become salient.

There is an apparent paradox in the attempt to use systems, such as the internet, which are essentially placeless and designed to provide access to global resources, in order to build a local net and a sense of local community. Schuler (1996) points out:

> While virtually all community network systems . . . offer access to at least some Internet services (e-mail at a minimum), the focus of a community network is on the local community.

To be effective mechanisms for building local social capital, local nets and other internet-based interventions need to act as bridges between the local and the global. Gurstein (2001: 281) sees this bridging function as being the most important characteristic of local nets and forecasts that,

> it is likely to be in the zone of interaction between the virtual and the real in communities that the future nexus of power and the recreation of citizenship

are likely to reside. Where physical communities are empowered by the global reach of the virtual and where the virtual is empowered by the physical force of the real is the point where the true resistance to the global and the globalising will develop and prevail.

Wellman and his colleagues have coined the neologism '*glocalisation*' to refer to the process in which the internet is used to enhance local interaction:

> The Internet both provides a ramp to the global information highway and strengthens local links within neighbourhoods and households. For all its global access, the Internet reinforces stay-at-homes. 'Glocalisation' occurs, both because the Internet makes it easy to contact many neighbours, and because fixed, wired Internet connections root users at their home and office desks.
>
> (Wellman 2001: 27)

Evidence produced by Hampton and Wellman (2000, 2002), in a study of a leading-edge wired suburb in Canada, and by Ferlander and Timms, in a study of a marginalised community in Sweden (2001, 2005), indicate that those who are most active online are often also most active in both the local community and the wider society. In the Canadian study, the middle-class residents connected with each other and the wider world from home and used the internet to further social and political activities. Those who were connected to the 'Net had more informal contact with their neighbours than those who were not connected and also maintained more contact with distant friends and family. Online relationships were used to provide social support and acted as bases for political action. In the Swedish study, following the demise of a subsidised intranet sponsored by the housing association, residents used an internet cafe to similar ends, combining online and offline forms of interaction. Users of the cafe expressed more trust, knew more people and had a more positive sense of local identity than those who were non-users. They also perceived less conflict and more commonality with fellow residents who had immigrant backgrounds. In both cases, social capital was enhanced through the use of the internet. A graphic expression of the effect is given in a poem composed by one of the users of the Swedish cafe (see the Appendix).

Building local community online

The internet provides a medium which can be used in a deliberate attempt to build community and enhance social capital. Kollock (1996), while noting that, 'There is no algorithm for community', suggests a number of guidelines for the development of online communities that are derived from more general studies of interpersonal collaboration. Among the factors stressed are continuity, 'Successful communities . . . must promote ongoing interaction', members must be able to identify each other and to establish clear group boundaries, they should have access to information about how partners have behaved in the past and they must be able to develop group norms.

Gurstein (2000, 2001) reports on a number of attempts which have been made to use local nets as a mechanism for building local communities within what has been termed the 'community informatics' approach. The emphasis is on making 'effective use' of ICT, providing services which are desired by residents and involving them in their management. The lack of a feeling of local ownership was a major reason advanced for the failure of the local net set up by the housing company in the stigmatised Stockholm suburb studied by Ferlander; conversely, the successful internet cafe in the same area involved active local participation and a sense of ownership (Ferlander and Timms 2005).

One tactic which may be adopted in the attempt to ensure effective use of the internet involves eLearning. This was the approach adopted in an EC project, SCHEMA (*Social Cohesion through Higher Education in Marginal Areas*). An account of SCHEMA is given on the project website (http://www.schema.stir .ac.uk/). Among the work-packages in the project, one was specifically concerned with exploring the potential of the Web to enhance a sense of community identity through participation in an online module, *Community Portraits*, based on the use of online collaboration in the production and sharing of community descriptions.

The Community Portraits module was developed as a means for exploring the use of the internet for community building among a number of diverse groups. In the initial pilot of the module, in 1999, participants were health and welfare workers living and working in geographically marginal areas (Lapland, East Germany, Scottish Highlands). The module was repeated with elderly visitors to an internet cafe in a stigmatised housing area in Stockholm in 2001–2002 and, dispensing with the spatial component of community, has been further developed for use with students presenting with disabilities in a number of Scottish universities in 2005.

The initial concentration on health and welfare workers was based on the belief that successful welfare practice requires understanding of the strengths and weakness of communities. Although this may seem an obvious perspective, much recent social work practice in the UK and Europe has been based on a relatively individualistic approach in which the community context has tended to be overlooked and the role of social capital downplayed.

A strong argument for a community-based approach to social work has been provided by Martinez-Brawley (1990, 2000), who notes that:

> Community-oriented social work depends on an attitude of mind that sees community as a potentially nourishing and important source of support and identity to its members. The notion that community nourishes its members is not commonplace. It is probably not an idea that is in the forefront of consciousness when social workers help clients make decisions.
>
> (Martinez-Brawley 1990: 216–217)

Community Portraits was designed to explore the capacity of online collaboration to develop both a community of practice amongst the course participants and an awareness of the community contexts in which they lived and worked, with an emphasis on the strengths of each community rather than weaknesses. The process involved comparing the distinctive features of each participant's own community with those presented by the others.

In its initial version, Community Portraits was presented online using a learning environment developed at the University of Oulu (*TELSIPro* now *Optima*). Participants were required to work collaboratively in small groups in order to produce comparative 'portraits' of the communities in which they worked. Groups of three participants, each from a different country, worked together to produce a comparative portrait of their three communities. Participants were expected to use their cultural and individual differences of perspective to sharpen each other's awareness of their community and to explore the positive as well as any negative features. The collaborative process was also expected to enhance the participants' awareness of their own, as well as each other's, perceptual frameworks and to encourage them to recognise the advantages of collaboration for extending ways of gathering and interpreting information, deepening understandings and developing ideas and innovations. Each participant was a looking glass for the others.

Despite a number of technical hitches, the results of the pilot were sufficiently encouraging to encourage further developments of the Community Portraits module (see Timms 1999 and www.odeluce.stir.ac.uk/docs/CoPor_Vienna1.doc). The first extension used the programme in the context of a stigmatised housing area in Stockholm, investigating the extent to which an attempt at community building online could contribute to the enhancement of social capital (for an analysis, see Ferlander 2004). The results were positive, suggesting that the use of the internet to build local communities online leads to an enhancement of community identity offline. Following the conclusion of the module, a number of related activities have sprung up based on smaller divisions – neighbourhoods – within the housing area.

A further extension of the approach has involved the substitution of a geographical basis for community with one based on another basis of identification: the attribution of a disability label. In the summer and autumn of 2005, groups of students in several Scottish universities undertook a version of Community Portraits designed to explore their experiences of disability and to encourage the development of a positive community identity. Further information is given on the website of the UNIVe project (www.e-uni.ee/Minerva/pdf/RDTG_manual_final_2.7.3.pdf).

Towards a non-local future?

There is now a considerable volume of research supporting the conclusion that the use of the internet by local communities is an effective means of enhancing community identity. Those who interact online also interact offline. The experience of online relationships within supportive virtual communities helps to build trust offline and can be used to enhance social capital in geographical communities.

There remain, however, many questions concerning the future impact of developments in computer-mediated communication on both local communities and social capital in the wider society. To date much use of the internet for inter-personal interaction remains text-based and has been tied to a physical address, the house or office in which access is available. With the development of high bandwidth wireless forms of communication in the developed world – the third generation of mobile telephony, encompassing broadband internet and mobile phones –

> computer-supported communication will be everywhere, but because it is independent of place, it will be nowhere . . . the person – not the place, household or workgroup – will become even more of an autonomous communication node.
>
> (Wellman 2001: 19)

Networked individualism is replacing previous forms of social connectedness and community. The internet and the mobile phone mean that we move from place-to-place forms of communication to person-to-person contact. As a result, the answer to the question 'Where are you from' or 'Where do you stay?' may become an email address and membership in one or many Web-based communities rather than a physical address. Membership in a single place-based community is being replaced by memberships in multiple communities, spread across space and time. Wellman's networked individualism provides the basis for the structural trans-formation of society, which Castells (1996) has described as 'The Rise of the Network Society'. The transformation has major consequences for both social organisation and the nature of personal identity. Castells suggests that 'our soci-eties are increasingly structured around the bipolar opposition of the Net and the Self' (1996: 3). Membership in varied communities provides the base for varied images of self and enables both personal and community identity to be negotiated and re-negotiated against a backdrop of continually changing interactions. The success or otherwise of the third generation of wireless communications may turn out to have far more than simply economic consequences for telecoms companies and their users and shareholders. Personal identity will still be related to community, but the basis for community may increasingly rest on electronic forms of communication rather than those involving physical co-presence.

Appendix

An IT-Cafe – a poem by Åsa Freij

Ett IT-café	Varandra
Är en bra idé	Och andra
Som blev gjord	lärde sig veta
Till ord	dock vad grannarna heta
Och till handling	och även att samarbeta
Varpå förvandling	och att sluta slåss
Skedde på en enslig ort	och så lite om själva datorn
Som smort	förstås
Gick sedan	Och om nätet
Integrering	Och litet förmätet
Och redan	Om världen därute
Känner många varann	Som från Skarpnäck
Ångest försvann	Öppnats
Vissa till och med fann	För oss

Åsa Freij 11.3.02

An IT-Café	Each other
Is a great idea	Which from Skarpnäck
That was made	And others
Into words	Learnt to know
And into action	The names of their neighbours
After which change	And even to co-operate
Occurred in a lonely place	And to stop fighting
Like clockwork	And also a bit about the computer
Happened then	itself
Integration	Of course
And already	And about the Net
Many knew one another	And became a little bolder
Agony disappeared	About the world out there.
Some even found	

(translated by Sara Ferlander)

References

Arnold, M. (2003) 'Intranets, community and social capital: the case of Williams Bay', *Bulletin of Science, Technology and Society*, 23(2): 78–87.

Beamish, A (1995) 'Communities online: community-based computer networks', unpublished Masters thesis, Massachusetts Institute of Technology, at: https://dspace.mit.edu/handle/1721.1/11860.

Blanchard, A. and Horan, T. (1998) 'Virtual communities and social capital', *Social Science Computer Review*, 16: 293–307.

Boase, J., Horrigan, J.B., Wellman, B. and Rainie, L. (2006) *The Strength of Internet Ties*, Washington, DC: Pew Internet and American Life Project, at: http://www. pewinternet.org.

Broom, H. and Selznick, P. (1977) *Sociology: A Text with Adapted Readings*, 6th edition, New York: Harper & Row.

Castells, M. (1996) *The Rise of the Network Society. The Information Age: Economy, Society and Culture, Vol. I*, Cambridge, MA and Oxford: Blackwell.

Castells, M. (2001) *The Internet Galaxy: Reflections on the Internet, Business and Society*, Oxford: Oxford University Press.

Cooley, C.H. (1902) *Human Nature and the Social Order*, New York: Scribners.

Dibbel, J. (1999) *My Tiny Life: Crime and Passion in the Virtual World*, London: Fourth Estate.

Doheny-Farina, S. (1996) *The Wired Neighborhood*, New Haven, CT: Yale University Press.

Etzioni, A. (ed.) (1998) *The Essential Communitarian Reader*, Lanham, MD: Rowman & Littlefield.

Fallows. D. (2004) *The Internet and Daily Life*, Washington, DC: Pew Institute.

Ferlander, S. (2004) 'The internet, social capital and local community', PhD thesis, University of Stirling, at: http://www.crdlt.stir.ac.uk/Docs/SaraFerlanderPhD.pdf.

Ferlander, S. and Timms, D.W.G. (2001) 'Local nets and social capital', *Telematics & Informatics*, 18(1): 51–65.

Ferlander, S. and Timms, D.W.G. (2005) 'Bridging the dual digital divide: a local net and an IT-cafe in Sweden', *Information, Communication & Society*, 9(2): 137–159).

Giddens, A. (1991) *Modernity and Self-identity*, Cambridge: Polity Press.

Gurstein, M. (ed.) (2000) *Community Informatics: Enabling Communities with Information and Communications Technologies*, Hershey, PA: Idea Group Publishing.

Gurstein, M. (2001) 'Community informatics, community networks and strategies for flexible networking', in L. Keeble and B. D. Loader (eds) *Community Informatics: Shaping Computer-mediated Social Relationships*, London: Routledge.

Hampton, K. and Wellman, B. (2000) 'Examining community in the digital neighbourhood: early results from Canada's wired suburb', in T. Ishida and K. Isbister (eds) *Digital Cities: Technologies, Experiences, and Future Perspectives*, Berlin: Springer-Verlag.

Hampton, K. and Wellman, B. (2002) 'The not so global village of a cyber society: contact and support beyond Netville', in B. Wellman and C. A. Haythornthwaite (eds) *The Internet in Everyday Life*, Oxford: Blackwell.

Kollock, P. (1996) 'Design principles for online communities', Harvard Conference on the Internet and Society, also published in *PC Update* 1998, 15(5): 58–60.

Kraut, R., Patterson, M., Lundmark, V., Kiesler, S., Mukopadhyay, T. and Scherlis, W. (1998) 'Internet paradox: a social technology that reduces social involvement and psychological well-being?', *American Psychologist*, 53: 1017–1031.

Martinez-Brawley, E. (1990) *Perspectives on the Small Community: Humanistic Views for Practitioners*, Washington, DC: NASW Press.

Martinez-Brawley, E. (2000) *Close to Home: Human Services and the Small Community*, Washington, DC: NASW Press.

Pew Internet and American Life Project (2005) *Internet: The Mainstreaming of Online Life*, at: http://www.pewinternet.org/pdfs/Internet_Status_2005.pdf.

Putnam, R.D. (2000) *Bowling Alone: The Collapse and Revival of American Community*, New York: Simon & Schuster.

Reid, E. (1998) 'The self and the internet: variations on the illusion of one self', in J. Gackenbach (ed.) *Psychology and the Internet: Intrapersonal, Interpersonal, and Transpersonal Implications*, San Diego, CA: Academic Press.

Rheingold, H. (1993) *The Virtual Community*, Reading, MA: Addison-Wesley. (Later editions at: http://www.rheingold.com/vc/book/.)

Schuler, D. (1996) *New Community Networks: Wired for Change*, New York: ACM Press.

Suttles, G. (1972) *The Social Construction of Community*, Chicago: University of Chicago Press.

Timms, L. (1999) 'Communities and welfare practice: learning through sharing', *New Technology in the Human Services*, 11(4): 11–17.

Wellman, B. (1997) 'An electronic group is virtually a social network', in S. Kiesler (ed.) *Culture of the Internet*, Mahwah, NJ: Lawrence Erlbaum.

Wellman, B. (ed.) (1999) *Networks in the Global Village*, Boulder, CO: Westview Press.

Wellman, B. (2001) 'Physical place and cyberplace: the rise of networked individualism', in L. Keeble and B. D. Loader (eds) *Community Informatics: Shaping Computer-mediated Social Relations*, London: Routledge.

Wellman, B., Boase, J. and Chen, W. (2002) 'The networked nature of community: online and offline', *IT & Society*, 1(1): 151–156.

Wirth, L. (1938) 'Urbanism as a way of life', *American Journal of Sociology*, 44(1): 1–24.

Chapter 7

The empirics of social capital and economic development

A critical perspective

Fabio Sabatini

Introduction

From a theoretical point of view, modern political economy has developed by depriving economic interactions of their social content. A typical example of this trend is given by the economy's working framework implied by Walrasian general equilibrium models. In this context, market interactions are reduced to the transmission of coded information through the auctioneer's agency. Agents never meet: they simply pass on to the auctioneer their purchase and selling proposals (Gui 2002). However, the economic activity is deeply embedded in the social structure, and agents' decisions are always influenced by a wide range of social and cultural factors. For example, most case studies show that enterprises devote an ever more relevant part of their financial resources to activities which are not directly related to production processes. Nurturing a co-operative climate inside the workforce and building trustworthy relationships with external partners generally constitute key tasks for management. On the other side, workers' satisfaction is ever more affected by the quality of human relationships among colleagues, and not only by traditional factors like wage and job conditions. According to Gui (2000), such relational assets contribute to firms' economic performance just like new machinery and warehouses. Growing attention has thus been devoted to the role that social norms, the diffusion of trust and logics of reciprocity play in shaping different kinds of transactions (Kahneman and Tversky 1979; Arnott and Stiglitz 1991; Berg et al. 1995; Fehr et al. 1997; Frey 1997; Fehr and Gatcher 2000; Sugden 2000). The growth literature is now pervaded by studies addressing the relationship between the economy's social and institutional fabric, the economic performance and development patterns (Kormendi and Meguire 1985; Barro 1996; Bénabou 1996; Collier and Gunning 1997; Knack and Keefer 1997; Temple and Johnson 1998; Whiteley 2000; Zak and Knack 2001; Gradstein and Justman 2002). Such voluminous strands of the literature may be interpreted as the sign of the emerging need to fill the gap that, in economics, still separates society from the economy.

The economic and sociological literature on social capital is another symptom of such need. In 1993, Putnam et al. tried to explain the different institutional and economic performance of the Italian regions as the result of the influence exerted by some aspects of the social structure, summarised into the multidimensional concept of 'social capital'. This study has received wide criticism in the social science debates of the 1990s. However, it posed a milestone for social capital theory, which registered an explosive development in the following decade, rapidly involving the attention of economists. As pointed out by Isham et al. (2002), a 'keyword' search in all journals in *EconLit*, the most frequently used database of references in economics, shows that citations for 'social capital' have grown rapidly over the last decade, doubling each year since the late 1990s. In 2000, social capital had about a quarter of the absolute number of citations. The so-called 'Italian work' (Putnam et al. 1993) has been pronounced by the editor of the mainstream *Quarterly Journal of Economics* as the most cited contribution across the social sciences in the 1990s (Fine 2001: 83).

During the last ten years, the concept of social capital has been invoked in almost every field of social science research, and has been used to explain an immense range of phenomena, from political participation to the institutional performance, from health to corruption, from the efficiency of public services to the economic success of countries. However, despite the immense amount of research on it, social capital's definition remains elusive and, also due to the chronic lack of suitable data, there is neither a universal measurement method, nor a single underlying indicator commonly accepted by the literature. From a historical perspective, one could argue that social capital is not a concept but a *praxis*, a code word used to federate disparate but inter-related research interests and to facilitate the cross-fertilisation of ideas across disciplinary boundaries (Durlauf and Fafchamps 2004). As pointed out by Brown and Ashman (1996), one of the primary benefits of the idea of social capital is that it is allowing scholars, policy makers and practitioners from different disciplines to enjoy an unprecedented level of co-operation and dialogue.

Even if conceptual vagueness may have promoted the use of the term among social scientists, it also has been an impediment to both theoretical and empirical research of phenomena in which social capital may play a role. This chapter provides an introduction to the concept of social capital, and carries out a critical review of the empirical literature on social capital and economic development. The survey points out six main weaknesses affecting the empirics of social capital. Identified weaknesses are then used to analyse, in a critical perspective, some prominent empirical studies and new interesting research published in the last two years. The review particularly lingers over the 'Italian work' carried out by Putnam et al. (1993), for two main reasons. Firstly, this research constitutes the seminal study of this voluminous strand of the literature. Secondly, its short-comings are 'critical', in that they repeatedly present themselves again in most of the following studies in the field.

The outline of this chapter is as follows: the second section briefly introduces the concept of social capital, and its relevance to economics. The third section presents a critical perspective on the empirics of social capital, pointing out the main weaknesses of existing measurement methods. The fourth section reviews the empirical literature on social capital and economic development. The chapter is closed by some concluding remarks and guidelines for further researches.

What is social capital and why is it relevant to economics?

Although it has been popularised only in the last decade, due to Bourdieu's (1980, 1986), Coleman's (1988, 1990) and Putnam's (Putnam et al. 1993, 1995a) prominent studies, the concept of social capital has a long intellectual history in social sciences. The sense in which the term is used today dates back to about 90 years, when Hanifan (1916) invoked the concept of social capital to explain the importance of community participation in enhancing school performance. After Hanifan's work, the idea of social capital disappeared from the social sciences debate (Seely et al. 1956; Homans 1961; Jacobs 1961; Loury 1977). Three decades before Putnam's work, Edward Banfield (1958) used the social capital concept to explain southern Italy's economic backwardness, but his study did not arouse interest in economic debates. Bourdieu (1980) identifies three dimensions of capital, each with its own relationship to the concept of class: economic, cultural and social capital. Bourdieu's idea of social capital puts the emphasis on class conflicts: social relations are used to increase the ability of an actor to advance his interests, and become a resource in social struggles: social capital is 'the sum of the resources, actual or virtual, that accrue to an individual or group by virtue of possessing a durable network of more or less institutionalized relationships of mutual acquaintance and recognition' (Bourdieu and Wacquant 1986: 119, expanded from Bourdieu 1980: 2). Social capital thus has two components: it is, first, a resource that is connected with group membership and social networks. 'The volume of social capital possessed by a given agent . . . depends on the size of the network of connections that he can effectively mobilize' (Bourdieu 1986: 249). Secondly, it is a quality produced by the totality of the relationships between actors, rather than merely a common 'quality' of the group (Bourdieu 1980). At the end of the 1980s, Coleman gave new relevance to Bourdieu's concept of social capital. According to Coleman, 'Social capital is defined by its function. It is not a single entity, but a variety of different entities, with two elements in common: they all consist in some aspect of social structures, and they facilitate certain actions of actors within the structure' (1988: 98). In the early 1990s, the concept of social capital finally became a central topic in the social sciences debate.

In 1993, Putnam et al. published their famous research on local government in Italy, which concluded that the performance of social and political institutions is powerfully influenced by citizen engagement in community affairs, or what, following Coleman, the authors termed 'social capital'. In this context, social capital is referred to as 'features of social life-networks, norms, and trust, that enable participants to act together more effectively to pursue shared objectives' (Putnam 1995b). Like other forms of capital, social capital is productive, making possible the achievement of certain ends, that in its absence would not be possible. But, in Coleman's words, 'Unlike other forms of capital, social capital inheres in the structure of relations between actors and among actors. It is not lodged either in the actors themselves or in physical implements of production' (Coleman 1988: 98). The use of the term 'capital' is criticised by several authors belonging to the field of economics, in that it refers to things that can be owned. For example, Bowles and Gintis sustain that the term 'community' would be more appropriate, because it 'better captures the aspects of good governance that explain social capital's popularity, as it focuses attention on what groups *do* rather than what people *own*' (2002: 422). By 'community', the authors mean a group who interact directly, frequently and in multi-faceted ways. This point is stressed by Arrow (1999), who sustains that 'capital' is something 'alienable', that is, its ownership can be transferred from one person to another. According to Arrow, it is difficult – as with human capital – to change the ownership of social capital.

The cited perspectives on social capital are markedly different in origins and fields of application, but they all agree on the ability of certain aspects of the social structure to generate positive externalities for members of a group, who gain a competitive advantage in pursuing their ends.

From a rational choice theory perspective, it is possible to describe social capital as an input of agents' utility and production functions. Becker (1974, 1996) describes social capital as a particular kind of intermediate good for the production of assets (the so-called 'commodities', corresponding to people's basic needs) entering as arguments in agents' utility functions. According to Becker, people invest rationally in social capital in the context of a utility maximisation problem. Becker's social capital is thus an individual resource, used within the context of utility maximisation problems by perfectly rational and informed agents. The role of social capital as a collective resource serving the achievement of macro outcomes is instead well explained by the new economic sociology perspective (Granovetter 1973, 1985). Granovetter identifies social capital mainly with social networks of weak bridging ties. According to the author, 'Whatever is to be diffused can reach a larger number of people, and traverse greater social distance, when passed through weak ties rather than strong. If one tells a rumour to all his close friends, and they do likewise, many will hear the rumour a second and third time, since those linked by strong ties tend to share friends' (Granovetter 1973: 1366). Social networks can thus be considered as a powerful means to foster the diffusion of information and knowledge, lowing uncertainty and transaction costs.

The problem of measuring social capital: a critical perspective

Despite the immense amount of research on it, the definition of social capital has remained elusive. Conceptual vagueness, the coexistence of multiple definitions, the chronic lack of suitable data have so far been an impediment to both theoretical and empirical research of phenomena in which social capital may play a role. In this regard, it is possible to observe that the problems suffered by empirical studies of social capital are, at some level, endemic to all empirical work in economics. Heckmann (2000) states that the establishment of causal relationships is intrinsically difficult: 'Some of the disagreement that arises in interpreting a given body of data is intrinsic to the field of economics because of the conditional nature of causal knowledge. The information in any body of data is usually too weak to eliminate competing causal explanations of the same phenomenon. There is no mechanical algorithm for producing a set of 'assumption free' facts or causal estimates based on those facts' (ibid.: 91).

However, according to Durlauf (2002: 22), 'The empirical social capital literature seems to be particularly plagued by vague definitions of concepts, poorly measured data, absence of appropriate exchangeability conditions, and lack of information necessary to make identification claims plausible.' In his article, the author reviews three famous empirical studies,[1] concluding that they do not help in understanding the socio-economic outcomes of social capital. Durlauf's critique is one step forward in respect to the position of some prominent economists, who doubt the possibility of providing credible measures, and question the opportunity itself to consider the concept as a useful analytical tool for economics. In his critique of Fukuyama, Solow (1995: 36) writes: 'If "social capital" is to be more than a buzzword, something more than mere relevance or even importance is required. . . . The stock of social capital should somehow be measurable, even inexactly.'

As a reply, it is possible to observe that, during the last ten years, empirical research has proposed a great variety of methods for measuring social capital and testing its ability to produce relevant social, economic and political outcomes. However, the empirics of social capital still suffer from a definite difficulty to address macro outcomes in a convincing way, and this strand of the literature seems to be chronically affected by some definite problems. In particular, we can identify five main shortcomings, as follows.

Firstly, *despite the great amount of research on it, the definition of social capital remains substantially elusive*. Following Coleman (1988: 98), the great part of the literature refers to social capital as all 'the aspects of the social structure that facilitate certain actions of actors within the structure . . . making possible the achievement of certain ends that, in its absence, would not be possible'. Such 'productive' aspects of the social structure can vary according to different environmental situations and agents' needs: 'A given form of social capital that is valuable in facilitating certain actions may be useless or even harmful for others' (ibid.). According to this approach, it seems virtually impossible to provide a single, universal, definition of what social capital is, and a unique, underlying, method of measurement to be used within the empirical research.

Secondly, *the idea that social capital is a multidimensional concept is now commonly accepted in the debate*. This allows each author to focus on a particular aspect of the concept, according to the aims and scope of his own study. Empirical work tends to address different dimensions of social capital, therefore adopting particular measures, derived from diverse data sources. This makes any general assessment difficult, due to incomparability in sampling designs and question wording (Wuthnow 2002). Furthermore, researchers cannot account for measurement error, which we would expect to find in the survey questions used to assess social capital (Paxton 1999).

Thirdly, *most empirical studies measure social capital through 'indirect' indicators, not representing the social capital's key components already identified by the theoretical literature* (commonly social networks, trust and social norms). Such indicators – for example, crime rates, teenage pregnancy, blood donation, participation rates in tertiary education – are quite popular in the empirical research, but their use has led to considerable confusion about what social capital *is*, as distinct from its *outcomes*, and what the relationship between social capital and its outcomes *may be*. Research reliant upon an outcome of social capital as an indicator of it will necessarily find social capital to be related to that outcome. Social capital becomes tautologically present whenever an outcome is observed (Portes 1998; Durlauf 1999). Of course, from a lexical point of view, it is possible to attribute the 'social capital' label to every aspect of the economy's social fabric providing a favourable environment for production and well-being. However, such definition poses a 'logic' problem: if social capital is everything that can make agents co-operate or markets work better, then any empirical analysis will find that social capital causes co-operation among agents and improves the efficiency of markets. This approach simply 'sterilises' the social capital literature, making it unable to foster the explanatory power of economic studies addressing the socio-cultural factors of growth.

Fourthly, *a great part of existing cross-national studies on the economic outcomes of social capital is based on measures of trust drawn from the* World Values Survey (*WVS*).[2] The WVS' way to measure generalised trust is the famous question developed by Rosenberg (1956): 'Generally speaking, would you say that most people can be trusted or that you can't be too careful in dealing with people?' Possible responses to this question are: 'Most people can be trusted', 'Can't be too careful' or 'Don't know'. The trust indicator resulting from this question is given by the percentage of respondents replying 'most people can be trusted', often after deleting the 'don't know' responses. Trust measured through surveys is a 'micro' and 'cognitive' concept, in that it represents the individuals' perception of their social environment, related to the particular position that interviewed people occupy in the social structure. The aggregation of such data, however, creates a measure of what can be called 'macro' or 'social' trust which loses its linkage with the social and historical circumstances in which trust and social capital are located. As pointed out by Foley and Edwards (1999), empirical studies based on cross-country comparisons of trust may be a *cul de sac*, because of their inability to address macro outcomes, in view of the absence of the broader context within which attitudes are created and determined. Fine (2001: 105) argues that 'if social capital is context-dependent – and context is highly variable by how, when and whom – then any conclusions are themselves illegitimate as the basis for generalisation to other circumstances'.

Also studies focusing on social networks instead of social trust generally do not take into appropriate account the multidimensional, context-dependent and dynamic nature of social capital. They usually analyse just one kind of network (for example, voluntary organisations), which is considered as representative of the social capital concept as a whole, through a single measure. However, a simple descriptive analysis of available data allows us to point out that, even if they constitute just one aspect of the multi-faceted concept of social capital, social networks are themselves a multidimensional phenomenon. They are characterised by different aspects, which can be described by a composite set of multiple indicators.

Fifthly, *following Putnam's hints, most studies focus on voluntary organisations as a proxy for measuring social capital.* The claim is that in areas with stronger, dense, horizontal and more cross-cutting networks, there is a spillover from membership in organisations to the co-operative values and norms that citizens develop. In areas where networks with such characteristics do not develop, there are fewer opportunities to learn civic virtues and democratic attitudes, resulting in a lack of trust. However, there are several reasons to doubt the efficacy of social capital measures simply based on the density of voluntary organisations. Firstly, even though individuals who join groups and who interact with others regularly show attitudinal and behavioural differences compared to non-joiners, the possibility exists that people self-select into association groups, depending on their original levels of generalised trust and reciprocity. Secondly, the group experiences might be more pronounced in their impact when members are diverse and from different backgrounds. According to some authors, if diversity matters for socialization of co-operative values, then voluntary associations might not be the measure to take into account, as such groups have been found relatively homogeneous in character. Voluntary associations indeed generally recruit members who already have relatively high civic attitudes (Popielarz 1999; Mutz 2002; Uslaner 2002). Moreover, in general, until now the literature has not provided a micro theory explaining trust's transmission mechanism from groups to the entire society, and the logic underlying the connection between social ties and generalised trust has never been clearly developed (Rosenblum 1998; Uslaner 2002). Thus, every finding on the correlation and/or the causal nexus connecting membership in civic associations to supposed social capital's economic outcomes must be handled with extreme caution.

The empirical literature on social capital and economic development: a critical review

After the publication of *Making Democracy Work* by Putnam et al. in 1993, economic research has produced a large volume of studies investigating the relationship between different aspects of the multidimensional concept of social capital and economic growth, usually represented by per capita income. For the purposes of this chapter, such an impressive amount of empirical studies can be partitioned into two main categories:

- Studies finding a positive relationship between social capital and economic development, but suffering from questionable methods for the measurement of social capital, as described in the five points listed in the previous section.
- Studies that, independently from the adopted measurement method, do not find a positive relationship between social capital and economic development, and some alternative, interesting, views.

Putnam and his disciples: the empirical literature on the positive relationship between social capital and economic development

The seminal study of this voluminous strand of the literature is the already cited 'Italian work' carried out by Putnam et al. (1993). In that research, social capital is measured by means of four main indicators of:

1   The number of voluntary organisations, including, for example, sports clubs and cultural circles.
2   The number of local newspaper readers. The idea for using this indicator is that newspapers, in Italy, constitute the most effective means to get information on local communities' problems and events. People reading newspapers are thus better informed and more likely to get involved in the community's life.
3   Voter turn-out at referenda. Since voting for a referendum does not imply immediate and direct advantages, such a behaviour cannot be founded on the pursuit of personal aims; therefore, it has to be considered as a signal of civic spirit or what, following Putnam, we can term 'civicness'.
4   The relevance of preference votes expressed by voters within political elections. This is interpreted as an indicator of civic backwardness, since, in the Italian political system, 'preference votes' have been historically used as a means for establishing client relationships and to obtain patronage favours.

The authors find a positive and significant correlation between these indicators and local institutions' performance. Moreover, citizen-initiated contacts with government officials in the south tend to involve issues of narrowly personal concerns, while contacts in the more trusting regions tend to involve larger issues, with positive implications for the welfare of the region as a whole. In a subsequent study, Helliwell and Putnam (1995) show that social capital, as measured through the same indicators, also positively affects the economic performance and, in the long run, the process of economic growth in the Italian regions. In the light of the arguments proposed previously in this chapter, it is possible to identify three main shortcomings in the 'Italian work'.

Firstly, the study relies on 'indirect' indicators as social capital measures. The number of newspaper readers, voter turnout at referenda and preference votes are not directly related to social capital's key components, which Putnam himself identifies with 'Features of social life-networks, norms, and trust, that enable participants to act together more effectively to pursue shared objectives' (Putnam 1995b). As pointed out previously, this may lead to considerable confusion about what social capital *is*, as distinct from its *outcomes*, and what the relationship between social capital and its outcomes *may be*. Research reliant upon an outcome of social capital as an indicator of it will necessarily find social capital to be related to that outcome. In this case, social capital – although previously defined by the authors as the complex set of trust and social networks – becomes tautologically present whenever an outcome, like newspaper diffusion and high voter turnout, is observed. The existence of such a relationship is not proved, nor analysed, within the study.

Secondly, the remaining indicator adopted by Putnam et al. (2003) is a measure of the density of that particular type of social network shaped by voluntary organisations. Some problems related to this measure have been briefly described above. In particular, even admitting the possibility for associations to exert a positive influence on trust and development, we have to state that, until now, theoretical studies have not provided an explanation of the mechanism through which trust within groups generalises to the entire society. Moreover, as already argued, an exploratory analysis of available data allows us to point out that, even if they constitute just one aspect of the multi-faceted concept of social capital, social networks are themselves a multidimensional phenomenon. Recent studies carried out on the Italian case (Piselli 2001; Andreotti and Barbieri 2003; Nuzzo and Micucci 2003; Sabatini 2005b) show that social networks and, within social networks, voluntary organisations, are both characterised by different aspects, which can be described only by a composite set of multiple indicators, or by latent indicators synthesising the different dimensions.

Thirdly, according to the measurements carried out by Putnam et al. (1993), the areas of Italy with the best institutional performance were those with left-wing local governments. This variable could be considered able to provide better explanations for institutional performance. This poses the problem of the role of omitted variables in the Italian work and, more in general, in all empirical studies of social capital. Moreover, social capital may be endogenous to institutional and economic performance, rather than a cause of them. A serious attempt to overcome these shortcomings could be made through the use of structural equation models (SEMs) as a means to carry out reliable empirical investigations, accounting also for omitted variables (Sabatini 2006). SEMs allow the taking into account of the joint effect of unknown exogenous phenomena on variables explicitly considered in the model. In addition, this technique provides a better evaluation of the form and direction of the causal relationship linking social capital to its supposed outcomes, making it possible to account for potential reverse effects (Jöreskog and Sörbom 1979; Bollen 1989).

I consider these points 'critical' because they repeatedly present themselves again in most of the following literature in the field. Knack and Keefer (1997) and La Porta et al. (1997) use data from the WVS to conduct cross-country tests of Putnam's hypotheses. These surveys include roughly 1,000 respondents in each of several dozen countries, and are intended to be nationally representative. Trust values for each country are calculated as the percentage of respondents who agree that 'most people can be trusted' rather than the alternative that 'you can't be too careful in dealing with people'. Knack and Keefer (1997) find that trust and civic norms are unrelated to horizontal networks and have a strong impact on economic performance in a sample of 29 market economies, suggesting that, if declining social capital in the United States has adverse implications for growth, it is the erosion of trust and civic co-operation, as documented by Knack (1992), that are of greater concern than the decline in associational life emphasised by Putnam (1995a, 1995b). La Porta et al. (1997) test the relationship between trust, income and firms' scale, regressing the revenues of the 20 largest firms as a proportion of GDP on per capita income, trust in people, and a measure of trust in family members. The authors find that the scale measure is unrelated to income, and strongly related to the two trust measures: positively for trust in people, and negatively for trust in family. These results are coherent with the early thesis of Banfield (1958) and, in particular, with the intuition of Fukuyama (1995), who stressed the relationship between social capital and industrial organisations. All these works have provided relevant hints to social capital research, but they all suffer from their way of measuring social trust at the national level. As already stressed, trust measured by the WVS is a 'micro' and 'cognitive' concept, in that it represents the individuals' perception of their social environment, related to the particular position that interviewed people occupy in the social structure. The aggregation of such data creates a measure of what can be called 'macro' or 'social' trust, which loses its linkage with the social and historical circumstances in which trust and social capital are located.

More recently, a notable study carried out by Guiso et al. (2004), focusing on the relationship between social capital and another aspect of economic prosperity, financial development, has received great attention in the economics debate. The authors' basic idea is that: 'One of the mechanisms through which social capital impacts economic efficiency is by enhancing the prevailing level of trust. . . . Since financial contracts are the ultimate trust-intensive contracts, social capital should have major effects on the development of financial markets' (ibid.: 527). Without providing a precise definition first, the authors measure social capital through blood donation and electoral participation, claiming that both measures 'are driven only by social pressure and internal norms, i.e. the fundamental components of social capital' (ibid.: 528). As already pointed out, this study measures social capital through indicators of what could be considered as one of its outcomes. The authors claim to have found a positive and significant relationship between social capital and financial development, but they rather prove the existence of a positive correlation between financial development, blood donation and electoral participation, without providing a credible explanation for such a relationship, nor for the supposed linkage between social capital and the variables adopted for its measurement.

Is social capital necessarily good for economic development?

Besides social capital's measurement problems, the empirical evidence on the linkage between economic prosperity and social capital is sometimes conflicting. Putnam (2000) and Costa and Kahn (2003) document the large decline in social capital in the United States in the twentieth century. However, it is hard to argue that the US economy did not flourish over this same period. On the other hand, the decline itself of US social capital has been widely questioned. For example, Paxton (1999) analyses multiple indicators of social capital in the US over a 20-year period. The results do not support Putnam's claims, showing instead some decline in a general measure of social capital, a decline in trust in individuals, but no general decline in trust in institutions, and no decline in associations.

The role of associational activity is a subject of greater contention. Putnam et al. attribute the economic success and governmental efficiency of northern Italy, relative to the south, in large part to its richer associational life, claiming that associations 'instil in their members habits of cooperation, solidarity, and public-spiritedness' (1993: 89–90). However, this co-operation and solidarity is invoked most commonly to resolve collective action problems at the level of smaller groups. If the economic goals of a group conflict with those of other groups or of unorganised interests, the overall effect of group memberships and activities on economic performance could be negative. Adam Smith noted that when 'people of the same trade' meet 'even for merriment and diversion' the result is often 'a conspiracy against the public' or 'some contrivance to raise prices'.[3] Similarly, Olson (1982) observes that horizontal associations can hurt growth because many of them act as special interest groups lobbying for preferential policies that impose disproportionate costs on society. Putnam's claims have also been widely questioned by empirical studies on Italy. In a recent paper, Peri (2004) provides a measure of social capital as civic involvement, given by the first principal component of three variables representing associational density, newspaper readers and voter turnout at a particular referendum. The author finds a positive correlation of civic involvement with measures of economic development in the raw data, but attributes it mostly to North–South differences: the correlation in fact does not survive checks of robustness and the inclusion of geographic controls. It is noteworthy that Peri's measurement of social capital follows a conceptual pathway very similar to that already covered by Putnam et al. also (1993), and suffers from the shortcomings described earlier.

Keefer and Knack (1997) provide some evidence for the conflicting influences of associational activity on growth, using a variable from Banks and Textor (1963) called 'interest articulation', which assesses (on a subjective scale ranging from 1 to 4) how effectively groups articulate their policy preferences to government. Although the ability of groups to articulate their interests is likely to be an important restraint on government, it also provides groups with a way to capture private benefits at the expense of society. Consistent with the view that these two effects tend to counteract each other, 'interest articulation' proves to be an insignificant predictor of growth when introduced into Barro-type cross-country tests. As pointed out in the previous section, Knack and Keefer (1997) find that trust and civic norms are unrelated to horizontal networks and have a strong impact on economic performance in a sample of 29 market economies.

Helliwell (1996) shows that trust, and an index of group memberships, are each negatively and significantly related to productivity growth for a sample of 17 OECD members. This sample omits the poor and middle-income nations for which trust has the largest effects.

The complexity of the relationship between social capital and growth is even more evident at the theoretical level. In particular, it is possible to argue that economic growth could be itself a factor of social capital's destruction: if people devote too much time to work and consumption, therefore sustaining growth, little time remains for social participation. Routledge and von Amsberg (2003) show that the process of economic growth is generally accompanied by higher labour turnover, which changes the social structure, increasing heterogeneity and affecting social capital. The authors focus on social capital as the aspect of the social structure influencing co-operative behaviour. In larger communities, which grow faster or are more efficient, social capital can deteriorate, making co-operative trade generally harder to sustain. By contrast, reduced labour mobility, which results in decreased labour efficiency, increases welfare by increasing the proportion of trades that are co-operative. In other words, 'the benefit of the increased social capital can outweigh the cost of lost efficiency' (ibid.: 172). This result is supported by Alesina and La Ferrara (2000), who show that in heterogeneous communities participation in groups that require direct contact among members is low, arguing that such a decline destroys social trust, therefore hampering economic growth. This study contains an interesting empirical result about substitution between social and private activities. The authors show that, controlling for individual and community level variables, 'moving from a full-time to a part-time job increases the propensity to participate' (ibid.: 880): working more brings about a reduction in social participation. Costa and Kahn (2003) show that this process has been particularly relevant for women in the last half century, since the enormous increase in their labour force participation rate, in the US as well as in other advanced societies, has subtracted from them much time previously available for social activities.

Devoting most time to work and consumption can also be interpreted as a 'defensive choice': Antoci et al. (2002) argue that the individual utility of social participation depends both on one's own and on aggregate participation, as well as on the opportunities available in the social environment. Agents may 'defend' themselves from a poor social environment by shifting to private activities, less exposed to external effects. The authors show that, 'If this strategy spreads over, private activities will be fostered, but at the expense of social activities. Since both effects accumulate over time, the outcome may be a joint occurrence of economic growth and social poverty' (ibid.: 23). By contrast, spending more time in social activities can lead to a richer social environment, but may act as an obstacle to private growth. However, the political science literature widely shows that social participation can foster the diffusion of trust (Almond and Verba 1963; Brehm and Rahn 1997; Stolle 1998; Stolle and Rochon 1998; Hooghe and Stolle 2003), therefore indirectly supporting economic growth. In other words, it is possible to argue that, if economic growth destroys social participation and trust, it can run faster, but is not sustainable in the long run.

All empirical studies reported in the former two sections present also a further, critical, limit: they do not take into appropriate account the very multidimensionality of the concept of social capital. Therefore, ignoring fertile insights provided by the sociological literature, the economics research on the empirics of social capital generally neglects the necessary distinction between different forms of social capital, e.g. 'bonding' and 'bridging social capital'. Studies in this field generally consider just from one to three of social capital's dimensions for carrying out empirical investigations on their effects on a few, definite, outcomes. According to such a limited scope of analysis, these studies in turn conclude that social capital is good or bad for economic growth.

Concluding remarks

Social capital is a multidimensional concept. Its most effective definition is that provided by Coleman, who stated that 'Social capital is defined by its function. It is not a single entity, but a variety of different entities, with two elements in common: they all consist in some aspect of social structures, and they facilitate certain actions of actors within the structure' (1988: 98). Such a vague definition, however, makes every attempt of empirical analysis difficult and hazardous. The review of measurement methods carried out in this chapter has pointed out six main weaknesses affecting almost all the empirical studies:

1   There is not a single, universal, definition of what social capital is, nor a unique, underlying, method of measurement to be used within the empirical research.
2   The use of different definitions, diverse indicators from various data sources, makes any general assessment difficult, due to incomparability in sampling designs and question wording.
3   The use of measures of trust drawn from the *World Values Survey* leads to the creation of indicators of 'social' trust losing their linkage with the social and historical circumstances in which trust and social capital are located.

4   The use of 'indirect' indicators, not representing social capital's key components as identified by the theoretical literature, may be misleading, and cause considerable confusion about what social capital *is*, as distinct from its *outcomes*, and what the relationship between social capital and its outcomes *may be*.
5   The difficulty of accounting for the multidimensionality of each of social capital's diverse facets, such as social networks.
6   The weakness of social capital measures simply based on the density of voluntary organisations.

Of course, from a lexical point of view, it is possible to attribute the 'social capital' label to every aspect of the economy's social fabric providing a favourable environment for production and well-being. Still, such an approach poses a 'logic' problem: if social capital is everything that can make agents co-operate or markets work better, then any empirical analysis will find that social capital causes co-operation among agents and improves the efficiency of markets. This approach simply 'sterilises' the social capital literature, making it unable to foster the explanatory power of economic studies addressing the socio-cultural factors of growth. The survey of the literature carried out in this chapter points out:

1   The need to acknowledge the multidimensional nature of social capital. It does not make sense taking into consideration just a single dimension, considering it as representative of the concept as a whole, and analysing its effect on economic performance. In contrast to what to date has been done by most cross-country studies, we have to be very cautious in carrying out international comparisons relying on just a single basic indicator (like trust levels). Each of social capital's dimensions may exert diverse effects on economic variables, in turn fostering or hampering growth and development. The need emerges to distinguish at least between 'bonding' and 'bridging social capital'. Bonding social capital is shaped by social ties fostering the pursuit of narrow – sometimes sectarian and contrasting with community's well-being – interests, and hampering the diffusion of knowledge and information. Bridging social capital is composed of weak ties, building bridges and connections between different types of networks, therefore fostering knowledge diffusion and socio-economic progress.
2   The expediency of focusing just on structural key dimensions of the concept therefore excludes by such measurement the toolbox of all indicators referring to social capital's supposed outcomes. Some recent studies advance the possibility of focusing on social networks, rather than on measures of perceived trust or on hazardous 'indirect' indicators. Such a strategy can foster the robustness of analysis without causing a relevant loss of generality. In this case, however, we must remember the existence of different types of social networks. Some of them do not necessarily play a positive role in the process of economic development and, at the micro level, in the agents' everyday lives.

Acknowledgements

I am deeply indebted to Elisabetta Basile and Claudio Cecchi for precious comments and suggestions. I wish to thank also Sergio Cesaratto, Benedetto Gui, Robert Leonardi, Raffaella Nanetti, Victor Sergeyev, Frans N. Stokman and Eric M. Uslaner for useful hints and conversations on my research topics. Needless to say, usual disclaimers apply. Useful materials for the study of social capital are available on the *Social Capital Gateway* website, providing resources for social sciences edited by the author of this chapter (www.socialcapitalgateway.org) (see Sabatini 2005a).

Notes

1 Durlauf's benchmark studies are Furstenberg and Hughes (1995), Narayan and Pritchett (1999) and Knack and Keefer (1997).
2 See, for example, Knack and Keefer (1997), La Porta et al. (1997), Zak and Knack (2001), Uslaner (2002), Beugelsdijk and van Schaik (2001) and Bjørnskov (2003).
3 This quotation is taken from Knack and Keefer (1997).

References

Alesina, A. and La Ferrara, E. (2000) 'Participation in heterogeneous communities', *Quarterly Journal of Economics*, 115(3): 847–904.
Almond, G. and Verba, S. (1963) *The Civic Culture*, Princeton, NJ: Princeton University Press.
Andreotti, A. and Barbieri, P. (eds) (2003) 'Reti e capitale sociale', *Inchiesta*, 139.
Antoci, A., Sacco, P.L. and Vanin, P. (2002) 'On the possible conflict between economic growth and social development', paper presented at the Conference 'Il valore economico delle relazioni impersonali', Milano-Bicocca, 24 September.
Arnott, R. and Stiglitz, J. (1991) 'Moral hazard and non-market institutions: dysfunctional crowding out or peer monitoring', *American Economic Review*, 81(1): 179–190.
Arrow, K. (1999) 'Observations on social capital', in P. Dasgupta and I. Serageldin (eds) *Social Capital: A Multifaceted Perspective*, Washington, DC: World Bank.
Banfield, E.G. (1958) *The Moral Basis of a Backward Society*, New York: Free Press.
Banks, A.S. and Textor R.S. (1963) *A Cross-polity Survey*, Cambridge, MA: MIT Press.
Barro, R.J. (1996) *Determinants of Economic Growth: A Cross-Country Empirical Study*, NBER Working Paper, 5698, Cambridge, MA: National Bureau of Economic Research.
Becker, G. (1974) 'A theory of social interactions', *Journal of Political Economy*, 82(6): 1063–1093.
Becker, G. (1996) *Accounting for Tastes*, Cambridge, MA: Harvard University Press.
Bénabou, R. (1996) 'Heterogeneity, stratification and growth: macroeconomic implications of community structure and school finance', *American Economic Review*, 86: 584–609.
Berg, J., Dickaut, J. and McCabe, K. (1995) 'Trust, reciprocity and social history', *Games and Economic Behavior*, 10: 122–142.
Beugelsdijk, S. and van Schaik, T. (2001) *Social Capital and Regional Economic Growth*, discussion paper Tilburg: Tilburg University, Center for Economic Research.

Bjørnskov, C. (2003) 'The happy few: cross-country evidence on social capital and life satisfaction', *Kyklos*, 56(1): 3–16.

Bollen, K. (1989) *Structural Equations with Latent Variables*, New York: Wiley.

Bourdieu, P. (1980) 'Le capital social', *Actes de la Recherche en Sciences Sociales*, 31: 2–3.

Bourdieu, P. (1986) 'The forms of capital', in J. G. Richardson (ed.) *Handbook of Theory and Research for the Sociology of Education*, New York: Greenwood Press, pp. 241–258.

Bourdieu, P. and Wacquant, L. (1986) *An Invitation to Reflexive Sociology*, Cambridge: Polity Press.

Bowles, S. and Gintis, H. (2002) 'Social capital and community governance', *Economic Journal*, 112(483): 419–436.

Brehm, J. and Rahn, W. (1997) 'Individual-level evidence for the causes and consequences of social capital', *American Journal of Political Science*, 41(3): 999–1023.

Brown, L.D. and Ashman, D. (1996) 'Participation, social capital and intersectoral problem solving: African and Asian cases', *World Development*, 24(6): 1467–1479.

Coleman, J. (1988) 'Social capital in the creation of human capital', *American Journal of Sociology*, 94: 95–120.

Coleman, J. (1990) *Foundations of Social Theory*, Cambridge, MA: Harvard University Press.

Collier, P. and Gunning, J.W. (1997) 'Explaining African economic performance', *Journal of Economic Literature*, XXXVII: 64–111.

Costa, D.L. and Kahn, M. (2003) 'Understanding the American decline in social capital, 1952–1998', *Kyklos*, 56(1): 17–46.

Durlauf, S.N. (1999) 'The case against social capital', *Focus*, 20: 3.

Durlauf, S.N. (2002) 'On the empirics of social capital', *Economic Journal*, 112(483): 459–479.

Durlauf, S.N. and Fafchamps, M. (2004) *Social Capital*, Berkeley: Centre for the Study of African Economies Working Paper Series, No. 214, Berkeley Economic Press.

Fehr, E. and Gatcher, S. (2000) 'Fairness and retaliation: the economics of reciprocity', *Journal of Economic Perspectives*, 14(3): 159–181.

Fehr, E., Gatcher, S. and Kirchsteiger, G. (1997) 'Reciprocity as a contract enforcement device: experimental evidence', *Econometrica*, 65(4): 833–860.

Fine, B. (2001) *Social Capital versus Social Theory: Political Economy and Social Science at the Turn of the Millennium*, London and New York: Routledge.

Foley, M.W. and Edwards, B. (1999) 'Is it time to disinvest in social capital?', *Journal of Public Policy* 19(2): 199–231.

Frey, B.S. (1997) *Not Just for the Money: An Economic Theory of Personal Motivation*, Cheltenham: Edward Elgar.

Fukuyama, F. (1995) *Trust: The Social Virtues and the Creation of Prosperity*, New York: Free Press.

Furstenberg, F. and Hughes, M. (1995) 'Social capital and successful development among at-risk youth', *Journal of Marriage and the Family*, 57: 580–592.

Gradstein, M. and Justman, M. (2002) 'Education, social cohesion and economic growth', *American Economic Review*, 92(4): 1192–1204.

Granovetter, M. (1973) 'The strength of weak ties', *American Journal of Sociology*, 78: 1360–1380.

Granovetter, M. (1985) 'Economic action and social structure: the problem of embeddedness', *American Journal of Sociology*, 91: 481–510.

Gui, B. (2000) 'Beyond transactions: on the interpersonal dimension of economic reality', *Annals of Public and Cooperative Economics*, 71(2): 139.

Gui, B. (2002) 'Più che scambi, incontri. La teoria economica alle prese con i fenomeni interpersonali', in P. L. Sacco and S. e Zamagni (eds) *Complessità relazionale e comportamento economico* (*Economic Theory and Social Interactions*), Bologna: Il Mulino.

Guiso, L., Sapienza, P. and Zingales, L. (2004) 'The role of social capital in financial development', *American Economic Review*, 94(3): 526–556.

Hanifan, L.J. (1916) 'The rural school community center', *Annals of the American Academy of Political and Social Sciences*, 67: 130–138.

Heckman, J.J. (2000) 'Causal parameters and policy analysis in economics: a twentieth century retrospective', *Quarterly Journal of Economics*, 115(1): 45–97.

Helliwell, J.F. (1996) *Economic Growth and Social Capital in Asia*, NBER Working Paper No. W5470.

Helliwell, J.F. and Putnam, R.D. (1995) 'Economic growth and social capital in Italy', *Eastern Economic Journal*, 21: 295–307.

Homans, G. (1961) *Social Behavior: Its Elementary Forms*, New York: Harcourt, Brace and World.

Hooghe, M. and Stolle, D. (eds) (2003) *Generating Social Capital: Civil Society and Institutions in Comparative Perspective*, New York: Palgrave.

Isham, J., Kelly, T. and Ramaswamy, S. (eds) (2002) *Social Capital and Economic Development: Well-being in Developing Countries*, Cheltenham: Edward Elgar.

Jacobs, J. (1961) *The Death and Life of Great American Cities*, New York: Random House.

Jöreskog, K.G., and Sörbom, D. (1979) *Advances in Factor Analysis and Structural Equation Models*, Cambridge, MA: Abt Books.

Kahneman, D. and Tversky, A. (1979) 'Prospect theory: an analysis of decision under risk', *Econometrica*, 47: 263–291.

Knack, S. (1992) 'Civic norms, social sanctions, and voter turnout', *Rationality and Society*, IV: 133–156.

Knack, S. and Keefer, P. (1997) 'Does social capital have an economic payoff? A cross-country investigation', *Quarterly Journal of Economics*, 112(4): 1251–1288.

Kormendi, R.C. and Meguire, P.G. (1985) 'Macroeconomic determinants of growth: cross-country evidence', *Journal of Monetary Economics*, 16: 141–163.

La Porta, R., Lopez-de-Silanes, F., Shleifer, A. and Vishny, R.W. (1997) 'Trust in large organizations', *American Economic Review*, Papers and Proceedings of the Hundred and Fourth Annual Meeting of the American Economic Association, 57(2): 333–338.

Loury, G. (1977) 'A dynamic theory of racial income differences', in P. A. Wallace and E. Mund (eds) *Women, Minorities, and Employment Discrimination*, Lexington, MA: Lexington Books.

Mutz, D. (2002) 'Cross-cutting social networks: testing democratic theory in practice', *American Political Science Review*, 96(1): 111–126.

Narayan, D. and Pritchett, L. (1999) 'Cents and sociability: household income and social capital in rural Tanzania', *Economic Development and Cultural Change*, 47(4): 871–897.

Nuzzo, G. and Micucci, G. (2003) 'La misurazione del capitale sociale. Evidenze da un'analisi sul territorio italiano' (The measurement of social capital: evidence from Italy), paper presented at the Symposium on 'Economie locali, modelli di agglomerazione e apertura internazionale', organised by the Bank of Italy and the University of Bologna, 20 November.

Olson, M. (1982) *The Rise and Decline of Nations*, New Haven, CT: Yale University Press.

Paxton, P. (1999) 'Is social capital declining in the United States? A multiple indicator assessment', *American Journal of Sociology*, 105(1): 88–127.

Peri, G. (2004) 'Socio-cultural variables and economic success: evidence from Italian provinces 1951–1991', *Topics in Macroeconomics*, 4(1).

Piselli, F. (2001) 'Capitale sociale: un concetto situazionale e dinamico' ('Social capital: a dynamic concept'), in A. Bagnasco, F. Piselli, A. Pizzorno and C. Trigilia (eds) *Il Capitale Sociale*, Bologna: Il Mulino.

Popielarz, P.A. (1999) '(In)voluntary association: a multilevel analysis of gender segregation in voluntary associations', *Gender and Society*, 13(2): 234–250.

Portes, A. (1998) 'Social capital: its origins and applications in modern sociology', *Annual Review of Sociology*, 24: 1–24.

Putnam, R.D. (1995a) 'Bowling alone: America's declining social capital', *Journal of Democracy* 6(1): 65–78.

Putnam, R.D. (1995b) 'Tuning in, tuning out: the strange disappearance of social capital in America', *Political Science and Politics*, 28: 664–683.

Putnam, R.D. (2000) *Bowling Alone: The Collapse and Revival of American Community*, New York: Touchstone Books.

Putnam, R.D., Leonardi, R. and Nanetti, R.Y. (1993) *Making Democracy Work*, Princeton, NJ: Princeton University Press.

Rosenberg, M. (1956) 'Misanthropy and political ideology', *American Sociological Review*, 21: 690–695.

Rosenblum, N.L. (1998) *Membership and Morals*, Princeton, NJ: Princeton University Press.

Routledge, B. and von Amsberg, J. (2003) 'Social capital and growth', *Journal of Monetary Economics*, 50(1): 167–193.

Sabatini, F. (2005a) 'Resources for the study of social capital', *Journal of Economic Education*, 36(2): 198.

Sabatini, F. (2005b) *Social Capital as Social Networks: A New Framework for Measurement*, Working Paper No. 83, Rome: Department of Public Economics, University of Rome La Sapienza.

Sabatini, F. (2006) 'The role of social capital in economic development: investigating the causal relationship through structural equations models', paper presented at the 'Social Capital, Sustainability and Socio-Economic Cohesion' conference, London School of Economics, 29–30 June.

Seeley, J.R., Sim, A.R. and Loosley, E.W. (1956) *Crestwood Heights: A Study of the Culture of Suburban Life*, New York: Basic Books.

Solow, R.M. (1995) 'But verify', *New Republic*: 36–39.

Stolle, D. (1998) 'Bowling together, bowling alone: the development of generalized trust in voluntary associations', *Political Psychology*, 19: 497–525.

Stolle, D. and Rochon, T.R. (1998) 'Are all associations alike? Member diversity, associational type, and the creation of social capital', *American Behavioural Scientist*, 42: 47–65.

Sudgen, R. (2000) 'Team preferences', *Economics and Philosophy*, 16: 175–204.

Temple, J. and Johnson, P.A. (1998) 'Social capability and economic growth', *Quarterly Journal of Economics*, 113(3): 965–990.

Torsvik, G. (2000) 'Social capital and economic development: a plea for the mechanism', *Rationality and Society*, 12: 451–476.

Uslaner, E.M. (2002) *The Moral Foundations of Trust*, Cambridge: Cambridge University Press.

Whiteley, P.F. (2000) 'Economic growth and social capital', *Political Studies*, 48: 443–466.

Wuthnow, R. (2002) 'The changing character of social capital in the United States, in R. D. Putnam (ed.) *Democracies in Flux: The Evolution of Social Capital in Contemporary Society*, Oxford: Oxford University Press.

Zak, P. and Knack, S. (2001) 'Trust and growth', *Economic Journal*, 111: 295–321.

Chapter 8

Co-operation, networks and learning regions

Network analysis as a method for investigating structures of interaction

Wolfgang Jütte

The notion of networks is currently in ascendancy within the field of adult and continuing education within Germany (see, for example, Loeper 2003: 186). Propagated in particular in the context of regional development, network concepts have been playing an increasingly important role since the end of the 1980s. The establishment of regional co-operation networks is expected to solve structural problems and offer innovation potential. The concept of the 'learning region' is a typical example of the promotion of more networking between the various providers of education, and is exemplified by German Learning Region initiatives.[1]

In discussions on continuing education, co-operation and networks are often associated with normative guidelines and idealistic descriptions. This would seem to be in contrast to the apparently naive descriptive-analytical approach of network analysis. Correspondingly, network-analytical work has been given a rather hesitant reception in continuing education research.

This chapter is based on my study, *Soziales Netzwerk Weiterbildung* (Social Network Continuing Education) (Jütte 2002), which was one of the first network analytical studies in the field of adult and continuing education in Germany. The study investigates the influence of social relationships in a local institutional landscape on the provision of continuing education. Interviews with those running, and working for providers of, continuing education were at the centre of this qualitative network analysis. In addition, a formal network analysis was carried out on the web of relationships between local institutions. This was, therefore, a qualitative network analysis in the sense of a mixed methods approach, as is often to be found in studies of pedagogical fields. The network visualisation proved to be an important 'translation step'. As will be explained in this chapter, visualising the network of relationships made it easier to refer the actors' patterns of interpretation and actions mentioned in the interviews to the regional structures of the local continuing education landscape. At the same time, visualisation also opened up opportunities for more far-reaching insights.

Inter-organisational co-operation in continuing education as a field of research

Starting point: observations on co-operation

The starting point for the study described here was the issue of co-operation in continuing education. Because this is a very particular system in comparison to other areas of education, there is a need for systematisation and organisation. Here, co-operation is seen as a key for the development of a 'system of continuing education'. Division of labour and co-operation between providers and institutions should lead to a co-ordinated joint achievement.

If, having considered the history of the concept of co-operation, one then takes stock of the actual co-operation; the effect is sobering. One of the everyday phenomena of continuing education is that providers and institutions do not know each other or do not co-operate as optimally as their mutual tasks require. Research literature paints a dubious picture, where successful co-operation seems to be the exception rather than the rule. Previous attempts to improve co-operation are considered to be far from optimal.

There are hardly any differentiated theoretical-methodical research designs to investigate co-operation in continuing education. Co-operation may be omnipresent as a normative objective (the political imperative of co-operation), but we have only an incomplete picture of the daily interactions between the actors in continuing education. Authors present their knowledge of the field and, on the basis of their experience, ideas on the potential and limits of co-operation are developed. Many of the generalisations made are founded on a narrow empirical basis; descriptions of approaches to co-operation developed by educational policy prevail. But how does co-operation take place on the level of practical everyday behaviour? The Research Memorandum for Adult and Continuing Education in Germany points out the need for an understanding of co-operation which is in touch with reality:

> Observations on competition, networking and its dynamics are not only part of a better scientific development of the field, but also provide a 'picture' which can guide practical behaviour and, furthermore, become the basis for both monitoring the system and advising policy.
>
> (Arnold et al. 2000: 23)

In spite of some critical field reports on model projects, there is a lack of investigation that would provide an adequate understanding of co-operation in everyday professional life. This incomplete picture of the everyday practice of co-operation in continuing education is also due to the theoretical and methodological deficits of research. Theory development on the issue of co-operation is to a certain extent restricted to regulatory policy. Research work often refers to objectives and planning documents of educational policy. Models of co-operation are developed and classified, only to conclude that they do not work in practice. Perhaps the analysis of co-operation reveals a normatively constricted concept of the system, as pointed out by Faulstich et al. (1997: 11): 'Current thinking in systems seems to still be attached to the Hegelian tradition of the German state philosophy.'

Starting point: networks as a strategy for modernisation

Analyses of present day society can no longer succeed without referring to networks. One of the characteristics of modern societies is that they form reticular (i.e. net-like structures) and increasingly organise themselves in the form of horizontal and open networks. 'Networks constitute the new social morphology of our societies' (Castells 1996: 469).

Networks represent the increasing differentiation and division of labour between sectors of society, which results in changing needs for co-ordination. New forms of organisation, which need changed mechanisms of control and co-ordination beyond hierarchy and market, are replacing the classic bureaucratic organisations.

The processes of change in society require a new structural logic, and networks appear to offer a suitable response. Great hopes are attached to networks as an innovative form of organisation. Network theories are gaining importance, not least against the backdrop of the crisis in the state's ability to control. In the face of financial cuts and a changing concept of the state, networking potential is being emphasised universally. This characterises the 'network economy in the welfare state' (Dahme and Wohlfahrt 2000).

The network metaphor is increasingly finding its way into literature on adult education, and many signs indicate that it may become a common expression. This is not least due to the fact that the idea of networking is in some way 'warming', because it is connected with relationships. Hopes are being pinned on networking, which conveys the impression that problems can be solved and a wide range of aims achieved. There are hardly any pilot schemes which do not emphasise their network character. Network has become the 'social metaphor for modernization' (Dahme 2000: 47) and has a lot to do with political orchestration.

The issue of system structure always involves consideration of available resources as well as their distribution. Here, various control (intervention) models exist simultaneously. In the practice of continuing education, a mixture of different forms of control can be observed. Great significance is attached to networks, especially by politicians and administrators. From the point of view of control theory, networks can be seen as 'a mixture of search, learning and negotiation systems, in which several actors cooperate and maintain discursive exchange relations. The state has an interest in such cooperation and networks taking place, because in this way it can gather information about autonomous associated actors or organisations acting in a subsidiary fashion, which it would not otherwise have access to' (ibid.: 50). Calls for networking are intended to counteract deficits in quality and control, but at the same time aim to optimise the use of resources and restrict costs or achieve savings. Networking is primarily discussed under the aspect of developing resources; genuinely pedagogical implications are often neglected.

Starting point: learning regions

At the end of the 1980s and the beginning of the 1990s, the status of the regions was enhanced in discussions concerning continuing education policy in Germany. Linked to regionalisation was the hope of strengthening the endogenous potential of a region. In this period, the governments of the various federal states (*Landesregierungen*) began to have their structures of continuing education evaluated by experts in order to find a framework for their further development. Models for regional co-operation and networking (i.e. the creation of networks) were also developed in the experts' reports. For example, the North Rhine-Westphalian Commission to evaluate continuing education suggested the creation of 'regional continuing education networks'. As far as their spectra of achievements are concerned, these networks are said to:

* promote regional needs assessment in cooperation with social, economic and cultural institutions,
* achieve the coordination of regional opportunities regarding the supply of needs,
* assure minimum standards of quality, as have been agreed or prescribed by the federal state (*Land*), for the institutions and the courses they offer and, where applicable, award marks of quality,
* improve the transparency of continuing education provision and promote continuing education through public relations work,
* safeguard and coordinate advice on continuing education,
* be involved, within the framework of integrated regional politics, in improving the cultural, social and economic structure.

(Giesecke et al. 1997: 193)

Numerous regional co-operation systems have been created in the past years. These are closely connected with the idea of 'learning regions', which are a response to the demand for stronger links between the various providers of continuing education and to the criticism of measures taken in isolation. In the concept of the 'lifelong learning region' promoted by the European Commission (2002), the network idea is connected very closely with the notion of closer partnership and co-operation between different stakeholders in formal, non-formal and informal settings (see Sankey and Osborne 2006).

The idea of concentrating and linking activities and actors remains of central importance. Through the increased co-operation of actors working within educational, employment and labour market policy, and other fields of politics, areas of education will become dovetailed and new interfaces and openings between the various areas of education will arise.

Network analysis: the case study

In the following section, an example is used to show how network analytical concepts can serve as a framework of reference and analysis for investigations. Here, I refer to my study of the local institutional landscape of continuing education in the North of Germany (Jütte 2002, 2006).

Distinction between networks as an organisational form and as an analytical construct

In the case of institutional networks in continuing education, we are usually dealing with the interaction-type inter-organisational network, i.e. it is 'understood as being a specific cooperation of several organizations which is planned to last for a longer period of time in order to achieve mutually defined goals and to gain added value for the individual participants' (Wohlfahrt 2002: 39).

Whereas the 'goal orientation of the network character' (Scheff 1999: 59) is part of the institutional network, the reference framework for the 'social network' is different. A network-analytical starting point has a heuristic function for investigating relational structures in continuing education. Thus the concept of the network approaches that of the system. The inter-relations between interacting actors as a whole form a local system.

Hereafter in this chapter, a social-scientific network concept is used which understands the network not as an organisational category but as an analytical category. Accordingly, a social network can be defined as a structure of social relations of units and the linkages between these. Clyde Mitchell, a founder of modern network analysis, calls it a 'specific set of linkages among a defined set of persons, with the additional property that the characteristics of these linkages as a whole may be used to interpret the social behaviour of the persons involved' (Mitchell 1969: 2).

In recent years, network analysis has 'taken off' scientifically and appeals to many disciplines. As an interdisciplinary research approach it is particularly widespread in the US and has developed its own organs of communication. The subjects investigated by network analysis are manifold. For example, business network research is directed at analysing company and production networks; psychological network research examines social networks, primarily with regard to their support function when coping with crises and illnesses; and network research can also be aimed at analysing many fields of politics.

However, network analysis is not simply a 'statistical instrument' but is also a 'perspective for theory' (Jansen 1999: 11). These rudimentary theoretical approaches are more likely to be a series of orientation hypotheses about the action of actors in socially structured contexts. In his theory of 'embeddedness', the American sociologist Mark Granovetter (1985) refers to how action is integrated in social relations. In order to map functional action in an appropriate way, the integration of the actors in the social structure must be taken into consideration.

Direct and indirect social relations open up opportunities or are obstacles to the actor's purposeful action. Network analysis views the behaviour of individuals against the backdrop of structural relations. Distinctions between 'strong' and 'weak' ties are just as relevant for network-theoretical assumptions and fields of investigation as the 'multiplexity' of relations and the creation of social capital.

Field of research, set of actors

In order to chart regional local continuing education as a social network of relations in an adequate manner, three levels can be distinguished analytically: the individual level, the level of social interaction and the level of the structure. Different units are the subject of the relational analysis on the various action levels (see Table 8.1). On the individual level, analysis is concerned with the individual actor. Here, explanations are sought in connection with the characteristics of a person (e.g. co-operative action-related orientation; the way a person sees himself in his professional role). On the level of social action, analysis is concerned with the processes of exchange between the actors (e.g. forms of co-operation; the forming of coalitions). On the structural level, the entire local system of continuing education is viewed (e.g. constellations of actors; structure of the actors' environment).

In the study described here, the landscape of continuing education examined was a medium-sized town which was given the name of 'Nordstadt' in the investigation. It is assumed that the ensemble of interacting actors as a whole and their inter-relations form a local–regional functional system. This includes the fact

Table 8.1 Multi-level analysis of the 'interaction system in continuing education'

Social level	Actor perspective	(Examples of) research aspects
(1) Individual level	Individual actors	• co-operative orientation of action • the way a person sees himself in his professional role • ...
(2) Level of social interaction	Relationships between the actors	• forms of working together • exchange relations • formation of groups • processes of co-operation • ...
(3) Level of the structure/ system	Structure of the network as a whole	• structural embedding • changing structures • constellations of actors • ...

that those acting there – as is the case in every system – are dependent on inter-action, communication and co-operation. This is what the term 'social network' implies: a network is said to be social when it is formed by relations.

The study was designed to be an analysis of a whole network in which the specific relations of all actors of a precisely defined and differentiated system or of a population are mapped. In the first step, 31 organisational actors who belong to the local system of continuing education were identified. This set of actors forms what is known as the basic entirety of the social system. However, gathering information on social relations poses difficulties because these relations can be defined differently depending on the content and context. Structures turn out to be a 'network of networks' (Jansen 1999: 20).

In the standardised survey, a fixed circle of actors was set for all 31 actors included in the investigation and they were asked to give information on the three dimensions of description:

- contact (How often are you in contact with actor X?),
- significance (How significant do you consider actor X to be?),
- liking (How much do you like actor X?).

This approach could be described as a sociometric analysis of the whole network. As far as the method is concerned, it is similar to the sociometry developed by Jacob Moreno in the 1940s for charting social relationships in groups (Moreno 1953).

For the mathematical-statistical analysis of the network of 31 actors, the data has to be organised in a special way. The notation of the network is conducted in square contact matrices (see Figure 8.1). The actor giving information is indicated in the columns and the actors who are being assessed in the rows. The data matrix forms the starting point for various network-analytical operations. The analysis of sociometric network data usually requires special software programs. One of the most common measures for nets is the density of the network. The density of the whole network is recorded by relating the number of actual ties to the number of ties which would potentially be possible. The density of relations says some-thing about the closeness and the frequency of mutual contacts between the actors. It gives an indication of the intensity of the inter-organisational communications structure and the exchange of knowledge between the actors, which are important prerequisites for co-operation. In closely woven networks, actors have direct communication. It can be assumed that a high density of relationships indicates co-operation. The more the actors in a region that are in contact with each other, the greater is the opportunity for co-operation. The density of a network is also seen as a measure of the proliferation of innovation (cf. Jansen 1999: 88).

By asking 'Who are you in contact with?', the direct institutional contacts within the system of continuing education are captured. The symmetrical matrix (Figure 8.1) represents the local web of contacts which is stretched between the institutions.

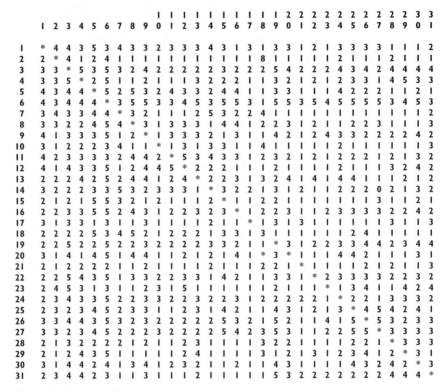

Figure 8.1 Matrix of the contacts.

If continuing education is regarded as an interacting system, the institutions maintain exchange relations with others, as the interaction matrix below shows. The contact matrix can be read as an indication of the exchange of resources or of the communication structure. Here, not only the structures of the contacts but also the barriers to communication are reflected.

Visualising networks as a mediation step between actor-related and structure-related interpretation

The study aimed to give a complete view of local continuing education by showing and outlining the dense network of relations. In doing so, both quantitative and qualitative forms of gathering and analysing data were used. Only through close combination of various multi-method research strategies (namely triangulation) were informative results expected to be yielded.

Co-operation as a social process must neither be attributed solely to personal characteristics nor solely to the structural context. In the interviews, actors gave information about their perception of the institutional landscape, about their own positive and negative choices regarding interaction partners and about the way they see themselves. Because these are actions in a social, interdependent system, it is informative to know more about the mutual interactions between several actors who refer to each other. Correspondingly, relational surveying of the local institutional landscape can contribute to a better understanding of the subjective interpretations and choices of individuals. Taking the individual perspective of the actors as a starting point, the entire structure is viewed in order to discover something about the participants' embeddedness.

Whilst attempting to explore structural ties and communicate the findings in a suitable way, I encountered network visualisation. Network analysis has always been associated with attempts to visualise structural data. Moreno (1953) attached great importance to graphic representations and developed coloured sociogrammes to represent group structures. But it was progress in data processing which opened up new possibilities for representing complex social structures. The graphic representations of network relations and constellations of actors for the study described were created in co-operation with Lothar Krempel of the Max-Planck Institute for the Study of Societies in Cologne and are described and shown below.

Network structures can be represented in various forms. Data regarding relations can be represented both in matrices and in graphs. As can be seen from the sociomatrix shown in Figure 8.2, the 'reality content of the data matrix' (Wienhold 2000: 127) is not directly apparent to the viewer. The 'empiristic language' makes it difficult to read. By representing complex structures of relations through the use of visualisations (cf. Krempel 2002, 2005), an important translation step is achieved. The special achievement of data visualisation is that it makes relations visible which would otherwise remain hidden or not be immediately apparent because of the large amount of data. In addition to this, the visualisation of complex structures of relations makes it easier to relate the actors' patterns of interpretation and action to structures. Looking at an actor's structural embeddedness provides a keener understanding for his subjective interpretations and choices.

In the qualitative network analysis described here, visualisation is used as a procedure for examining the macro-relations more closely. The visualisation of data concerning relations provides an image of the situation which helps the viewer to see the actor in his relational and spatial contexts and thus to gain insight into his local 'anchoring'. By considering the institutional landscape holistically, the actors' relational environment can be better taken into consideration in the interpretation of relations. The visualisation sensitises the viewer for the relational 'anchoring' of actors as members of the local community.

Figure 8.2 shows the functional and structural relations which exist between the 31 actors in the local system of continuing education. The complex interconnections form the complete configuration of local continuing education. Although one of the strengths of network visualisation is its intuitive readability, the layout and patterns of features used are described here. The actors are represented by nodes. Different colours are used to represent the different groups of actors. The stronger

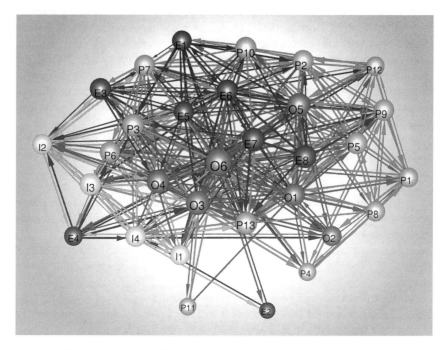

Figure 8.2 Contacts in the local institutional landscape.

the actors are connected to each other or the closer their contact to each other is, the nearer together they are. Actors who have no direct or only indirect contact are located more remotely from each other. The overall location is a result of the centrality of the actors; the central actors are arranged in the middle. At the same time, the number of direct ties an actor has (degree) plays a role. The degrees of the actors are reflected in the size of the node.

Let's look again in more detail at the location of the actors in the whole structure. Who are the central actors? This question of sociometric status is an old one. Specific opportunities and obstacles result from the location of the actor in the whole network. The figure expresses an evaluation. The units are arranged in concentric circles according to their status. The closer an actor is to the centre, the higher is his sociometric value. Correspondingly, this is weaker the further a unit is towards the periphery. The measures of centrality reveal that there are 'visible' institutions, i.e. those which are in the middle of the network. However it is not possible to deduce the 'significance' or 'desirability' directly from this. Institutions located on the periphery, which operate in monopolies or niche markets, may well have a comfortable life. However, there is something to be said for the network analytical assumption that central actors have advantages in terms of information. They have a better overview of the whole network in all its diversity. Central organisations are characterised by a great knowledge of resources ('knowing who does what where'); in uncertain environments in particular, it is possible that this results in greater certainty.

If we look at the peripheral actors, the first organisation which stands out is that of the Danish minority, P11 (bottom centre in Table 8.1). A special feature here is that there is a Danish and a German sub-system, each of which exists relatively separately from the other. A further peripheral actor is P4 (bottom right in Table 8.1), an organisation providing training for carers for the elderly, whose head, Herr Preisle, refers to himself as being not so 'central', as he covers mainly special interests:

> ... I feel slightly exotic, because we really only provide this one type of training. So I can't evaluate the co-operation between providers here on a local level and don't know much about it. I know that we have good connections to the family education centre; we have good connections to the town authorities.

As this statement shows, actors *position* themselves in the local structure. They were provided with the evaluation scheme of 'core/peripheral' with which they could characterise how they relate to their system. They were able to use this code not only for others but also for themselves. Peripheral actors commented on their remote position.

In the following section, the status of peripheral actors will be taken into closer consideration. This is done with the aid of a new form of network visualisation. One of the various forms for exploring structures and patterns (cf. Krempel 2001: 221) is selection. Here the layout is re-calculated and the 31 actors are maintained; however, only certain actors and pieces of information are inserted. In this way representations are created which are greatly simplified, but at the same time 'specific and systematic analyses of the whole information' are facilitated (ibid.). Once the location of the actors (in their spatial distribution) has been determined, the constellations of actors can be explored more extensively, for example through considering further information about certain distributions of characteristics. In Figure 8.3, for example, edge attributes for liking (closeness, distance) have been included (actors E3 and O2). These are represented additionally by what are known as zone symbols, which yield information about the primary environment. In the graphic containers two hemispheres have been included. The upper hemisphere shows the incoming relations and the lower one the outgoing relations. They give information about the actor's structural embeddedness. The different coloured portions stand for the affective evaluation. Blue sections indicate a reserved relationship, whereas red stands for closeness/liking. Because the sections are represented in different colours, it is easier to make comparisons.

Actors with monopoly-like positions represent a counterpoint to these 'isolated' actors, who to a large extent lack relationships to others. The organisation E2, a 'one-man company' which has been located in the town for over 15 years, is an example of a solitary figure in the local structure of relationships (cf. bottom

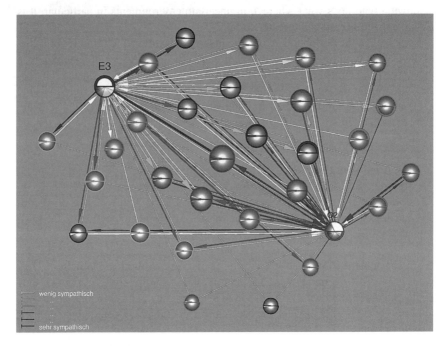

Figure 8.3 Peripheral actors.

right in Figure 8.3). Herr Eggerle, the head of this small continuing education organisation, personifies the autonomous self-employed provider who has a certain detachment from the other providers of continuing education. This is due both to his claim to independence and to the size of the organisation, which does not give him much chance to make himself heard in the concert of the large operators:

> At the beginning I didn't make any effort to co-operate, I just started. I wasn't looking for co-operation, I didn't want anyone to interfere [. . .] I just wanted to do my own thing here . . . carve my niche and just be left to work in peace without any connections which would also have restricted me.

It is not clear to what extent Herr Eggerle actually chose this modest solo strategy and to what extent it was a case of adapting to local circumstances. However, a glance at the network visualisation leaves no doubt that he has a relatively isolated position in the overall structure.

Strengths and limits of network analysis

If one is in favour of a stronger empirical orientation in continuing education research, network analysis is an important instrument which can be used in many ways to analyse relational data. Here, I would like to focus on two dimensions which represent the strengths of a network analytical approach. On the one hand, it can act as a sensitising concept for revealing structural connections and inter-dependencies. On the other hand, it mediates between an actor-related and a structure-related interpretation. However, it is also important to realise the specific barriers to reception presented by network analytical work.

Network analysis as a sensitising concept for institutionalisation processes

Network analysis serves as a conceptual framework for describing and analysing inter-organisational relations in continuing education. As a sensitising concept it can reveal structural connections and interdependencies.

Apart from the organisational and co-operative structures of networks, there is also the more profound reality of informally networked interactions between actors in continuing education. Schäffter (2001: 3) has described these dense informal networks as 'latent social networks [as] an expression of institution-alization processes with long-term effects for structuring'. Accordingly, it is necessary to 'become perceptive for the latent networks which already exist, in order to recognize them as an asset, activate them for particular plans and in order to be able to take the building of structural networks into account as a criterion of quality for organizations in continuing education' (ibid.: 1).

Network analyses provide the prerequisites for recording the potential of relations. At the same time, they provide numerous starting-points for co-operative networks. When shaping formal types of co-operation, it is often a case of consciously taking up existing networks.

Combining the perspectives of action and structure

In research work on co-operation in continuing education, structural and personal paradigms of explanation are usually listed alongside each other. Often the tension between these is released unilaterally by arguing that co-operation depends on the person. By analysing relations, co-operation is neither seen solely as the result of individual actions nor solely attributed to the prevailing structural conditions. By taking a network analytical view, it becomes apparent that co-operative action by actors in continuing education is dependent on social and structural realities. The options for action are influenced by structural contexts and one's own compe-titive and co-operative styles of communication by structures. The attractiveness and efficiency of qualitative network analysis lie in this linking and particular accentuation of dimensions relating to the actor and the system.

Barriers to reception

The innovative potential of social scientific network concepts for educational research is to be found, on the one hand, in their interdisciplinary approach. On the other hand, however, there remains the necessity to tailor network-analytical concepts and their operationalisations (trust, social capital) more specifically to the relevant educational field of action. All too often stale ideas are applied generally and simplistically, and thus do not provide sufficient benefits in discussions. One barrier to its reception by potential beneficiaries of research is perhaps to be found in the social-technological bias attached to network analysis. Sociometry has already been hindered by this perception. The transition from the mere description of social relationships to practical, organisational change, for example to the improvement of political implementation strategies, is also by no means easy. Recording inter-organisational and interpersonal relationships is a powerful tool which makes the actors' knowledge of relationships more transparent. However, the expense and complexity of many research instruments also act as a barrier here. Fürst (2003: 22) points out how empirically complicated and difficult it is to analyse learning regions, because it is not only a case of recording networks but also of including the contents of the communication. Here, there are many methodological traps which the researcher can fall into.

The challenge is to develop pragmatically oriented research instruments, for example a 'self audit tool' (cf. Osborne and Sankey 2006). This also raises the question, in which form structural insights into the field can be fed back to the actors.

Note

1 See http://www.lernende-regionen.info/dlr/1_141.php for information relating to a Federal Ministry of Education programme entitled, 'Learning Regions – Providing Support for Networks'.

References

Arnold, R., Faulstich, P., Mader, W., Nuissl von Rein, E. und Schlutz, E. (2000) *Research Memorandum on Adult Education*, Frankfurt am Main: German Society for Education Science.

Castells, M. (1996) *The Rise of the Network Society – The Information Age. Economy, Society and Culture, Vol. 1*, Cambridge, MA: Blackwells.

Dahme, H.-J. (2000) 'Kooperation und Vernetzung im sozialen Dienstleistungssektor. Soziale Dienste im Spannungsfeld diskursiver Koordination' und systemischer Rationalisierung' ('Cooperation and networks in the social service sector: social services in the area of conflict of discursive cooordination and systemie rationalisation'), in H. J. Dahme and N. Wohlfahrt (eds) *Netzwerkökonomie im Wohlfahrtsstaat. Wettbewerb und Kooperation im Sozial- und Gesundheitssektor* (*Network Economy in the Welfare State: Competition and Cooperation in the Social and Health Sector*), Berlin: Sigma.

Dahme, H.-J. and Wohlfahrt, N. (2000) *Netzwerkökonomie im Wohlfahrtsstaat. Wettbewerb und Kooperation im Sozial- und Gesundheitssektor* (*Network Economy in the Welfare State: Competition and Cooperation in the Social and Health Sector*), Berlin: Sigma.

European Commission (2002) *Call for Proposals (EAC/41/02): European Networks to Promote the Local and Regional Dimension of Lifelong Learning (the 'R3L' Initiative)*, Brussels: Commission of the European Communities.

Faulstich, P., Schiersmann, C. and Tippelt, R. (1997) 'Weiterbildung zwischen Grundrecht und Markt' ('Continuing education between basic right and market'), in U. A. Krüger (eds) *Sonderheft der Zeitschrift für Pädagogik*, Kongress der DGfE in Halle, Opladen: Leske u. Budrich.

Fürst, D. (2003) 'Lernende Region' aus Sicht der Regionalwissenschaft' ('learning region from the perspective of the regional science'), in U. Matthiesen and G. Reutter (eds) *Lernende Region – Mythos oder lebendige Praxis? (Learning Region – Myth or Living Practice?)*, Bielefeld: W. Bertelsmann Verlag, pp. 13–34.

Gieseke, W., Lenz, W., Meyer-Dohm, P., Schlutz, E. and Timmermann, D. (1997) *Evaluation der Weiterbildung (Evaluation of Continuing Education)*, Soest: LSW.

Granovetter, M.S. (1985) 'Economic action and social structure: the problem of "embeddedness"', *American Journal of Sociology*, 3: 481–510.

Jansen, D. (1999) *Einführung in die Netzwerkanalyse: Grundlagen, Methoden, Anwendungen*, Opladen: Leske und Budrich.

Jütte, W. (2002) *Soziales Netzwerk Weiterbildung. Analyse lokaler Institutionen-landschaften (Social Network Continuing Education: Analysis of Local Institutional Landscapes)*, Bielefeld: Bertelsmann.

Jütte, W. (2006) 'Netzwerkvisualisierung als Triangulationsverfahren bei der Analyse lokaler Weiterbildungslandschaften' ('Visualisation of networks as method of tri-angulation in the analysis of local continuing education landscapes'), in B. Hollstein and F. Straus (eds) *Qualitative Netzwerkanalyse (Qualitative Network Analysis)*, Wiesbaden: VS Verlag für Sozialwissenschaften, pp. 199–220.

Krempel, L. (2002) *Netzwerkvisualisierung: Prinzipien and Elemente einer graphischen Technologie zur multidimensionalen Exploration sozialer Strukturen (Visualisation of Networks: Principles and Elements of a Graphic Technology as a Means of Multi-dimensional Exploration of Social Structures)*, introduction and overview available in English, at: http://www.mpi-fg-koeln.mpg.de/~lk/netvis/onlinepdf/englishintro1. pdf.

Krempel, L. (2005) *Visualisierung komplexer Strukturen. Grundlagen der Darstellung mehrdimensionaler Netzwerke (Visualisation of Complex Structures: Basic Principles of Representation of Multidimensional Networks)*, Frankfurt am Main: Campus.

Loeper, J. (2003) 'University continuing education in Germany', in M. Osborne and E. Thomas (eds) *Lifelong Learning in a Changing Continent*, Leicester: NIACE.

Mitchell, J.C. (1969) 'The concept and use of social networks', in J. C. Mitchell (ed.) *Social Networks in Urban Situations: Analyses of Social Relationships in Central African Towns*, Manchester: Manchester University Press, pp. 1–50.

Moreno, J.L. (1953) *Who shall survive? Foundations of Sociometry, Group Psychotherapy and Sociodrama*, New York: Beacon House.

Sankey, K. and Osborne, M. (2006) 'Lifelong learning reaching regions where other learning doesn't reach', in R. Edwards et al. (eds) *Researching Experiential and Community-based Learning*, London: Routledge.

Schäffter, O. (2001) *In den Netzen der lernenden Organisation (In the Networks of the Learning Organisation)*, Dokumentation KBE-Fachtagung,'Vernetzung auf allen Ebenen' vom 10 November, at: http://www.treffpunkt-ethik.de/download/KFT_Lernende_Organisation.pdf.

Scheff, J. (1999) *Lernende Regionen. Regionale Netzwerke als Antwort auf globale Herausforderungen* (*Learning Regions: Regional Networks as an Answer to Global Challenges*), Vienna: Linde Verlag.

Wienold, H. (2000) *Empirische Sozialforschung. Praxis und Methode* (*Empirical Social Research: Practice and Method*), Münster: Verlag Westfälisches Dampfboot.

Wohlfart, U. (2002) 'Zur Geschichte interorganisatorischer Netzwerke' ('History of interorganisational networks'), *DIE Zeitschrift für Erwachsenenbildung*, 1: 39.

Chapter 9

Communities of practice and purpose

Making knowledge work in the university industry interface

*Tony Hall, Deirdre Hogan, Eamonn McQuade,
Emma O'Brien and Rhona Sherry*

Introduction

The recent history of Ireland's economic development has been characterised by unprecedented growth and expansion. The key indicators combine to paint a very positive picture for the current status of the Irish economy. At the time of writing, there is full employment in the Irish economy (unemployment is less than 5 per cent); government debt (as a percentage of GNP) is at 34 per cent, down from 93 per cent in 1993; and GDP and GNP per capita are ahead of the related EU-15 measures. Furthermore, notwithstanding the recent economic downturn, which particularly affected software engineering and internet-related sectors, the Irish economy has continued to demonstrate impressive growth, and furthermore continues to attract considerable FDI (foreign direct investment) in the high value adding areas of information and communications technology (ICT), biomedical engineering and pharmaceuticals. However, there are growing concerns, despite these successes, about Ireland's ability to maintain this level of economic growth, and also remain competitive in the face of intensifying international competition, particularly in the manufacturing and services sectors.

Ireland has a relatively small number of successful, outwardly investing companies and employment in Ireland is heavily dependent on the indigenous sector that accounts for approximately 80 per cent of the Irish workforce. Thus, in the future, the Irish economy will be more dependent on its ability to create and support innovation-based, exporting small and medium-sized enterprises (SMEs) and indigenous companies and industries. This will necessitate a workforce with high-level skills, expertise and knowledge, matched with the ability and strategy to turn this knowledge into commercially successful employment creating businesses and wealth. Ireland is therefore challenged with making a transition from low to high value-added activities, which require adaptability and flexibility in worker re-training. Through tax breaks and other incentives, Ireland's FDI strategy has led to the development of a large number of graduates with world-class knowledge and expertise in manufacturing, particularly in ICT, all of whom are now particularly vulnerable to the effects of economic restructuring. These graduates would benefit from developing new skills and competencies – both generic and sector-specific – in order to ensure their continued employability in the emerging global knowledge economy.

In order to realise a culture of lifelong learning that effectively supports the workforce and particularly graduates in up-skilling and professional development, key economic, financial and social issues will need to be addressed (Duke et al. 2005). Ireland's future economic competitiveness will be enhanced by increasing both the employment potential of the country and the employability of the individual. The aim of the Programme for University Industry Interface (PUII) is to contribute to this goal with a particular focus on the individual graduate.

The Programme for University Industry Interface

The Programme for University Industry Interface (PUII) was initiated in June 2003 as an action research project with the objective of identifying the needs and up-skilling requirements of graduates employed in the manufacturing and ICT sectors in Ireland, in order to develop their employability within a rapidly changing economy. The focus of PUII has been on the manufacturing and ICT sectors because, from an Irish perspective, these sectors are in particular facing increasingly intense international competition. PUII was established as an interface between the various stakeholders in graduate development – individuals, industry and educational institutions – to investigate the issues of employability, employment, and education in the overall context of the national need.

Successful economic strategies, such as tax breaks, and investment in education and training over the past number of years have developed Ireland into a very attractive location for foreign direct investment, with the result that many high-tech manufacturing companies have located their operations in Ireland. These strategies have contributed to Ireland becoming one of the most successful economies in the world and a highly regarded location for world-class manufacturing. Manufacturing is still a key industry sector for Ireland and is the largest sectoral employer, employing more than 300,000 (16.1 per cent) of the Irish workforce in 2004 (EGFSN 2005).

Manufacturing industry in Ireland, however, is currently facing a changing market. While employment in manufacturing grew between 1999 and 2004, the rate of growth was slower compared to the average annual growth rate of 2.9 per cent for that period (ibid.). Ireland's FDI manufacturing base is facing intense competition from lower cost countries, with the result that many companies are now choosing to move or to locate their operations overseas:

> The trend will continue towards more off shoring of jobs – and not just in manufacturing, but also in 'impersonal services'. . . . Richer countries with higher wage levels will need to shift their workforces away from these impersonal services and manufacturing and towards personal services.
>
> (*Irish Times* 2006)

It is against this background for the manufacturing sector in Ireland that PUII has two main aims:

1 To identify the skill sets and technical competencies needed by individuals so they are in a position to contribute to the future economic development of Ireland.
2 To research and pilot new and innovative learning models that will deliver in-company education and training for next generation employability.

PUII methodology

To address the issues effectively, PUII has adopted the Community of Practice (COP) approach, a method that is growing in popularity in the education and training fields. It is increasingly being employed in domains such as IT design for business settings and instructional design of educational applications and systems (Barab et al. 2004). The basic structure of the COP is predicated on an apprenticeship model of learning and social capital. The term used to describe this process is *Legitimate Peripheral Participation* (LPP) (Lave and Wenger 1991). What LPP essentially means is that a new participant in a community, a workplace for example, is a novice who starts off from a peripheral position. But as they develop and become more competent, through learning and interaction with more experienced colleagues, they move more towards the centre of the organisation. Their increased participation is legitimised by their growing expertise in the community. The end result is that their identity is transformed through the process of enculturation; they become a member of the COP, speaking and acting in ways that mark them as a community member:

> An assumption underlying Community of Practice theory is that learning occurs not only as a cognitive change in the learner but also as a social trajectory within a group. The social identities of learners change as the learners become recognized as experts within a social group that shares a set of practices.
>
> (Job-Sluder and Barab 2004: 377)

Increasingly, COP is being used to examine and understand intra-organisational learning, and furthermore how institutions, companies, public sector bodies, and so on, interact with their external social partners. For example, Barrett (2004) has employed the COP approach, combined with ethnographic methods, to understand the learning culture, particularly the hidden but crucially important informal aspects of how employees learn, within a high-tech manufacturing firm and foundry environment. Barrett examined how learning is mediated in this setting, and the affects of the social milieu (employees' background and the organisational context) on the learning that occurs within the company. One of the interesting findings of this research was the disparity, in certain areas of the organisation's learning culture, between *espoused* and *lived* institutional values. The experience of one employee, Lyle, is illustrative; he was responsible for creating the company's formal training system, including training manuals and schedules. However, this became a 'window-dressing' exercise rather than meaningful and transformative organisational learning. Lyle: 'I started realising that I was missing out on, um, I was documenting a learning process, but I wasn't living a learning process' (Barrett 2004: 116) As the researcher comments, 'Ironically, producing the documentation appeared to be the emphasis instead of learning' (ibid.). Through application of the COP approach, Barrett was able to identify important areas for redress within the organisation, aspects that would need to be improved upon in order to enhance intra-organisational collaboration and learning.

A typical COP consists of a group of people informally bound together by shared expertise; a passion for joint enterprise; and a mutual or common concern or interest (Wenger and Snyder 2000). Members share knowledge and use their creativity and resourcefulness to address relevant problems and identify best practice. The work of the COPs within the PUII programme of research is integrated with and supported by a number of PhD students and post-doctoral researchers. The strength of a COP is that it reflects the members' own understanding of what is important. The terms of reference for the COPs allow for modifications of the aims and objectives as determined by the COP team.

PUII has undertaken research through the establishment of five COPs since 2003, two of which are still operating. The work of the COPs has been produced in the form of a series of reports. Specific outputs of PUII to date have included the identification of:

1   Skills and competencies required for next generation employability (COP1 Report[1]).
2   Future landscape for manufacturing and ICT in Ireland (COP1 Report).
3   Current use of technology in up-skilling within companies in Ireland (COP2 Report).
4   Successful models for technology-based training within organisations (COP2 Report).
5   Competencies required to enhance the capacity of small and medium-sized enterprises (SMEs) (COP3 Report).
6   Barriers encountered in the delivery of training and up-skilling within SMEs (COP3 Report).
7   Competency development frameworks for the development of technical, transferable and business skills in individuals within companies (COP4 Report).

The PUII COPs have been structured in such a way as to ensure that all important stakeholders are involved: industry and commercial interests, governmental agencies and academics. PUII is directed by an Executive Board and assisted by an Industrial Advisory Board and an Academic Advisory Board. These boards consist of key executives from industry, development agencies and representatives from the international academic community. The boards guide and monitor the research agenda of PUII. In the case of PUII, a typical COP is comprised of seven to nine individuals from industry, supported by a COP manager; an academic consultant (PhD student); a research consultant (post-doctoral fellow); a University of Limerick patron; and the PUII project manager.

In addition to using COP for eliciting up-skilling, lifelong learning and social capital requirements from graduates in industry, PUII has also focused on generating a set of deliverables and actionable items, which will help to move Ireland along in terms of graduate development and education. PUII has developed a model for graduate up-skilling and professional development, Productive Citizenship, and a roadmap for graduate education in Ireland, MAP: a Modular Accreditation Programme, which will be implemented by the Higher Education Authority in September 2007.

Results and findings: Productive Citizenship, MAP and GAP

The outcomes of PUII's research, based on capturing the 'authentic voice of industry', are a clear understanding of the skills and competencies needed for next generation employability and the models and approaches that are needed to support the lifelong learning of graduates. Central to PUII's philosophy is an appreciation of learning and work as complementary activities and the potential represented by lifelong learning to realise this relationship to the benefit both of the individual and society.

PUII's research has led to the development of the Productive Citizenship Model (PCM), an innovative model for the delivery of next generation skills and competencies into the workplace. This model has influenced the proposed development of a national MAP for the delivery of up-skilling and the enhancement of management capability within organisations.

The PCM is an instrument for sustaining and developing the exchange value of the individual's knowledge, skills and competencies at a number of levels, including deep specialist knowledge, e.g. PhD; transitional knowledge, e.g. graduate diplomas; and just-in-time knowledge, e.g. partial modules or a small numbers of modules. The model is designed for the self-directed, autonomous learner. It provides learner support in the form of a decision support system and learning advice. It underscores financial support, Recognition of Prior Learning (RPL) for exemption and access to courses, Paid (Educational) Study Leave (P(E)SL), and flexible delivery methods. It emphasises reward for learning, whether in the form of qualification, credits or certificates of attendance/completion. Its implementation will require the combined expertise and resources of universities, other third-level institutions, private education institutions, training providers and in-company training. Funding this strategy will involve an integrated, tripartite approach involving government, employers and the individual.

In order to facilitate the individual learner in engaging with the PCM it is crucially important that they are adequately supported in a number of respects. Through its research and collaboration with key stakeholders – companies (both multinational and SME), social partners and government agencies, PUII has identified the skills and competencies that are required to sustain the employability of graduates in Irish manufacturing. Furthermore, PUII has distilled the dilemmas and challenges that must be faced in order to implement the model effectively.

Dilemmas of the Productive Citizenship Model

Mismatch of timescales

One of the principal dilemmas that must be faced in implementing the Productive Citizenship Model is the mismatch between timescales in academe and industry. Companies operate within shorter production cycles than third-level educational providers, and this creates a disparity between the amount of time one must ordinarily complete to gain a qualification, and the more immediate, day-to-day requirements of the workplace. This situation exists particularly in SMEs, where the pressure on resources and time is perhaps even more pressing than in larger companies, which are somewhat insulated by economies of scale. Addressing this issue is central to providing flexible training to individuals in the workplace – education providers need to transform their access and pedagogical structures to become more responsive to the individual in this respect. Through its modular approach, illustrated in the Ladder of Progression (Figure 9.1), PUII outlines various possible study paths, which will enable graduates to select modules with different modes of accreditation, certification and varying levels of resource and time commitment. This affords individual graduates sufficient options and possibilities to engage in lifelong learning in a way that suits their respective requirements.

Individual development needs versus company training needs

A conflict exists between the individual and the company in terms of training and development requirements. The PCM focuses on developing knowledge, skills and competencies with high exchange value in the emerging knowledge economy, thus enabling individuals to transfer between job role, company and industry. On the other hand, companies invariably prioritise training that aligns with the company strategy and day-to-day running of the organisation rather than that which enhances employability of employees.

'Productive Citizenship' versus 'Contributing Citizenship'

PUII's concept of Productive Citizenship does not imply that those not represented in the framework are economically or otherwise unproductive. Rather, it is there to mark a distinction within the labour force, and say that the approximately

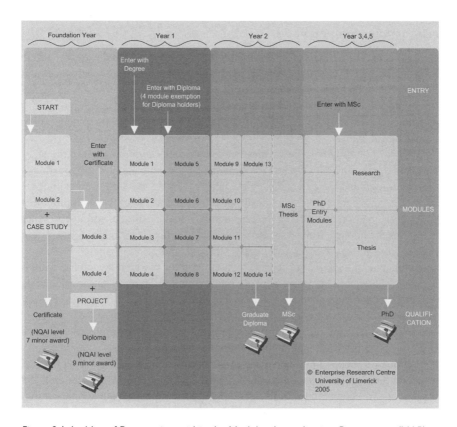

Figure 9.1 Ladder of Progression within the Modular Accreditation Programme (MAP).

78,000 individual graduates, who are involved in Irish manufacturing, and who are facing major sectoral changes in their industry, need to engage with a particular process of lifelong learning in order to remain as employable and thus productive as they can be, within the Irish economy.

This raises the dilemma or question of how we can foster the economic capacity and thus the employability of the individual graduate, but in a way that does not discount or impinge upon the other important non-economic, social contributions they might make. Although this debate is not easily resolved, it needs to be flagged as an important dilemma to be addressed in any process that seeks to implement Productive Citizenship or similar lifelong learning initiatives.

Payment

In terms of paid study leave, there is a triad of stakeholders involved, the individual, the employer, and the government. PUII proposes that payment should be related to and commensurate with the benefit gained by each stakeholder.

Ireland's Graduate Advancement Programme (GAP) for economic development

In addition to the Productive Citizenship Model and national Modular Accreditation Programme, PUII has also developed GAP, the Graduate Advancement Programme, which identifies key aspects of the broader educational and socio-economic context that need to be addressed in order to enhance the employability of graduates, and thereupon ensure Ireland a leading role in the emerging global knowledge economy.

Over the past 40 years, Ireland has made enormous commitments to the technical and intellectual development of its people. The establishment of the Institutes of Technology and the expansion of the universities, in areas of strategic importance, was an element of a national strategy designed to increase the employment and wealth creation potential of the country. This had the aim, in addition to other initiatives, of making Ireland an attractive location for foreign direct investment (FDI). This strategy has proven highly effective and has contributed to Ireland becoming one of the most successful economies in the world today, and a location for world-class manufacturing. Equally important is that Ireland has developed its capacity for innovation and is a leader in this within the OECD economies (Florida and Tingali 2004).

Competition from many other economies that aspire to emulate Ireland's success, presents a challenge to the sustainability of the country's economic prosperity. One response to these challenges has been to initiate a new strategy based on strengthening Ireland's research potential. Science Foundation Ireland, the Programme for Research in Third Level Institutions and the recent announcement of a further investment of 3.8 billion in research are evidence of strategy in action. Through such means, Ireland aims to become a most attractive location for inward investment in research and development, to complement the existing strong but threatened FDI manufacturing base; and furthermore to build an indigenous capacity for employment and wealth creation based on leading edge research and product development. However, the success of these will require a complementary strategy to prepare the labour force so that Ireland is in a position to benefit economically from the implementation of the research strategy.

In order to ensure this success continues and that graduates in manufacturing and ICT are in a position to be able to meet the requirements for higher productivity, to compete with lower cost locations and to operate in the multicultural global environment, PUII has identified the strategic need for a national GAP. This programme, which is predicated on the Productive Citizenship model and MAP (which will be implemented nationally in September 2007), will be a multidisciplinary one, with the potential to incorporate learning related to any sector or subject in order to address immediate and identifiable requirements for skill and competencies; to enhance the employability of graduates in those areas and their contribution to the knowledge economy and to the success of Ireland as a leading knowledge society. The programme will also address the need for additional PhD candidates, by preparing people at work to undertake action-based research in industry at PhD level.

Features of GAP

From a structural point of view Ireland is one of the few EU countries that does not have formal paid study leave provision. Having such a provision would encourage individuals to participate in GAP while encouraging companies to relate paid study leave to company business or personnel development goals. Other issues, such as incentives for company participation and a framework for financing lifelong learning, need to be considered.

Third-level institutions need to be much more flexible in meeting the needs of learners who are combining learning and work in a very busy and demanding environment. The institutions must have processes in place to recognise that individuals may have developed significant knowledge and expertise during their career worthy of academic recognition. The Bologna Accord and the European Credit Transfer System (ECTS) provide agreed structures to guide this. However, third-level institutions should also be incentivised to engage with these initiatives and the flexible delivery of learning opportunities. PUII's research shows that a much closer working relationship between industry, the development agencies and academic institutions is needed in order to develop good practices for employees and companies participating in GAP.

The indigenous SME sector, particularly those companies engaged in exporting and cutting edge innovation, needs particular consideration. There are many factors that inhibit the participation of SMEs and their personnel in lifelong learning,[2] including the perceived risk of losing key people and intellectual property. Thus in designing the GAP programme for graduates, special care needs to be taken to incorporate responses to the needs of SMEs.

The objective of GAP is to accelerate the development and deployment of professionals in employment and of graduates by addressing known resource and knowledge shortfalls in industry, research and education.

The specific features of GAP are as follows:

- *Facilitation participation*:
    - national formal paid study-leave provision
    - convenient and accommodating registration and administration
    - academic recognition of prior knowledge and experience
    - recognising the need for people to balance their work, lifestyle and learning commitments
    - flexible delivery and participation in duration, time, location and communication media
    - modules/courses available from multiple institutions and including private providers

- *Financial arrangements*:

    - incentives for those in employment, companies, institutions and private providers
    - a supportive national taxation regime
    - scholarships for full-time participation
    - recognition and rewards for achievement

- *Learning environment*:

    - benchmarked against best in class MBA and PhD programmes
    - comprehensive tutorial support
    - a blend of best practice approaches, including distance learning and ICT support
    - a flexible modular programme
    - international experts' and practitioners' involvement in curriculum design and delivery
    - case studies based on best practice industrial practices
    - cross-sector and cross-discipline engagement
    - access to experts in related disciplines
    - opportunities for shared learning between groups of learners
    - innovative application of network technology for learning, mentoring and management

- *Redeployment in the workplace*:

    - GAP participants and graduates highly valued in career planning and progression, recruitment and in employment in industry, research and education
    - specific openings that are targeted at newly qualified GAP graduates
    - GAP graduates become champions and active promoters of the programme
    - GAP graduates sought out for employment by leading companies and research institutions.

Conclusions

PUII has conducted a substantial amount of research over the past four years into the needs and requirements of individuals within the manufacturing and ICT sectors. This research indicates that the approximately 78,000 graduates in Irish manufacturing and ICT need to augment their skills and competencies in order to be able to meet the current requirements for higher productivity, to compete with lower cost locations and to operate in the multicultural global environment. One of the strategies proposed by the Irish government to deal with this is to strengthen the research potential of the country. Recent announcements of an investment of 3.8 billion in research between 2007 and 2013, will give Ireland the opportunity to build an indigenous capacity for employment and wealth creation based on leading edge research and product development. This strategy is crucial in order to keep Ireland internationally competitive, to ensure that it continues to develop its growing knowledge economy and to attract and retain world-class manufacturing operations. According to the Expert Group on Future Skills Needs, cost competitiveness is no longer a basis on which Ireland will be able to attract FDI: 'It is now the availability of a suitably skilled and experienced workforce and a supportive infrastructure in the broad sense of the term that are underpinning [Ireland's] continued success' (EGFSN 2005).

PUII's research to date has highlighted the need for long-term structural solutions to build Ireland's capacity for wealth creation and product development, particularly for those employed in manufacturing industries. PUII is aware that, as the economy continues to develop, new demands and new sectors will present different requirements to those of the currently dominant industries. PUII has thus developed innovative learning models: Productive Citizenship and national Modular Accreditation and Graduate Advancement Programmes to assist not only individuals, but also the education sector and industry to deliver the required training and up-skilling to Ireland's graduates in order to ensure their continued employability into the future. Ongoing collaboration between industry, the government and the education sector is seen as crucial in this regard:

> The exploitation of knowledge and commercialisation of research must become embedded in the culture and infrastructure of the higher education system. This requires continued emphasis on new campus company start-ups, a pro-innovation culture of intellectual property protection and exploitation, programmes in entrepreneurship, consulting services, information services, new forms of graduate development programmes and greater links between higher education institutions and private enterprise. This role should be actively encouraged and incentivised
>
> (Enterprise Strategy Group 2004)

Finally, PUII has pioneered the use of Communities of Practice and Legitimate Peripheral Participation to engender enhanced social capital in the area of university industry collaboration, in order to identify ways in which we can enhance graduate education and professionalisation in Ireland. The COP and LPP methodologies have proven highly effective in enabling the stakeholders to collaborate and also to identify how best to facilitate lifelong learning for graduates in Irish industry. Therefore, following from PUII's experience, COP and LPP have much to commend them as research methodologies.

What makes LPP such a powerful concept is that the participants, through their involvement in the community, assume ownership of an issue or problem, and there is a strong commitment to change and innovation. In addition to LPP, there are other facets of the COP approach that make it particularly suitable to address the types of questions that the PUII has been endeavouring to answer. Firstly, what distinguishes COPs are their intrinsically collaborative focus: a core idea is to have the key stakeholders involved. One of the benefits of this particular aspect to academia is that it helps academics to collaborate actively with practitioners in the field: industrialists, governmental agencies and so forth. It offers the opportunity to ground theory in practice.

The Community of Practice methodology is an effective framework to enable individuals in industry and academia/researchers to come together to share experience, knowledge and insight. With the guidance and support of an overarching Executive Board and Industrial and Academic Advisory Boards, and support from background research, they can be used to develop a best practice solution for a given problem, enabling participants to better leverage their collaborative strengths. What has been particularly distinctive about the PUII Community of Practice approach has been its facilitation of innovative extra-university collaboration, where the university can identify and start to address effectively the requirements of industry. This is proving particularly important in the Irish context as manufacturing evolves from its traditional roots to knowledge-based, high-value strategic activity.

It is envisaged that the products of the PUII research – Productive Citizenship, MAP and GAP – will contribute considerably to the further development of graduates' intellectual and social capital, and thus also to Ireland's continued, future economic and societal prosperity.

Acknowledgements

The authors would like to thank the many stakeholders who have contributed to making PUII a successful programme of action research, both our academic and our industrial partners. In particular, we would like to express a special thank you to our Academic and Industrial Advisory Boards. Finally, we would also like to thank our funders, the Higher Education Authority and the Department of Enterprise, Trade and Employment for their continued support of PUII.

Notes

1   All COP reports are available at http://www.ul.ie/~puii/Reports.php.
2   PUII (2005) *Moving Small Companies Towards Next Generation Employability*, www.ul.ie/~puii

References

Barab, S.A., Kling, R. and Gray, J.H. (eds) (2004) *Designing Virtual Communities in the Service of Learning*, New York: Cambridge University Press.

Barrett, A. (2004) 'Organizational learning and communities of practice in a high-tech manufacturing firm', unpublished PhD thesis, University of Idaho.

Duke, C., Osborne, M. and Wilson, B. (eds) (2005) *Rebalancing the Social and Economic: Learning, Partnership and Place*, Leicester: NIACE.

Enterprise Strategy Group (2004) *Ahead of the Curve – Ireland's Place in the Global Economy*, Dublin: Forfás.

Expert Group on Future Skills Needs (EGFSN) (2005) *National Skills Bulletin*, Dublin: FÁS.

Florida, R. and Tingali, I. (2004) *Europe in the Creative Age*, Creative Class Online, at: http://www.creativeclass.org/rfcgdb/articles/Europe_in_the_Creative_Age_2004.pdf.

Irish Times (2006) 'Workplace must reflect pace of global change', 14 April.

Job-Sluder, K. and Barab, S.A. (2004) 'Shared "we" and shared "they" indicators of group identity in online teacher professional development', in S. A. Barab, R. Kling and J. H. Gray (eds) *Designing Virtual Communities in the Service of Learning*, New York: Cambridge University Press.

Lave, J. and Wenger, E. (1991) *Situated Learning: Legitimate Peripheral Participation*, New York: Cambridge University Press.

Wenger, E. and Snyder, W.M. (2000) *Communities of Practice: The Organizational Frontier*, Boston, MA: Harvard Business School Press.

Chapter 10

Beyond the social capital rhetoric – an investigation of the use of social networks in the co-ordination of intra-enterprise activities

A case study of small-scale rural non-farm enterprises in Zimbabwe

Jethro Zuwarimwe

Introduction

Frequently within social capital discourse it is reported that people increasingly identify with their local communities, using their local relationships as an important foundation for economic and social action (Duke et al. 2005). For the past decade social capital has become instrumental in economic policies and development programmes. In fact, the reading of Granovetter (1985) that social capital is both a glue and lubricant has reinforced the views of some scholars and convinced others that economic processes cannot be fully explained by pecuniary variables and rational behaviour alone. Against this backdrop many researchers have been investigating the role of social capital in various aspects of human engagements, which include economic activities.

An interesting area where social capital has attracted wider application is the investigation of economic agents' social learning behaviour. The acknowledgement in the economics corpus of the inherent weaknesses of the market as an institution to facilitate co-ordination of activities of economic agents has invoked and reinvigorated more interest in social capital research. Careful investigations by Bibow et al. (2005), Dew et al. (2004) and Lawson (1993) have revealed that, faced with economic problems of co-ordination and contracting, entrepreneurs devise social networks, conventions and mimetic behaviour so as to make their actions more predictable. What can be distilled from emerging literature is that social capital and learning are closely related, as people who are actively involved in social networks are more informed and thus more able to adopt new approaches in conducting their businesses (Duke et al. 2005). As Duke et al. (ibid.) also observed, social networks and sociability are important ingredients in any coherent strategy for developing learning and a sustainable economy. Researchers have established interesting and significant relationships between social capital and economic outcomes (Barr 2000; Johnson et al. 2002; Duke et al. 2005; Granovetter 2005) and some scholars are being tempted to use such social capital perspectives in the investigation of various socio-economic phenomena (Isham 2000; Tiepoh and Reimer 2004; Nyangena 2005; Sanchez et al. 2005; Katungi 2006).

However, though the academic treatise of social capital and the benefits from social networks is indeed convincing, specifically how small-scale entrepreneurs in Zimbabwe use social capital to ease co-ordination friction in their enterprises is yet to be fully investigated. While Fafchamps (1997, 2001, 2004) pioneered work with respect to mobilisation of financial resources and reduction of market access transaction costs, there is yet to be substantial follow-up work specifically on the use of social networks in intra-enterprise activities. This is despite mounting global indications that small-scale entrepreneurs will continue to dominate the economic landscape in the foreseeable future and that social capital facilitates some economic benefits to individuals through improved information flows.

Building upon the pioneering work of Putnam (1993), Grootaert (1999), Barr (2000), Masuka (2003), Fafchamps (2004), Akerlof and Kranton (2005), Dasgupta (2005) and Granovetter (1985, 2005), this chapter aims to explore the use of social capital by small-scale entrepreneurs within a rural context. The specific questions to be investigated are: What use do small-scale entrepreneurs make of social networks in their enterprises and how do the entrepreneurs facilitate the development of such networks in their respective enterprises? What are the implications for policy on small-scale enterprise development?

Other than contributing to academic knowledge concerning the role social capital plays in economic development, policy makers stand to benefit in the designing of sustainable small-scale entrepreneurship support policies and pro-grammes. Institutions supporting small-scale entrepreneurs need to be constantly enlightened on how to design strategies in which social learning and social networks are appreciated. By and large the established and prospective small-scale entrepreneurs stand to benefit if they are informed concerning which social learning platforms they can use for their development.

The chapter is organised in the following way. The second section provides the conceptual framework of the arguments in this chapter. The third section condenses the arguments from literature about social networks and intra-enterprise activities, and concerns the data used in the study. The fourth section presents and discusses results from the research. The fifth section summarises the findings, pointing out possible policy implications of the results.

Conceptual framework

After establishing an enterprise and setting the goals to be achieved, the next step is to set up the intra-enterprise operational framework where the various operations function in synergy. Contracts with workers to perform various functions have to be drawn up, and because they have different knowledge stocks, expectations and different functions they are remunerated differently.

While mainstream economics postulates situations of complete contracts formulation by rational economic agents, modern economics shows that there are transaction costs to be met in the process. In that regard, bounded rationality and incomplete contracting take place to ease the friction of transaction costs within economic agents. Because entrepreneurs do not have complete *ex post hoc* information needed to design complete contracts, they come up with negotiated incomplete contracts that the parties can mutually co-ordinate with minimum problems (Foss and Foss 1999). To this end, entrepreneurs rely on their social networks as well as facilitating the creation of more familial environments where workers are psychologically contracted to the enterprise. Entrepreneurs therefore use their social networks to ease co-ordination problems within their various enterprises. It is within this framework that social networks are discussed in the chapter.

A brief overview of the social capital and intra-enterprise activities literature

Adam Smith in his thought-provoking book *The Wealth of Nations* defines an entrepreneur as a benevolent economic agent who transforms demand into supply for profits. Casson (2006) defines an entrepreneur as someone who organises and assumes the risk of a business in return for profit. Chen (2005) quoted Schumpeter as defining an entrepreneur as someone who carries out new combinations of factors of production to produce new goods or services or introduces new products to the markets or even creates new organisations.

Given the above, entrepreneurship entails at least three stages that call for information search and co-ordination. Firstly: identifying, tracing and developing an economic opportunity demand requires some dexterity to recognise, perceive and evaluate information about the opportunity. The second stage entails mobilising resources to transform the opportunity into a product. Given that an entrepreneur generally needs the co-operation of others, the final stage involves co-ordination of sustainable production processes.

Information about an economic opportunity does not exist at one place nor is it within a single individual but is spatially distributed and within different people. An entrepreneur has to enlist support from others to harness and organise the information into a coherent economic programme before other astute entrepreneurs capture it. Moreover, he or she has to mobilise resources – material and human capital – to effectuate the opportunity. More often than not he or she does not command all the resources and has to borrow in order to start the project. Research by Fafchamps (1997) shows that formal financial institutions are not an option for such new entrepreneurs as they are viewed as high-risk investments. New entrepreneurs also do not have all the technical expertise to manage the operations of the enterprise. Instead, they enlist voluntary co-operation from employees through mutual co-ordination activities within an enterprise and such social networks are crucial in promoting and improving the learning curve of entrepreneurs when conducting their business.

Social networks and co-ordination within enterprises

In this knowledge driven economic era, individuals who are actively involved in learning have better chances to realise more value from a given bundle of resources. It is therefore little wonder that Elsner (2005: 19) argues that a more realistic understanding of economics today has to start from the two socio-economic phenomena of dilemma prone interdependencies and strong uncertainty among agents. These also entail ubiquitous or potential co-ordination failure, and hence the redefining of economics as a science of effective co-ordination. It is in this light that social networks and sociability have emerged as twin pillars in building a learning society and robust economies.

Research shows that firms stand to benefit significantly by organising economic activities in such a way that workers voluntarily co-operate with each other (Rob and Zemsky 2002; Akerlof and Krantan 2005; Goette et al. 2006). When workers co-operate, their different talents complement each other, and this positive learning facilitates mutual information flow and eliminates 'free riding' at the workplace. It is in the best interest of entrepreneurs to discover and devise strategies that foster internal linkages, which in turn encourage network development. The question is: What conditions encourage workers to remain integrated and voluntarily co-operating in cases where they have different functions and status levels in a firm?

Conventional economic literature explains this from the perspective of pecuniary incentives, namely, wages and performance bonuses. With well-designed rules, codes of conduct to be followed by workers and financial rewards, entrepreneurs may believe that they can achieve total commitment and co-operation from workers. However, research shows that monetary incentives and written codes alone remain a blunt instrument to motivate workers because they are imperfect measurements of individual effort based only on variables observed by management. Production processes at any enterprise depend on collective team efforts (Akerlof and Krantan 2005). To use financial rewards as the sole tool for enlisting co-operation of workers creates differentiated social status; this can threaten and sever ties between workers, risking the survival of collectivity (Kosfeld and von Siemens 2006). Lack of strong intra-group connectedness and social learning is likely to impede co-ordination and productivity at workplaces as workers also seek intangible rewards and recognition.

The limitations of controlling workers' behaviour completely by pecuniary incentives have led researchers to investigate in social environments those strategies that enlist workers' willingness to take unselfish co-operative and efficiency enhancing actions. Corporate culture (Rob and Zemsky 2002) and workers' identity alteration (Akerlof and Krantan 2005) have emerged to describe atmosphere at firms where workers co-operate. While the importance of direct interdependency in enterprises has previously been recognised in economics, it has now been given new dimensions by the social capital discourse.

Akerlof and Krantan (2005) established that strategies which inculcate a sense of identity and attachment of employees with the firm make them behave in concert with the organisation's goals. Such strategies ensure that workers are willing to put in more effort even for less financial remuneration. When workers identify with an enterprise they become insiders who do not require large differences in monetary rewards to induce them to contribute. This leads to a lower wage bill, ultimately making it profitable for the firm to invest in the identity fostering programmes for the workers.

This idea of differentiated social structures has now been repackaged in economics as 'corporate culture development'. Corporate culture within a firm changes beliefs and persuades employees to behave and believe that members of their own group are more likely to co-operate in efforts towards the group goals (Goette et al. 2006). After an investigation of group dynamics at enterprises, Goette et al. concluded that the social capital of organisations yields important benefits such as fostering of efficiency behaviour including individual workers' willingness to co-operate.

Literature from management sciences suggests that corporate culture results in more cohesive, highly motivated workers with fewer barriers in interpreting, transferring and diffusing of valuable information. Different trajectories of individual members' goals are realigned towards one mutual goal, where group goals will prevail over individual aspirations. There is mutual approval of individual efforts with respect to planning for strategies to sustain future employability. This has been central in the social networks and collective action discourse and Elsner (2005) argues that by fostering cohesion within workers, intra-enterprise networks make feasible the planning of future-oriented collective action at firms.

Heywood et al. (2005), in a study of UK high performance workplaces, concluded that workers perform better when they are in a family environment where mutual information exchange is facilitated. They established that such familial work environments foster a psychological contract between workers and management. Such familial relationships act as cost-effective self-monitoring mechanisms where workers and employers share information more openly, leading to high levels of productivity. A high level of worker participation in decision making during strategic planning sessions enlists more worker commitment than mere financial rewards.

The Japanese are renowned for having successfully converted workplaces into an extended family and other Asian, and in particular Chinese, success in business is believed to be a result of the conversion of their strong families into viable corporate entities (Pun et al. 2000). Running through the leading arguments in the social capital debate is the idea that a good economic institution must be one rich in social capital that promotes lifelong learning.

The data

Data for the study reported here was collected in a survey of 130 small-scale entrepreneurs in the Chimanimani district of Zimbabwe between November 2004 and July 2005. Of the 130, 51.5 per cent were male-owned, 27.7 per cent female-owned and 20.8 per cent family-owned businesses. The nature of businesses was categorised as trading, construction, carpentry and welding, craftwork and restaurants, dressmaking and salons, electronics and repair services, agro-processing and small-scale manufacturing, graphics and design services, office services and phone shops, vehicle servicing and spare parts sales, and others.

Male entrepreneurs are involved in all the categories of business, with the female businesses mainly being in craftwork and restaurant activities, dressmaking and salons and trading. On the other hand, family-owned enterprises mainly consist of trading, carpentry and welding, agro-processing and office services. The data was collected in a survey that was conducted amongst small-scale rural non-farm entrepreneurs in Chimanimani district, with the assistance of local research assistants. The data was captured by means of a modified World Bank Social Capital Assessment Tool (designed by Krishna and Shrader (1999)). This tool was used during the interviews with the owners of the enterprises.

Results and discussion

Social networks and intra-enterprise activities organisation

Casson (2006) observed that entrepreneurs stand to benefit if their workers are bonded together by strong intra-enterprise social networks. This, together with sociability, is an important ingredient for a sustainable organisation of operations in a firm. Therefore responses were sought on how the entrepreneurs use their social networks when seeking who to employ and how they revitalise development of such networks. This was to investigate the benefits of and use to which entrepreneurs put their social networks whilst carrying out the activities of their enterprises. Further investigations concerning benefits of socialising the workplace and strategies employed to encourage development of intra-enterprise social networking were undertaken.

The results show that 69.4 per cent of the female entrepreneurs, 36 per cent of the family-run enterprises and 33 per cent of the male entrepreneurs prefer to employ friends and relatives. The remaining proportions in each category prefer to employ anyone who qualifies for the job. Those who prefer to employ friends and relatives were further asked why they prefer that option, with interesting responses. Figure 10.1 shows whom the entrepreneurs prefer to employ.

When asked to give reasons for each preference, the responses given varied. Among these were that relatives and friends are not difficult to work with and they are sympathetic even if the business is not doing well. Furthermore, problems can be solved amicably using social systems, as relatives and friends want to share in the business's success. As was also established by Johnson et al. (2002), entrepreneurs who employ relatives and friends are assured of greater commitment, as well as the greater possibility of forging less financially demanding contracts between them and their employees.

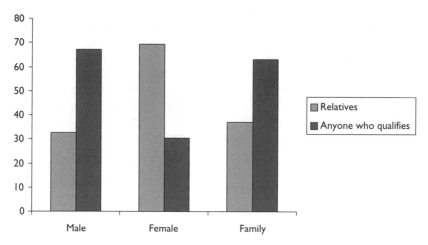

Figure 10.1 Sources of employees in the enterprises.

It is easy to negotiate contracts with friends and relatives who are willing to share information that helps in the enterprise's growth, whose commitment to carrying out enterprise activities does not necessarily come from monetary remunerations alone, as well as being willing to accept lower remunerations should the enterprise encounter hard times financially. Entrepreneurs' use of previously developed relational ties and social mechanisms to solve problems at the enterprise reinforce this view. In this regard, entrepreneurs rely on the psychological contract between them and their workers for co-ordinating operations at the enterprises.

In this light, the entrepreneurs reduce transaction costs related to setting up elaborate supervision mechanisms because the familial ties between them solicit co-operation. Relational ties developed prior to engagement in commercial activities become important ingredients for developing and co-ordinating a sustainable economic unit (Duke et al. 2005). Such results concur with the views of Hite and Hesterly (2001), that new entrepreneurs resort to engaging workers they have some previous ties with to reduce contractual challenges. Such social ties act as both glue and lubricant, as was also established by Johannisson et al. (2002). As glue they bind the relatives and friends to render their total commitment to the entrepreneur and as a lubricant the social relations make it easier to co-ordinate the activities at the enterprise.

Reliance on relatives and friends concurs with the significance of strong social networks to economic outcomes of Granovetter (1973, 1985, 2005), Burt (1992) and Lin (2000). Entrepreneurs benefit by recruiting from similar homogeneous social categories because previous repeated interactions lead to the development of trust and mutual understanding. Moreover, those entering a firm through previous personal contacts are not likely to compromise such networks and will preserve co-operation and promote consummate performance. According to Granovetter

(2005), some entrepreneurs deliberately recruit relatives and friends so as to benefit from the loyalty and social control that already exist between them. In such social relations are what Dasgupta (2005) terms 'installed channels', that create trust to freely share tacit knowledge between employees and entrepreneurs.

There are a number of possible explanations why more female entrepreneurs than family-run enterprises and male entrepreneurs prefer to employ relatives and friends. In the study, female entrepreneurs tend to operate generally smaller enterprises compared to the other two categories. The mean value of male-, female- and family-owned enterprises, respectively, were ZIM$6,000,000.00, ZIM$4,500,000.00 and ZIM$10,000,000.00.[1] The smaller size of the enterprises run by females deterred them from attracting and employing qualified employees. Their option then was relatives and friends who will be more 'helping hands' than being full-time employees. Alternatively, female entrepreneurs could be more risk averse than others so they prefer to employ people they know and trust, who in this case are friends and relatives. Perhaps most female entrepreneurs employed relatives and friends to complement their human capital shortcomings, as most of them have relatively fewer years in school than the other two categories of entrepreneur.

Intra-enterprise bonding motivation strategies

The challenge for any enterprise is to nurture and foster strong internal linkages and networks to facilitate diffusion of new skills and knowledge sharing. The development of such intra-enterprise knowledge sharing platforms is a critical part of a broader workplace strategy (Heywood et al. 2005). For this reason, the entrepreneurs were asked how they forge familial networks among workers and the responses given are shown in Table 10.1.

An interesting observation was that most of the entrepreneurs use non-pecuniary forms of motivation, such as providing lunch and breakfast to workers, end of year parties, being open and transparent with the workers and providing on-the-job training. Financial support given to an employee who encounters a social problem

Table 10.1 Forms of bonding strategies used

	Male frequency	Female frequency	Family-run enterprise frequency
On-the-job training	9	5	4
Being transparent to workers	18	11	5
Personal use of enterprise resources	2	2	4
Financial support in case of social problem	31	8	8
Giving generous leave days	5	2	8
Offering transport allowance to workers	6	1	2
Providing breakfast and lunch	7	6	11
Setting production targets	2	10	4

such as the death of a family member topped the forms of motivation used. Awards and bonuses, including giving discounts to workers when buying from the enterprise, also emerged as a significant way of motivating employees. The responses are indicative of deliberate efforts made to create a family environment and strong psychological contract within the enterprise.

Male entrepreneurs dominated those who provide financial support to employees who would have encountered a social problem, as well as giving production bonuses. Female entrepreneurs cited end of year parties, awards and production bonuses, and being open and transparent. Family-run enterprises mainly motivate their workers by providing lunch and breakfast, giving generous leave days, offering financial support in case of social problems, awards and production bonus incentives. Figure 10.2 below shows the frequencies of the motivation methods cited by the different categories of entrepreneurs.

In the previous section it was observed that male entrepreneurs mostly prefer to employ anyone who qualifies for the job. By the same token, offering financial support to workers who would have encountered social problems as well as being open and transparent assists them in creating a familial relationship with their employees. A related phenomenon is that most female entrepreneurs prefer to employ relatives and friends. In this regard, hosting annual family parties, setting production targets, offering awards and bonuses as well as being open and transparent to their workers are better strategies to cement their strong social ties. Ironically, few female entrepreneurs provide financial support to their employees. The explanation could be that any social problem encountered by a relative or friend (who they mostly employ) is integral to their personal behaviour and not reported as part of their entrepreneurial life. Production targets, end of year parties, awards and being open to the workers will motivate workers to increase production as they will anticipate a large end of year celebration with its associated awards and bonuses. For family-run enterprises ('that want to keep the wealth in

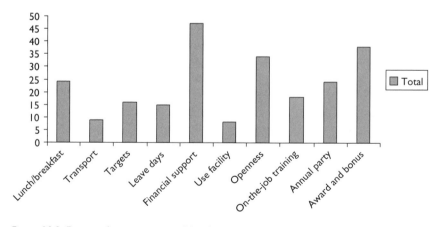

Figure 10.2 Forms of motivation used by the entrepreneurs.

the family' as one respondent indicated), having lunch and breakfast together is a platform for making decisions.

Looking at the motivation methods through a social capital lens, what can be discerned concurs with results from other research. For instance, the results concur with Davidssan and Henig (2003), Rob and Zemsky (2002) and Granovetter (2005) that such loyalty fostering systems are used to elicit co-operation, as such intense socialisation homogenises workers. Such intense social relations based on extended family and friendships are likely to ease co-ordination at such enterprises.

This is collaborated by Heywood et al.'s (2005) findings that traditional monetary incentives are not the sole mechanisms that can enlist total commitment and co-ordination of workers. They established that a culture of shared perceptions of mutual obligation and trust within the workforce forge a psychological contract between entrepreneurs and their workers. A conclusion that can be drawn is that strong relational exchanges forge a psychological contract that makes it easier for knowledge generation and diffusion. With respect to sourcing subtle tacit information, entrepreneurs would rather rely on people they know, most possibly these being relatives and friends in whom they have some confidence.

Socialising within the workplace

With the understanding that entrepreneurs get significant benefits if production is organised such that workers voluntarily co-operate, efforts have been directed at fostering workers' preferences for co-operation and in how to socialise the workplace. In this study, entrepreneurs were then asked how they facilitate socialisation of their workplaces. In the survey, 92.3 per cent indicated that they conduct planning sessions with their workers and only 7.7 per cent saw no value in planning with their workforce. All family-run enterprises plan with workers, with 88 per cent of the male entrepreneurs and 94 per cent of the female entrepreneurs also doing the same.

How often they meet annually for planning sessions is shown in Table 10.2. Almost 70 per cent of the respondents meet between 48 and 96 times a year. A majority of the family-run enterprises (62.97 per cent) meet four times a month, with 58.82 per cent of female entrepreneurs meeting eight times a month or two times a week. When probed on the benefits they derive from engaging in such time-consuming planning sessions, a number of insightful responses were given. The major benefits in order of priority were correcting mistakes, tapping into workers' knowledge, developing a shared vision and setting realistic goals, and meeting of targets. Davidssan and Henig (2003) observed that friends and relatives increase entrepreneurs' access to more diverse knowledge and entrepreneurial intelligence as such bonding social capital is positively associated with successful exploitation of opportunities.

Whereas male- and family entrepreneurs mainly benefit from tapping into ideas from workers, female entrepreneurs mainly benefit in terms of correcting mistakes. Female entrepreneurs are the majority of those with lower levels of education, and

Table 10.2 Frequency of planning with workers per year

No. of meetings per year	Male (%)	Female (%)	Family-run enterprises (%)	Total (%)
1–6	0	8.82	3.70	3.33
12	16.95	8.82	7.41	12.5
24	0	0	3.70	0.83
48	28.81	17.65	62.97	33.33
72	1.7	0	.00	0.83
96	37.29	58.82	11.11	37.5
288	15.25	8.88	11.11	11.67
Total	100	100	100	100

thereby such social planning platforms augments shortcomings in human capital. What emerges is that entrepreneurs use intra-enterprise planning networks to set goals and vision, important hallmarks of learning institutions. Entrepreneurs plan with workers so as to tap into the diverse knowledge stocks in their workforce. Figure 10.3 is a synthesis of the benefits that accrue from planning with workers.

Planning with workers is a way of providing them with broad goals and information about where the enterprise is going, as well as tapping into the enclaves of workers' tacit knowledge that is dispersed amongst the individuals making up a productive unit. Mantzavinos et al. (2003) defined this as a collective learning process, where there is modification of the mental models of the individuals according to the feedback received from the social environment. Such planning sessions create an environment for two-way collective learning within an enterprise unit. Such collective learning provides a framework for collective solutions to problems and this is the main reason for the plasticity of human behaviour where interactions with other individuals give rise to change and growth in society, polity, economy and organisations (Nonaka et al. 2000; Mantzavinos et al. 2003; Steiner 2004; Pierguiseppe and Giuseppina 2005).

That a significant number of entrepreneurs plan with their workers shows that efforts are made to facilitate knowledge sharing and exchange through intra-enterprise social networks. The planning platform lubricates the interaction of productive agents, making it easier to co-ordinate the diffusion of tacit knowledge. As Mantzavinos et al. (2003), Nonaka et al. (2000), Pierguiseppe and Giuseppina (2005) and Steiner (2004) established, a conducive learning environment is key for entrepreneurs to attain and maintain a competitive edge. Similarly, as Steiner (2004) established in the Austrian province of Styria, industrial cluster networks and social learning platforms are crucial in knowledge generation and diffusion as they facilitate economic co-operation and knowledge exchange within a firm. Findings from that study also confirm Giuliani's (2005) observation that knowledge of firms' processes resides in its workers and can be effectively co-ordinated through social processes such as planning engagements.

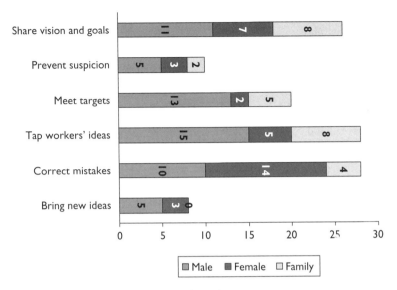

Figure 10.3 Benefits from planning with workers.

Such intra-enterprise bonding creates a psychological contract binding workers to carry their duties with little supervision as well as binding entrepreneurs not to cheat their workers, for example with respect to wages. Resources that would otherwise have been devoted to monitoring and evaluation will then be put to other productive functions in the enterprise. Planning with workers as stakeholders of the enterprise generates trust for the workers to adhere to contractual obligations. It was also established by Masuku (2003) that trust-based contractual relationships facilitate the smooth performance of members to a contractual arrangement. Such social motivation persuades workers and entrepreneurs to demonstrate organisational citizenship behaviour (Heywood et al. 2005).

However, research elsewhere has established that in the long run, benefits from strong social networks will have limited effects if a majority of the employees are relatives and friends as they have the same stock of knowledge (Dasgupta 2005; Duke et al. 2005). While such strong ties facilitate co-ordination of intra-enterprise activities, they tend to preclude workers from accessing outside ideas. However, because most small-scale entrepreneurs do not have research and development components as part of their enterprises, such intra-enterprise social networks become very useful in facilitating knowledge sharing and diffusion.

Finally, the respondents were asked who they would leave in charge of the business should they be away for some time. Table 10.3 shows the responses: 53 per cent indicated that they would leave the business in the hands of a friend or relative, 46 per cent would leave an assistant in charge, and less than 1 per cent indicated that they would close their business. From these results it appears that

Table 10.3 Who will be in charge of business when the owner is away

	Male	Female	Family-run enterprise	Total
	% [n=68]	% [n=35]	% [n=27]	% [n=130]
Relative or friend	34.3	75	70.4	53.05
Assistant	64.2	25	29.6	46.15
Close shop	1.5	0	0	0.8
Total responses	100	100	100	100

75 per cent of the female entrepreneurs and 70 per cent of the family-run enterprises have confidence in their relatives and friends. However most male entrepreneurs (64 per cent), most of whom previously indicated that they prefer to employ anyone who qualifies, prefer to leave the business in the hands of an assistant. The above observations should be viewed in relation to other factors, such as the size of the business and the nature of activities being carried out. Since most of the enterprises are small in scale, it becomes logical to leave a trusted friend or relative or alternatively an informed assistant in charge. However, some activities like carpentry and craftwork are such that for continuity's sake only those who have some knowledge of them should be left to run the enterprise.

The majority of the entrepreneurs appear to rely on their strong relational ties that make it easier to organise the operations and activities of their enterprises. Their management style revolves around their strong ties, and is similar to Chinese management culture, which is based on strong familial ties in which the family is the basic building block in business. According to Pun et al. (2000), the Chinese management culture, influenced by Confucian philosophy and the *guanxi* system, stresses the importance of the family in the socio-economic hierarchy. Perhaps this, together with the economic environment of Zimbabwe as a developing country, explains why most of the enterprises are small and, as in the Chinese case, based on sole proprietorship. However, it may be as Yamagishi et al. (1998) claim: intense familial trust and ties prevent trust from developing beyond the confines of the family and as a result we observe the development of small enterprises with limited capital to expand.

Male entrepreneurs leave their assistants in charge perhaps to reinforce workers' identification with the enterprise given that most of them employ those with appropriate qualifications. By extending such responsibility to workers, they are developing trust that will then make it easier to co-ordinate enterprise activities. Their management style leans strongly towards the approach of American management, in which businesses can be left in the hands of assistants who do not necessarily have to be relatives and the belief is that anyone can be a successful entrepreneur (Yamagishi et al. 1998; Pun et al. 2000). In the final analysis, intra-enterprise social networks and sociability are seen as important pillars in the economic development of small-scale enterprises.

Summary and policy implications

This chapter has examined the role of social capital with respect to its use by small-scale enterprises for intra-enterprise co-ordination. Rural non-farm enterprises mostly prefer to employ relatives and friends, though others employ those who have the qualifications. Most of the entrepreneurs in the study resort to using non-financial resources to motivate employees, as well as planning with their workers as a way to share information and knowledge. When the entrepreneurs in the study were asked whom they would leave in charge of business should they be absent, most female- and family-owned enterprises would be left in the hands of a relative or friend, while most male-owned enterprises would be left in the hands of an assistant.

The chapter has established that social networks are important ingredients in the economic development of small-scale entrepreneurs with respect to co-ordinating intra-enterprise processes. There are differences between male-, female- and family-run enterprises with respect to how they use social capital. Unlike male entrepreneurs, who mostly employ anyone who qualifies, female entrepreneurs prefer to employ relatives and friends, mainly as a means to alleviate co-ordination of intra-enterprise activities. While most male entrepreneurs employ anyone who qualifies, they also employ relational networks as mechanisms for reinforcing motivation and these create a sense of corporate citizenry and a psychological contract between them and their workers.

There are several policy suggestions from the results. Firstly, the results show that unlike the conventionally held notion that entrepreneurs are homogeneous, there are clear differences between male-, female- and family-run enterprises. The implication for policy is that entrepreneurial support programmes should be designed to reflect such social realities, rather than designing 'one fits all' policy programmes.

Results show that the entrepreneurs benefit from intra-enterprise social networks with respect to co-ordination and information generation and diffusion. While such strong networks are beneficial in 'getting started' and the immediate needs of the entrepreneurs, as Burt (1992) has established, more diverse and richer knowledge stocks come from bridging and linking social networks. For policy purposes, entrepreneurs' wider knowledge sharing platforms in the form of business trusts and business expos should be facilitated as a platform for wider networking and learning. More entrepreneurship education should be availed upon and facilitated in communities so that the entrepreneurs benefit from an informed labour force. However, while cohesive strong intra-enterprise networks benefit the entrepreneurs with respect to co-ordination of intra-enterprise activities, care should be taken, otherwise they will be prevented from seeing and appreciating benefits of wider network formation.

Business education establishments, in designing entrepreneurial support programmes, should analyse and identify beneficial social networks to balance both social and economic requirements of economic agents; enterprises should become not simply the locus for social engagement (important though this is), but also must be the drivers for economic growth. As was also established by Davidssan and Henig (2003), the needs of entrepreneurs outstrip the capacity of the generalist business advisor. However, such policy advice should encourage ways of maintaining active social relations within and between entrepreneurs, but within a wider platform where entrepreneurs share information and strategies. Business associations and trusts can surely play a significant role, but methods should be established to factor in the understanding of social capital in their training programmes.

Acknowledgements

The author gratefully acknowledges the support from the WK Kellogg Foundation that made this study possible. The study also contributes to the Foundation's mission in support of the development of healthy and sustainable communities in Southern Africa. He also acknowledges wise guidance from Professor J Kirsten of the Department of Agricultural Economics, Extension and Rural Development, University of Pretoria. The author also would like to acknowledge very useful comments and technical assistance from Professor Mike Osborne.

Note

1 During the survey period the official government exchange rate was 1US$ = ZIM$824.00.

References

Akerlof, G.A. and Krantan, R.E. (2005) 'Identity and the economics of organizations', *Journal of Economic Perspectives*, 19(1): 9–32.
Barr, A. (2000) 'Social capital and technical information flows in the Ghanaian manufacturing sector', *Oxford Economic Papers*, 52: 539–559.
Bibow, J., Lewis, P. and Runde, J. (2005) 'Uncertainty, conventional behavior and economic sociology', *American Journal of Economics and Sociology*, 64(2): 507–532.
Burt, R.S. (1992) *Structural Holes*, Cambridge, MA: Harvard University Press.
Casson, M. (2006) *Entrepreneurship: The Concise Encyclopaedia of Economics*, at: http://www.econlib.org/library/Enc/Entrepreneurship.html.
Chen, A. (2005) *Entrepreneurship: What Does it Really Mean?*, at: http://www.firstquatermain.com.
Dasgupta, P. (2005) 'The economics of social capital', an expanded version of the A. C. Mills Lecture delivered at the Annual Conference of Australian Economists, University of Sydney, September.
Davidsson, P. and Henig, B. (2003) 'The role of social and human capital among nascent entrepreneurs', *Journal of Business Venturing*, 18: 301–331.
Dew, N., Velamuri, R. and Venkataraman, S. (2004) 'Dispersed knowledge and an entrepreneurial theory of the firm', *Journal of Business Venturing*, 19: 659–679.

Duke, C., Osborne, M. and Wilson, B. (2005) *Rebalancing the Social and Economic Learning, Partnership and Place*, Leicester: National Institute of Adult Continuing Education.

Elsner, W. (2005) 'Real world economics today: the new complexity, coordination and policy', *Review of Social Economy*, 63(1): 19–52.

Fafchamps, M. (1997) 'Trade credit in Zimbabwean manufacturing', *World Development*, 25(5): 795–815.

Fafchamps, M. (2001) 'Networks, communities and markets in sub-Saharan Africa: implications for firm growth and investment', *Journal of African Economies*, 10(AERC Supplement 2): 109–142.

Fafchamps, M. (2004) *Market Institutions in Sub-Saharan Africa: Theory and Evidence*, Cambridge, MA: MIT Press.

Foss, K. and Foss, N. (1999) 'Entrepreneurship, margins and contract theory', presented at the Austrian Economics and the Theory of the Firm Conference, 16–17 August, Copenhagen, Denmark.

Giuliani, E. (2005) *The Structure of Cluster Knowledge Networks: Uneven and Selective, not Pervasive and Collective*, Aalborg and Copenhagen: Danish Research Unit for Industrial Dynamics, working paper No. 05–11, at: http://www.druid.dk/index.php?id=22.

Goette, L., Huffman, D. and Meier, S. (2006) *The Impact of Group Membership on Cooperation and Norm Enforcement: Evidence using Random Assignment to Real Social Groups*, Boston: Centre for Behavioural Economics and Decision Making, Federal Reserve Bank of Boston, working paper No. 06–7.

Granovetter, M. (1973) 'The strength of weak ties', *American Journal of Sociology*, 78: 1360–1380.

Granovetter, M. (1985) 'Economic action and social structure: the problem of embeddedness', *American Journal of Sociology*, 91(3): 481–510.

Granovetter, M. (2005) 'The impact of social structure on economic outcomes', *Journal of Economic Perspectives*, 19(1): 33–50.

Grootaert, C. (1999) *Social Capital and Household Welfare and Poverty in Indonesia*, working paper No. 6, Washington, DC: World Bank.

Heywood, J.S., Siebert, W.S. and Wei, X. (2005) *High Performance Workplaces and Family Friendly Practices: Promises Made and Promises Kept*, discussion paper No. 1812, Bonn: Institute for the Study of Labour.

Hite, J.M. and Hesterly, W.S. (2001) 'The evolution of firm networks: from emergence to early growth of the firm', *Strategic Management Journal*, 22: 275–286.

Isham, J. (2000) *The Effect of Social Capital on Technology Adoption: Evidence from Rural Tanzania*, IRIS center working paper No. 235, at: SSRN: http://ssrn.com/abstract=260053.

Johannisson, B., Ramirez-Pasillas, M. and Karlsson, G. (2002) 'The institutional embeddedness of local inter-firm networks: a leverage for business creation', *Entrepreneurship and Regional Development Journal*, 14(4): 297–315.

Johnson, N., Suarez, R. and Lundy, M. (2002) *The Importance of Social Capital in Colombian Rural Agro-enterprises*, CAPRi, working paper No. 26, Washington, DC: IFPRI.

Katungi, E. (2006) 'Social capital and technology adoption on small farms: the case of banana production technology in Uganda', PhD thesis, Department of Agricultural Economics, Extension and Rural Development, University of Pretoria, South Africa.

Kosfeld, M. and von Siemens, F. (2006) 'Competition, cooperation, and corporate culture', paper prepared for the Priority Programme on Foundations of Human Social Behaviour: Altruism versus Egoism Research, University of Zurich.

Krishna, A. and Shrader, E. (1999) *Social Capital Assessment Tool*, prepared for the World Bank Conference on Social Capital and Poverty Reduction, Washington, DC, 22–24 June.

Lawson, T. (1993) 'Keynes and conventions', *Cambridge University Review of Social Economy Publication* 51: 174–200.

Lin, N. (2000) 'Building a network theory of social capital', *Connections*, 22(1): 28–51.

Mantzavinos, C., North, D.C. and Shariq, S. (2003) *Learning, Institutions and Economic Performance*, working paper series of the Max Planck Institute for Research on Collective Goods, at: http://ideas.repec.org/s/mpg/wpaper.html.

Masuku, M.B. (2003) 'The role of contractual relationships in the performance of supply chains: a case of the sugar industry in Swaziland', PhD thesis, Department of Agricultural Economics, Extension and Rural Development, University of Pretoria, South Africa.

Nonaka, I., Toyama, R. and Nagata, A. (2000) 'A firm as a knowledge-creating entity: a new perspective on the theory of the firm', *Industrial and Corporate Change*, 9(1): 1–20.

Nyangena, W. (2005) 'Essays on Soil Conservation, Social Capital and Technology Adoption', PhD thesis, Department of Economics and Commercial Law, University of Gotenborg, Sweden.

Piergiuseppe, M. and Giuseppina, T. (2005) *What Makes Small and Medium Enterprises Competitive: An Investigation into the Italian Manufacturing Sector*, Foggia: Dipartimento di Scienze Economiche, Matematiche e Statistiche Universita` degli Studidi Foggia.

Pun, K.F, Chin, K.S. and Lau, H. (2000) 'A review of the Chinese cultural influences on Chinese enterprise management', *International Journal of Management Reviews*, 2(4): 325–338.

Putnam, R.D. (1993) *Making Democracy Work: Civic Traditions in Modern Italy*, Princeton, NJ: Princeton University Press.

Rob, R. and Zemsky, P. (2002) 'Social capital, corporate culture and incentive intensity', *RAND Journal of Economics*, 33: 243–257.

Sanchez, P., Rodriguez, M.A. and Ricart, J.E. (2005) *Social Embeddedness in Low Income Markets: Influential Factors and Positive Outcomes*, Navarra: Centre for Business in Society, University of Navarra.

Steiner, M. (2004) 'The role of clusters in knowledge creation and diffusion – an institutional perspective', paper presented at the 44th European Congress of the Regional Science Association, Porto, 25–29 August.

Tiepoh, M.G.N. and Reimer, B. (2004) 'Social capital, information flows, and income creation in rural Canada: a cross-community analysis', *Journal of Socio-Economics*, 33: 427–448.

Yamagishi, T., Cook, K.S. and Watabe, M. (1998) 'Uncertainty, trust, and commitment formation in the United States and Japan', *American Journal of Sociology*, 104(1): 165–194.

Chapter 11

Lifelong learning

Institutionalisation and regulating mechanisms

Kornelia Eftimova Ilieva

Introduction

Recent research has shown that there is an important gap between the acceptance of Lifelong Learning (LLL) concepts and their application in policy (Osborne and Thomas 2003) in different European countries. It can be seen that in many countries within Europe, diverse activities have been introduced in different parts of each national education and training system under the umbrella of LLL. Research also has shown that in different national contexts, considerable debate and controversial opinions on LLL issues are evident (Coffield; UNESCO 2001; Medel-Anonuevo 2003a, 2003b). For the purpose of this chapter on LLL, Field's (2006) distinction between concept, policy and practice will be considered. The analysis in this chapter broadly adopts Field's differentiated approach and sees LLL not only as an abstract theory or ideology, but draws on the complicated interplay between all its forms by focusing on particular everyday practices of actual people.

The next problem appears in the way we understand the institutionalisation process itself. I will show how in the Bulgarian case, historically the particular process of the institutionalisation of an informal educational activity into a formal organisational system has happened. I aim to describe what constitutes sufficient conditions for an educational field to overcome that crucial social change required to become an example – 'a good practice'. In this case, I propose an alternative social construct of *social networks* in this context.

The main thesis proposed here is that the 'new educational order' needs to be institutionalised in entirely different structures, such as social networks, in order to guarantee the flexibility of the system in a fast-changing environment.

The theoretical framework

This chapter is extensively drawn on the conclusions made by Podolny and Page (1998) and their definition of social networks:

> We define a network form of organization as any collection of actors (more than 2) that pursues repeated, enduring exchange relations with one another

and, at the same time, lacks a legitimate organizational authority to arbitrate and resolve disputes that may arise during the exchange.

Although I use mostly social network analysis (Scott 1991), the chapter is most likely to be seen as a theoretical bricollage in using different approaches *to explain* (in Weber's terms) the particular case which finally can be seen as 'a good practice' in LLL institutionalisation.

Institutionalisation is a very complex issue (Scott 2001), and readers will recognise within this chapter some aspects of a neo-institutionalism (Di Maggio and Powell 1991; Levy 2004), organisational studies (Stensaker 2004), as well as the theory of structuration (Giddens 1984) and even ethno-methodology (Garfinkel 1967). The reason for this mélange is that the goal of this chapter is not to be theoretically 'pure' as there is no single perspective or approach which can explain all social and cultural phenomena (see Merton 1968).

According to Scott (2001), institutionalisation deals with the historical process of establishing and legitimating formal and rational organisational structures, and sustainable practices, with their associated social roles providing stability and social order. However, there is a contradiction in that there is an initial assumption that in periods of crucial social change stability may actually impede such a change. Thus, the challenge is how to maintain a balance such that the desired social change is not hindered. In this context, what is needed is the institutionalisation of dynamic structures over which some control can be exerted.

For this purpose I will use the explanatory power of 'new institutional theory' (NIT) combined with social networks as the social reality of organisational type. NIT is chosen here because of the three main assumptions it represents. First, with regard to NIT, Scott (2001: 44) makes the assumption that 'the newer conceptual models emphasize cognitive over normative frameworks and have focused primary attention on the effects of cultural belief systems operating in the environments of organisations rather than intra-organizational processes.' The specific utility of NIT from an analytical point of view is that it is concerned with the level of analysis of the 'organisational field', namely a 'set of diverse organisations engaged in a similar function' (ibid.: 137). Second is a very important assumption which stresses the dynamic aspect of institutional processes: NIT explains 'not only how institutions arise but how they undergo change' (ibid.: 50). The third main assumption of NIT is that, 'institutions are embodied in individual experience by means of roles' (Berger and Luckman 1967: 73–75, quoted in Scott 2001: 58). In conclusion, drawing on the above conceptual model we can see the LLL sphere as 'an organisational field of educational providers'.

The purpose of this chapter is to demonstrate what might be sufficient conditions for the institutionalisation of LLL. Social networks are seen here as being at the meso-level of social structure (Hedström 1994). They are a form of organisation between hierarchies and the market, and represent a unique alternative possessing not only its own logic (Powell 1990), but also providing a number of advantages over alternatives, such as the fostering of learning, representing a mechanism for the attainment of status or legitimacy, providing a variety of economic benefits, facilitating the management of resource dependencies, and offering considerable autonomy for the employees as participants in learning. Burt (2004) has described the analysis of social networks themselves as a methodology, but my approach here is to take the network itself as a unit of analysis rather than the nodes within networks or transactions in which these nodes are involved. Furthermore, the nodes in my study are not different human beings; rather, in this particular case, they are mostly small educational providers such as local learning centres. Very often the centre itself is represented by only one person, but he or she acts not as an individual, but mostly as an institutional actor where personal and institutional interests are merged. This factor is of crucial importance when there is crisis or change in the given educational organisation or educational field. This approach to analysis is helpful as a way to establish when 'educational order' should be re-ordered (Field 2005).

Due to the lack of factual information and available archives, the logic of the research emanates from the ethnomethodological tradition of Garfinkel (1967), and the interplay between agency and structure (Giddens 1984). Its sources are people and their actual everyday practices. The shift to the more generalised level is made by the case study method, which has been used here to show the real process of institutionalisation and institutional transformation to what could be defined as a LLL – an organisation at the time of crucial social change embracing political, economic and cultural-cognitive change.

In an increasingly globalised world the choice of a national case could be questioned, and of course in Europe, the Bologna process[1] leads to an internationalisation of higher education in particular. However, the reality is that it is still predominantly the nation state which is in the position of determining its educational policies, using national financial mechanisms to support or reject different educational activities. As Green (1990: 48) puts it: 'National education explained the ways of the state to the people and the duties of the people to the state.' It is also worth stressing here that although the case considered here is national (Bulgaria), the research clearly shows sub-national and international aspects within the issues studied.

The method

I suggest that the most adequate method for this particular research is the case study. It is an appropriate approach to use in situations where specific qualitative methods cannot give depth for the understanding of social phenomena. I propose here a new approach within this area of methodology – the *multi-level case study*. When considering a very complex social phenomenon, it is difficult to limit the borders of the case study. Choosing a particular factor or object we might blind ourselves to those 'outside' the case, legitimating in this way the particular body, institution, person or concept. The case study methodology is usually one within which one or more qualitative methods are utilised within a constrained set of defined borders. It has limitations with the main critique concerning subjectivity and possibility of providing a generalising conclusion. However, it can be used as an experimental prototype and, following Yin (1994), must satisfy the main conditions of qualitative methods: describing, understanding and explaining. To overcome the limitations of the methodology, mainly its subjectivity, the researcher should be very reflective and pay attention to details, using multiple sources of data. Yin proposes, in order to guarantee the validity of evidence, using at least six sources of data:

- documents
- archival records
- interviews
- direct observation
- participant observation
- physical artifacts.

The Bulgarian case: lost in translation

There is no such expression directly translated into Bulgarian language as lifelong learning. Although there are some popular proverbs and folk concepts arguing that 'one is learning during all one's life', it is almost impossible to translate this term successfully. However, currently many providers in their everyday practices with formal, non-formal and informal education are engaged in what could be described as LLL. These include agencies in many different sectors of society, including: enterprises, non-profit making organisations, trade unions' training organisations, teacher training organisations and schools. How have these practices arisen given that there is no clear definition or discussion about LLL? Is LLL something new in Bulgarian society or are there traditions in this field?

Furthermore, given that there is no common definition at a national level for LLL in Europe despite the European Union's generalised statements (see Osborne and Thomas 2003), the problem of a lack of clear meaning is accentuated for Bulgaria, a former socialist country that entered the EU in 2007. The ascension countries are 'in a *doubled* transition'. Firstly, in moving from a socialist totalitarian regime to a market economy, they face huge problems in adapting their educational systems to the new economic situation. Simultaneously and secondly, they are constrained to adopt the educational goals and approaches of their national educational systems to that of a globalising (Europeanising) world.

Asking what is the shape and substance of LLL in Bulgaria, I started with the only available artifact: the event, *LLL days – Bulgaria*, which has taken place yearly since 2001. This event includes participants of all types of educational providers and it is organised by the IIZ/DVV[2] Sofia Bureau in Bulgaria based within a EU Gruntdvig 4 initiative, the *Adult Learning Week*, in which the UK National Institute of Adult and Continuing Education (NIACE) also takes part. The number of the participants varies each year but one of the main co-organisers is the

Federation of Societies for Dissemination of Knowledge, *Znanie*.[3] This is a large network (more than 30) of non-profit organisations, spread all over the country dealing with the provision of different educational activities. Although the official website says that the organisation was established in 1991, research has shown that to the great extent this is the former National Society for Spread of Knowledge 'Georgi Kirkov',[4] established by an order of the Central Committee of the Bulgarian Communist Party in December 1971. This organisation existed for the period from 1971 to 1989 when socialism collapsed. During this initial period the Society provided a wide range of educational, but mainly propaganda, activities.

Surprisingly after 1989, the same organisational structure was kept and two years later the new organisation was registered. The old structure was transformed into the new federation, *Znanie*, consisting of 30 different NGOs in 1991. Detailed national-level longitudinal research was commissioned by the Federation (Boyadjieva et al. 1994) about 'consumers'' attitudes towards educational 'services'. The NGOs of the Federation immediately adapted to new market conditions and responded to demand by providing vocational training, language courses and certificates in specific professional areas, such as computing. The Federation is now one of the important actors in the Bulgarian educational market, providing certified and non-certified vocational and personal education courses focused around leisure pursuits.

The importance of learning and education during the socialist period in Bulgaria

Education within a state-driven, centralised, totalitarian system in Bulgaria during the socialist period from 1944 to 1989 had a significant role in forging identity and bringing people together. My initial assumption was that learning is a proven mechanism for successful social inclusion. Education as a socialising process provided by particular educational institutions helps people 'to gain socially valued skills, knowledge, capabilities, and credentials' (Wotherspoon 2002: 17). However, it is necessary to embed checks and balances at a system level in order to avoid negative ideological and propaganda consequences.

Generally speaking, recently propagated concepts of LLL as a new policy for education are based on a presumption of involving all types of formal, non-formal and informal educational practices in a wide-ranging learning environment. This is illustrated in the European Commission's Memorandum on Lifelong Learning (EC 2001). The Commission and its member states have defined lifelong learning, within the European Employment Strategy, as all purposeful learning activity, undertaken on an ongoing basis with the aim of improving knowledge, skills and competence. This is the working definition adopted in this memorandum as a starting-point for subsequent discussion and action. Lifelong learning is no longer just one aspect of education and training; it must become the guiding principle for provision and participation across the full continuum of learning contexts (ibid.).

The reasons, purposes and consequences of this presumption are beyond the scope of this chapter, but practically it means the total coverage of human life by learning activities. It is important, however, to stress the specificity of terms when we are speaking about formal, non-formal and informal education in the Bulgarian case. All these educational forms were to the great extent 'formally' established and developed by the state during the socialist period. That is why I am using the well-known English terms only to define different types of implementation of educational activities; but we must have in mind that all these activities in the Bulgarian case do not have the same characteristic features as in Western countries. Non-formal and informal educational activities were well known and scientifically developed and implemented in Bulgaria during the socialist period within propaganda activities. The department *Propaganda I Agitazia* (Propaganda and Agitation) was established immediately after the Communist Revolution in 1944, and over the years the department was associated with different departments depending on the specific aims it sought to achieve.

If we literally translate the content of different LLL concepts and activities of the Bulgarian socialist period, they would be like the structure of the Propaganda and Agitation department from September 1944 as shown in Figure 11.1. Over the years the structures were merged or separated but the department continued to be the most important department of Agitation and Propaganda of the Central Committee of the Bulgarian Communist Party (CCBCP). This department implemented the governance of the whole activity of the Party connected with:

- organisation and direct governance of the verbal and printed propaganda of Marxist-Leninist ideas,
- help and governance of the local party's councils and preparation of theses, lectures and reports for public propaganda and celebrations,
- organising printed propaganda through periodicals – journals and everyday newspapers,
- organising and directly implementing agitation – enlightenment activity among the mass population,
- organising and celebrating historical events,
- organising printed and visual agitation – leaflets, brochures, slogans, posters, caricatures, diagrams, as well as public lectures.

After 1948, and following reorganisation and renaming of sectors, the structure was as shown in Figure 11.2. Continuing with the reorganisation, reshaping and renaming of the sectors, the structure ten years later was as shown in Figure 11.3 and the sub-sectors were called 'problem-solving groups'. Within the last sub-group and until the end of the 1960s, the 'Lecturers' group' was created. This group was the prototype and the main initiator of the establishment of the 'Georgi Kirkov' society.

Ideological marginalisation was one of the main categories of exclusion and inequality in the 'equal totalitarian' Bulgarian society. All educational forms, such

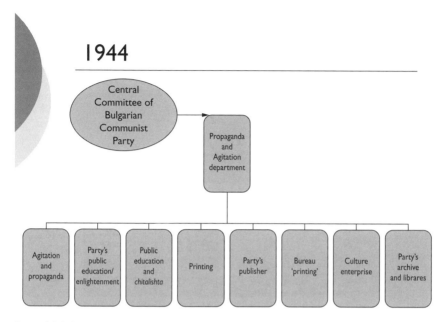

Figure 11.1 Structure of Propaganda and Agitation, 1944.

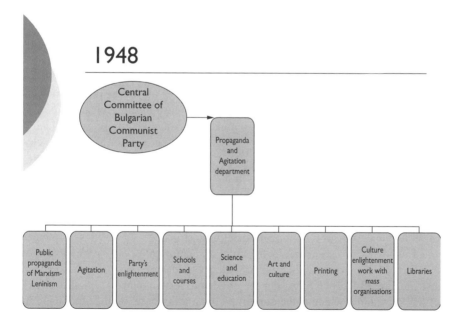

Figure 11.2 Structure of Propaganda and Agitation, 1948.

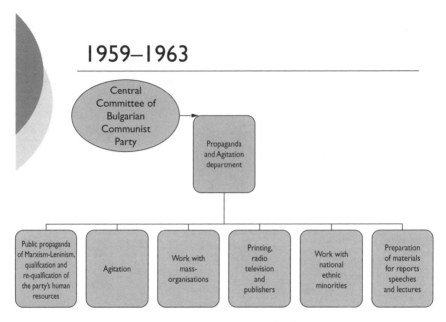

1959–1963

Figure 11.3 Structure of Propaganda and Agitation, 1959–1963.

as flexible short time courses, on- and off-the-job training, lectures, speeches, conversations, events, celebrations, mass-libraries and museums, were used as propaganda mechanisms for spreading socialist and Marxist dialectical materialist ideas. All these activities were also used in an informal way as an 'opinion poll' for feedback to the state. There was an additional and detailed analysis of questions asked by the audience and opinions expressed beyond the educational purposes of activities. In this case, Marxist propaganda played the role of a powerful mechanism for social inclusion in the rapidly industrialising Bulgarian society, molding and unifying an increasing population. Although equity was officially proclaimed from the first decades of socialist governance, a lot of discrepancies in economic, educational and ideological origin were observed. That is why it was of vital importance and necessity to use the socialisation impact of education and learning processes in order to keep individuals' attention pointing towards the 'right direction'. The official formal system for adult education in Bulgaria was practically unavailable during this period, but in order to educate people towards a new 'view of life' through socially constructing their realities (cf. Berger and Luckman 1967), specific non-formal and informal organisations to cover all society were indispensable. By providing the idea of a new social order, the state accomplished two aims. On the one hand, it maintained the homogeneity of the population, which is the aim of the totalitarian state; on the other hand, it consolidated human resources for the modernising processes in one particular direction – that of the Socialist State.

The activities of the Propaganda and Agitation department aimed to overcome the natural stratification process caused by industrialisation (Giddens 1984) and they formed mental attitudes toward equality and unity. Institutionalised forms of the propaganda mechanisms become the backbone of the diversified society and one of the basic fundamentals for social integration. The 'top-down' centralised institutionalisation of non-formal and informal educational practices not only sustained social cohesion, but provided the reproduction of the desired social order. However we should note this integrity was ideologically maintained. It was achieved by the specific (borrowed from the USSR) model of institutional organisation characterised by centralisation, bureaucratisation, strong hierarchical order and a predominantly top-down flow of information.

Various forms of mass communication, as the most influential channels for manipulation, were also used extensively from the beginning of the 1970s. It is also important to underline that propaganda activities through educational programmes grew in parallel with television, in basically an environment of exclusively public broadcasting. However, the extensive processes of modernisation[5] lead to individualisation and fragmentation which contradicted the aim of total control of the command-administrative socialist state.

Due to well-developed educational practices in all forms (formal, non-formal and informal) in 1989, at the end of the socialist era, Bulgarian society entered the market-led economic period with a well-established educational structure and quite a large number of educational providers, as follows:

- secondary and higher education oriented towards young people in full-time programmes; a system of school and university education,
- the system of continuing professional education (CPE) was well developed also, principally in the field of teacher training for secondary school. Also after the 1959 Education Act, centres for CPE within the universities and polytechnics were established in order to support fast changing and dynamic industrial development. The well-developed system of re-qualification was also organised within trade unions as well as at local municipal centres for short-course vocational training,
- non-formal education, predominantly in the field of music, languages, dancing, painting and art activities as a whole, was organised on a local level by municipal authorities and *chitalishta*[6] – local cultural organisations providing the whole range of educational activities. All these courses were on a short-term basis and regular – once or twice a week,
- informal activities – public lectures, speeches, conversations, events, celebrations, mass-libraries, museums, excursions all over the country, predominantly at historical places. The informal sector reached all citizens – children, youths and adults.

Adult education in Bulgaria was well developed during the socialist period but it was poly-centric and not within the formal educational system. Furthermore, it was not oriented toward the basic literacy of the people. And, most importantly, non-formal and informal educational activities were strongly ideologically overburdened under the umbrella of the Propaganda and Agitation department. It is important to stress that all of these activities are institutionalised in a very dynamic and flexible form. They had been changed regularly over the years and their content was changeable and oriented towards problem-solving for the state at a given time. Once the context had been changed, new activities were related to changed environmental conditions and demands.

Organisational structure for provision of propaganda and agitation activities in Bulgaria during the socialist period

Following Kulich (1989):

> Consistent with the ideological, political and economic system established in the Soviet Union after 1917 and in Eastern Europe since 1945, all forms of adult education have to fit into the prevailing social system and planned economy. Adult education is considered an important ideological tool and throughout the region it is subject to Communist Party and state control.

However, the socialist period in Bulgaria is still being researched. It is almost impossible to find archives of most of the structures and organisations – they are lost, burnt, or access is very often denied. The same is the case with most of the public organisations. There were many professional unions and public organisations during the socialist period in Bulgaria, so called *Massovi organizatzii* (mass organisations). They operated in a top-down fashion and in most cases were centrally controlled and governed by the Communist Party in order to avoid 'wrong' attitudes. The Party had the full control of all types of education at all levels. This control was wielded by the Party and the state agencies at the national, provincial or state and also at the district and local levels. Mass organisations were considered important in ideologically-driven educational activities for citizens. Universities were not directly involved as organisations in this process.

For the purpose of this chapter I will present the specific case of *Drujestvo za razprostranenie na nauchni znania 'Georgi Kirkov'* (the National Society for Dissemination of Scientific Knowledge 'Georgi Kirkov'), this being the main form of non-formal and informal educational provision. During the period of my research, no archive for this organisation has been found and it seems not to be available. For this reason the research has been carried out focusing on different and multiple sources of data: mainly by participant and direct observation for more than two years and interviews with 20 ex- and current employees. For the purpose of ethical concerns all respondents are anonymised. A content-analysis of the official newspaper, *Rabotnichesko delo*, for the period 1970 to 1990 and some partially available documents of the CCBCP (Fund 1B, the State Archive), as well some of the numbers of the official society's journal, *Lekzionna propaganda*

(*Lecturers' propaganda*), has been undertaken. Of course, there are still many gaps which could be filled in the future and a new source or document could change the whole logic of the analysis presented here.

The National Society for the Dissemination of Scientific Knowledge 'Georgi Kirkov' was part of a large supra-national network within the socialist bloc. The only Soviet bloc country which did not have such a society was Yugoslavia. All other countries in the region (Bulgaria, Czechoslovakia, German Democratic Republic, Hungary, Poland and Romania) created the same structures based on the model of the *Znanie* society established in the Soviet Union in 1947 as a Society for the Dissemination of Political and Scientific Knowledge.

The Society for the Dissemination of Scientific Knowledge 'Georgi Kirkov' was established in Bulgaria in 1971. The objective of the association was to assist the Communist Party of Bulgaria in the education of the future active builders of the socialist society – persons who will be highly conscious from the ideological point of view, with a solid morality and good physical health, and keen awareness of their duty and responsibilities (Micheva et al. 1982: 57).

A national assembly with the status of a highest governing body represented by the Council of the Republic, consisting of 81 representatives of the Bulgarian Communist Party and scientists from the universities and Bulgarian Academy of Science was created at a national conference in December 1971. More than 400 people – intelligentsia, lecturers and organisers of lectures – were present. A month earlier, in November 1971, the *Sauz na nauchnite rabotnizi* (Union of Scientific Workers) had decided to fully participate in the activities of the 'Georgi Kirkov' society. As a consequence of a decision of this conference, all local municipalities were obliged to establish local centres under the order of the CCBCP, which were to be controlled by this Council of the Republic. There were established approximately 28 local centres because they represented one per administrative region,[7] with a main central town in each region. As interviewees say, the aim was to establish such centres in the smaller villages too, but this was unsuccessful. Respondents reported that there were few appropriate people (either qualified and/or loyal to the Communist Party) available. Furthermore, in the countryside, because of the more traditional attitudes and a focus on agricultural activities, interest towards such activities was lower. All local 'Georgi Kirkov' centres were connected, but not hierarchically. They functioned on a principle of a social network, organised by the same ideas that established socialist order in Bulgaria as a whole, but with a high level of autonomy at the local level. Each had one and the same function, but the actual content of the activities was decided at a local level. The centres had mainly controlling, co-ordinating and representative functions. They had only a few permanent paid staff, whose salaries were ensured, centrally, by the Council of the Republic. Their institutionalisation and regulation was top-down, given the quite abstract ideology of 'building the Socialist State' and the 'Socialist Human Being'. They functioned on the basis of individual projects (rather than offering a definite number of lectures) and applied to a single financing centre in order to receive support to co-ordinate visits of lecturers to enterprises and other organisations. For example in 1974, one of the districts signed 220 contracts. It is notable that these lectures were obligatory for employees; failure to attend would mean threat of sanction or even loss of their job. However, the many respondents in this research stated that some of the lectures 'were very interesting and useful'.

The local centres were much more institutionally embedded into the local district than on the national or party level, although a national conference took place every five years, with participants from all over the country. This ensured regular horizontal reciprocal action. Over the years the city centres of the society played the role of the brokerage between political decision makers, financial institutions, lecturers and educational providers, as well as providing an audience for the already planned lectures. The thematic clusters under the slogan of the *Generalnata Linia* (General Line) in building the 'Socialist Society' were mainly in economics, Marxist–Leninist philosophy and sociology, international relations and health education. For this purpose the national society and each local society possessed a large database of lecturers. The society was also obliged to help methodologically and thematically in support of already existing forms of education, including folk universities, and were involved in planning of courses, workshops, seminars, theoretical conferences, lectures and thematic cycles, by providing yearly plans and programmes. This was within a programme created in 1974 entitled *Sistema za upravlenie I koordinazia na masovata propaganda* (A system for direction and co-ordination of the mass lectures propaganda). It was not possible to find exactly how many lectures and people were involved in this activity for the whole period, but for example in 1973, in just one of the 28 administrative districts, 7,517 lectures had been presented. This local society had 1,317 members, including 1,151 with higher education level qualifications (including three professors, 22 research fellows and 17 PhD students), with 69 research officers and 166 people with secondary-level education.

Whilst in the 1970s Bulgaria developed into an industrialised society with its main characteristics, including increased leisure time for a wider range of people, these activities were still attended by a large number of citizens. For example, as recently as 1981, over one million[8] people attended training courses. Human resource and expert knowledge in the field of adult non-formal and informal education was widely spread and well developed. It should be stressed that all these activities were centrally financed and the provision of courses and lectures was free to all.

That explains Boyadjieva et al.'s (1994) findings that Bulgarian society was (and still is) characterised by high educational levels,[9] high levels of literacy and very positive attitudes toward all educational activities. Bulgarian people are 'trained' to use the whole range of formal, non-formal and informal educational activities in their different forms and types. To a great extent in Bulgarian society there is the habit of attending educational and cultural events. However, despite this tendency, in modern Bulgaria there are problems for a number of reasons. Firstly, courses are no longer free and because of economic transformation many people don't have enough resources to pay for provision; secondly, there is still an entrenched view that all adult education should be freely provided. In addition, all these systems and activities, because of the Cold War period, were developed in an isolated fashion. Although the concrete practices at everyday level were similar, they were named differently in order to distinguish them from the practices of Western experts and their traditions in the field. For example, the Bulgarian *chitalishta* (reading houses) are very similar to the community centres in the UK, although the literal translation has a different connotation. On the other hand, many of the lectures provided by the centrally governed Georgi Kirkov society can be compared to 'public lectures' in the UK universities – especially those in local history, economies, national history or other topics in the field of science and humanities. The same is the case with different educational and learning activities in the field of social inclusion targeting the ethnic minorities, marginalised groups and disabled and disadvantaged people.

The network of educational providers in the conditions of the market economy

In 1989, after the fall of communism, all the Party structures, legislation and regulations were annulled. Consequently, all organisations working under the Party's umbrella have been closed. However, a large network of educational providers and qualified experts in teaching and learning activities and human resources was available. On the other hand, there was a high level of market demand for new specific educational activities. The local centres of the Georgi Kirkov society in different towns, which were not already sponsored by the state, continued to function and re-directed themselves to educational activities within the private and NGO sector. They started to offer fee-based courses responding to market demand, such as language and computing courses, preparation for entry to secondary school and professional colleges, as well as to universities. Simultaneously, the tradition of being oriented towards project-based funding helped professionals to apply for European funding and quickly transform the networks from national state financing to EU financing.

Using the neo-institutional approach to analysis, it would appear that this network of educational providers is no longer embedded in any institutional context and field. Being separate from the formal educational system structure, it was thrown into the new post-communist conditions without any centrally provided laws or regulations. The network was quite autonomous and not bounded by the national institutional context. The network was absolutely free to work as an enterprise in the conditions of the market economy.

But it was still an informal network of people who have been interested in preserving their professional identity as educational providers. The new economic and political situation destroyed not only their formal organisation; but also was a real threat to their professional identity. At the heart of this identity are the competences for delivering *flexible* educational provision and the methodology and know-how of organising, co-ordinating and providing *any* type of educational activity (my italics). As Field (2005: 128, my italics) states:

> The interplay between networks and learning is not simply part of a process by which skills and techniques are shared, and information is passed around. It is also an active part of *the process of making sense of the world* . . .

In this way, by preserving the network through communication and information channels, they not only maintain their identity, but provide themselves with social and economic benefits relying on the trust-based relationships established during the preceding period of 20 years.

To quote Field (ibid.: 68), 'Much knowledge – including many practical applications – is tacit, or embedded in specific social networks with their largely unquestioned routines; indeed these networks are often creating and re-creating knowledge, rather than simply engaging in a series of one-way knowledge transfer.' The latter is the case with the school teachers, for example. Despite the ideal type of professional identity for the school teacher, who is very often embedded into the particular content of the exact transfer of specific knowledge, the representatives of the Georgi Kirkov society are predominantly suppliers and co-ordinators between the supply-side (lecturers, experts, university representatives) and demand-side (specific groups of people with specific learning attitudes and interests).

In 1991, through a bottom-up process of institutionalisation, a new Federation of the Societies of Dissemination of Knowledge (*Znanie*) was created, consisting of 30 local NGOs. In most cases, the centres are situated in the same building, and the people employed are the same. What is different is the juridical registration and status, and the substance of courses and services provided. Each local NGO offers provision specific to the particular region and its demands, but the programmes have changed from non-certified propaganda and civic education lectures to certified vocational qualifications and other short-term professional courses.

However, some national programmes take place, principally funded within EU-financed projects, such as 'Second Chance'[10] (a literacy programme for adult Roma citizens) and 'X-pert'[11] (a European certificate in computing). Nevertheless, it is up to each separate centre to decide what to offer or not to offer, how and in what form and timespan. Each local centre is free to enter into different partnerships and can decide to participate or not in the joint Federation-level activities. The Federation provides co-ordination and information. Being a larger network for learning activities in Bulgaria, the network has attracted the German-based IIZ/DVV (see Note 2) and other foreign educational providers. In this way, IIZ/DVV is a co-organiser of the event 'LLL Days in Bulgaria', and the main organiser of the event in 2006 (27–29 October).

It should be stressed here that the national formal educational system (secondary and higher education) is still characterised by centralisation, bureaucratisation, and a strong hierarchical order with a predominantly top-down flow of information (Dimitrov 2004). In this way, it is still not in a position to transform itself towards the new order of the market economy and was unable to successfully access the new EU and World Bank finance mechanisms. Evidence of the state administration not being able to adapt itself to the new environmental requirements and the lack of the expert knowledge in the field is demonstrated by the failure of the World Bank project for 'The modernization of the education in Bulgaria'. The first stage amounted to $US15.4m, but after monitoring this first phase of the project the World Bank canceled the rest of the project.[12]

Conclusions

Being research in progress, currently I have established the following critical aspects on the questions posed. Educational institutions, public, private and non-profit, make use of the different discourses of LLL depending on the project they are participating in. The private and non-profit sector have internalised the different discourses of LLL concepts, whilst as of mid-2006 on a national level there is still no national strategy for LLL. Although being rather abstractly defined at EU level, the concept has been used in two typical ways:

- 'bottom-up' – when there are some problems or specific requirements predominantly on a local administrative municipal level. The existing NGO or private companies organise different types of short-term fee-paying courses – mainly languages and vocational training. Under various EU education programmes, sometimes they provide free services for the participants and also attract different local authorities.
- 'top-down' – when there are specific projects which provide financial support and experts look for target groups and legitimate them. The concrete example is Romas (gypsies) as a target group in Bulgaria who were not consolidated as such as a group previously.

There is no consensus on the terminology used for LLL by the Ministry of Education, Ministry of Labour and Social Policy, the National Agency for Vocational Training and Education, or the Institute of Education[13] (now a former structure as it has been closed as an organisation during the research period). Every state institution uses different reference documents and definitions depending on its specific activity. In many cases discrepancies on an international level are transferred to a national level. As different organisations such as the EC, European Training Foundation, OECD, World Bank and UNESCO are using in a different way the LLL concept, so too are Bulgarian governmental institutions.

The Ministry of Education uses the concept quite literally, by issuing formally different types of documents and strategies in order to adapt the legislation to EU standards[14] (Republic of Bulgaria 2006). The Ministry of Labour and Social Policy is the most active actor in using EU funds. It tries to provide national policy in the field of LLL mainly in the field of vocational training and to combat unemployment, a major consequence of economy transformation (Republic of Bulgaria 2003). The National Agency for Vocational Training and Education works on establishing new state educational standards in vocational training by providing basic characteristics for different professions. This institution accredits Centres for Vocational Training with the Leonardo da Vinci and Socrates programmes of the EC as the basic channels for co-funding. In addition, currently it supports the publishing of an Educational Glossary, which will consolidate the terms on a national level.

The formal educational system in Bulgaria is still not in a position to open itself to new concepts. A Strategy for LLL is forthcoming, but there is still a debate as to which ministry or state agency will be responsible for funding. Higher education institutions, including universities, due to their partial autonomy, have succeeded in participating as partners in different international projects (mainly within Education and Training frameworks of the EU) related to LLL concepts. Unfortunately to the author's knowledge there is no institution which is a main co-ordinator of its own project.

The LLL concept is a product of modern industrialised society (Osborne et al. 2005). The concept and globalisation tendencies are mutually connected (Osborne et al. 2004) and neither exists without the other. The LLL concept is a strong mechanism for consolidating people within the new society of Europe, but there is no consensus at a national level within the EU on what the LLL concept is. As such, it is a shell within which every country puts its own specific educational or social problems. The only consensual point is the centre for financing. The LLL discourse strongly depends on the specific understanding of a sponsoring organisation.

Using learning nowadays as an inclusion mechanism is a process very similar to those used at a national level during the twentieth century by each industrialising European nation state. These processes are more visible in socialist countries as there the processes were more forced and not historically natural. There are, however, very particular challenges for Bulgaria in the future, as illustrated in a recent World Bank report:

> First Bulgaria's working age population is shrinking much more rapidly than in many countries in the EU, placing even greater demands on higher labour productivity – and thus the ready availability of a skilled labour force – as a key determinant of economic growth. Second, despite its high levels of educational attainment and tremendous progress in recent decades, there are still gaps with EU countries. At the same time, some recent trends – on quality and participation – raise concerns. Third, inequalities in access to good quality education are still high. Low income groups, rural residents and ethnic minorities are at risk of economic and social exclusion in the future.
>
> (World Bank 2005: 1)

In brief, LLL institutionalisation in Bulgaria during the socialist period 'formally' happened simultaneously though both top-down and bottom-up principles. There were appropriate social conditions, including leisure time, and high levels of literacy and education during the socialist period, which supported the emergence of LLL practices. However, most importantly there was a state apparatus which provided learning activities within the direction of civic (citizenship) education. New LLL (re)institutionalisation uses already existing social networks which were formally destroyed in 1989, but which have informally existed through the individual contacts, and through communication and information channels. On this basis new formal networks providing educational and learning activities have been established as a NGO network. The experts of the former professional and educational organisations are the basis for these networks and participants in the LLL debate representing both state agencies and the new NGO and private educational providers. The challenges posed by accession to the EU, and achieving the goals of the Lisbon Agenda 'to become the most competitive and dynamic knowledge-based economy in the world, capable of sustainable economic growth with more and better jobs' are particularly stringent for Bulgaria when viewed in the context of the World Bank's analysis. The sustaining of a LLL network may be crucial in this process by providing new policy documents and the forthcoming Strategy in LLL with a real base for the development of the sustainable educational practices and activities. The lack of official formal policy in this field makes the available networks invisible and is partly the reason for the omission of this activity by supra-national bodies such as the World Bank.

Notes

1 The Bologna process is a brief general term describing the political process to establish a European area of Higher Education by 2010. The Bologna Declaration was signed on 19 June 1999. The process aims 'to make the higher education systems in Europe converge towards a more transparent system whereby the different national systems would use a common framework based on three cycles'. This is to achieve 'the most competitive and dynamic knowledge-based economy in the world'. See http://ec. europa.eu/education/policies/educ/bologna/bologna_en.

2 IIZ/DVV is Institute for International Co-operation of the German Adult Education Association.

3 The word 'Znanie' means 'knowledge' in English.

4 Georgi Kirkov is the name of very famous party and communist politician from the middle of the twentieth century.

5 Bulgaria has the demographic and educational characteristics of a well-developed industrialised society. The age structure of the Bulgarian population is as follows: 0–14 years: 14.4 per cent; 15–64 years: 68.5 per cent; 65+ years: 17.1 per cent. Urban inhabitants in 2001 were 69 per cent of total population (Nationalen statističski institut: Bălgarija 2005).

6 The *chitalishta* of Bulgaria are a specific type of cultural and educational institution, which have a long tradition in the history of the country and are closely related to the development of civil society within the country before the totalitarian regime (1944). Since the nineteenth century, almost all villages and towns in Bulgaria have had at least

one *chitalishte*. The *chitalishta* offer a wide range of cultural activities (concerts, festivities, films, etc.), as well as educational courses (foreign languages, music, drawing, painting, folklore, singing and dancing). *Chitalishta* organise different study groups according to participants' interests, regardless of gender, age, religion, social status or ethnic background. Nowadays, the *chitalishta* are often the only places where older people are able to gather, study, exchange their experiences and knowledge, and establish social and cultural contacts with other people. Many *chitalishta* are a stepping stone to further community participation and offer a wide variety of activities, such as amateur theatre, singing lessons, cookery, needlework and woodcarving. They are the place where traditional region-specific, and often special events, are organised and sustained and where participants can present the skills and knowledge they have acquired. This might be viewed at a European level as an example of 'good practice' in LLL. The other main characteristics of these institutions are that they are a type of NGO and are charity institutions. They work on a local principle and supply inter-generational contacts between members and participants. Currently a network of 500 centres exists (see http://www.chitalishte.bg/).

7 Currently the administrative territory separation is quite different.
8 The population of Bulgaria at the beginning of the 1980s was about 8.5 million, with over 60 per cent urban inhabitants (Nationalen statističeski institut: Bălgarija 1981).
9 Later studies report that 98.2 per cent of the total population of Bulgaria had a level of basic literacy in 2003 (United Nations Development Report (UNDP) 2005: 259). It is the more highly educated who are historically more oriented to continuing education and LLL activities (Boyadjieva et al. 1994).
10 This was a project providing a methodology, train the trainers module and education period for low-income Roma citizens to achieve a primary education certificate.
11 This is a certified training course in basics of the MS Office and Windows applications, which is benchmarking the computer literacy for the euro-passport system.
12 The report of this project, with ratings that 'the outcome was unsatisfactory, the sustainability was unlikely, the institutional development impact was negligible, and the Bank and borrower performance were both unsatisfactory' can be found at the World Bank website (http://www-wds.worldbank.org).
13 This was the main research institute on the national level under the governance of the Ministry of Education providing the expert knowledge about the policy in the field of education.
14 This is additionally quite strange as EU standards as a homogeneous system no longer exist.

References

Berger P. and Luckman T. (1967) *The Social Construction of Reality: A Treatise in the Sociology of Knowledge*, London: Penguin.
Boyadjieva, P., Gerganov, E., Dilova, M., Paspalanova, E. and Petkova K. (1994) *Education beyond the School Doors*, Sofia: Gal-Iko.
Burt, R.S. (2004) 'Structural holes and good ideas', *American Journal of Sociology*, 110: 349–399.
Coffield, F. (ed.) (2000) *Differing Visions of a Learning Society, Vols 1 and 2*, Bristol: Policy Press.
Di Maggio, P.J. and Powell, W.W. (eds) (1991) *The New Institutionalism in Organizational Analysis*, Chicago: University of Chicago Press.
Dimitrov, G. (ed.) (2004) *Darjavata sreshtu reformite (The State Against Reforms)*, Sofia: Iztok-Zapad.

Duke, C., Osborne, M. and Wilson, B. (2005) *Rebalancing the Social and Economic: Learning, Partnership and Place*, Leicester: NIACE.

EC (2001) Making a European Area of Lifelong Learning a Reality, at: http://ec.europa.eu/education/policies/111/life/index_en.html.

Field, J. (2005) *Social Capital and Lifelong Learning*, Bristol: Policy Press.

Field, J. (2006) *Lifelong Learning and the New Educational Order*, 2nd edition, Stoke-on-Trent: Trentham Books.

Garfinkel, H. (1967) *Studies in Ethnomethodology*, Englewood Cliffs, NJ: Prentice Hall.

Giddens, A. (1984) *The Constitution of Society: Outline of the Theory of Structuration*, Berkeley: University of California Press.

Hedström, P. (1994) 'Mesolevel networks and the diffusion of social movements: the case of the Swedish Social Democratic Party', *American Journal of Sociology*, 106(1): 145–72, also at: http://www.nuffield.ox.ac.uk/users/hedstrom/ajs3.pdf.

Kulich, J. (1989) 'Provision in Eastern Europe and Soviet Union', in C. Titmus (ed.) *Lifelong Education for Adults: An International Handbook*, Oxford: Pergamon Press.

Levy, D.C. (2004) *The New Institutionalism: Mismatches with Private Higher Education's Global Growth*, PROPHE Working Paper No. 3, at: http://www.albany.edu/~prophe.

Medel-Anonuevo, C. (2003a) *Lifelong Learning Discourses in Europe*, Hamburg: UNESCO Institute for Education.

Medel-Anonuevo, C. (2003b) *Citizenship, Democracy, and Lifelong Learning*, Hamburg: UNESCO Institute for Education.

Merton, R.K. (1968) *Social Theory and Social Structure*, New York: Free Press.

Micheva, P., Bizkov, G. and Petkov, I. (1982) *Adult Education in the People's Republic of Bulgaria*, Prague: European Centre for Leisure and Education.

Nationalen statističeski institut: Bălgarija (1981) *Socialno i ikonomičeskoto razvitie*. (Social and economic development), Sofia: NSI, annual publication, at: http://www.nsi.bg.

Nationalen statističeski institut: Bălgarija (2005) Socialno i ikonomičeskoto razvitie. (Social and economic development), Sofia: NSI, Annual publication, at: http://www.nsi.bg.

Osborne, M. and Thomas, E. (2003) (eds) *Lifelong Learning in a Changing Continent*, Leicester: NIACE.

Osborne M., Gallacher, J. and Crossan, B. (eds) (2004) *Researching Widening Access to Lifelong Learning – Issues and Approaches in International Research*, London: Routledge.

Podolny, J.M. and Page, K.L. (1998) 'Network forms of organization', *Annual Review of Sociology*, 24: 57–76.

Powell, W.W. (1990) 'Neither networks nor hierarchy: networks form of organisation', in B. Staw and L. L. Cummings (eds) *Research in Organizational Behavior*, Greenwich, CT: JAI Press.

Republic of Bulgaria (2006) *Obrazovanie i Obučenie 2010. Prinos na R. Bălgarija kăm săvmestnija doklad na Evropejskata komisija i săveta 2006* (Education and Training 2010. Contribution of the Republic of Bulgaria to the joint report of the European Commission and Council 2006), Sofia: Republic of Bulgaria.

Republic of Bulgaria, Ministry of Labour and Social Policy (2003) *Employment Strategy 2004–2010*, adopted by the Council of Ministers on 6 November, Sofia: Republic of Bulgaria.

Scott, J. (1991) *Social Network Analysis: A Handbook*, London: Sage.

Scott, R.W. (2001) *Institutions and Organizations*, London: Sage.

Stensaker, B. (2004) *The Transformation of Organizational Identities: Interpretations of Policies Concerning the Quality of Teaching and Learning in Norwegian Higher Education*, Enschede: CHEPS.

UNDP (2005) *Human Development Report*, New York: UNDP, at: http://hdr.undp.org/reports/global/2005/.

UNESCO (2001) *National Education Policies and Programmes and International Cooperation*, Paris: UNESCO.

World Bank (2005) *Bulgaria – Education and Skills for the Knowledge Economy: A Policy Note, executive summary*, at: http://siteresources.worldbank.org/INTBULGARIA/Resources/EducationPolicyNote_EN.pdf.

Wotherspoon, T. (2002) *The Dynamics of Social Inclusion and Exclusion – Public Education and Aborginal People in Canada*, Toronto: Laidlaw Foundation.

Yin, R. (1994) *Case Study Research: Design and Methods*, 2nd edition, Beverly Hills, CA: Sage.

Chapter 12

Place-centric and future-oriented learning in the local village context

Erik Wallin

This chapter draws on the recently completed *CoLabs.eu* project funded within the R3L initiative on 'European Networks of Learning Regions' (European Commission 2002),[1] which involved some local social experiments in order to 'make the village a virtual campus'. The motivating background for the project was the need for major *educational process re-engineering* in order to work effectively within the remit of the *third mission* of universities; that is, to engage in the development of suitable competences of relevance to the surrounding society. The objectives for the project included the design and implementation of local 'collaboratories'. A *collaboratory* was our concept for an ICT-supported facility for combined learning and project work in a local context. In the project, such facilities were called *CoLabs* and the key objective was to design and implement such CoLabs to support local learning initiatives and exchange of experiences between the project partners. The outcomes of the experiments and the general results achieved are discussed in more general terms with some recommendations on how to make villages not only 'learning villages', but also innovative and creative, signalling the need for a new framework for knowledge creation where place and people really matter.

Background and motivation

In Sweden and in most other EU-member states, there is a need for dedicated methods, facilities and organisational models to support the third mission of universities. In this context, the third mission is considered to be the application of knowledge to existing regional problems, to contribute to the generation of competences to solve such problems and to contribute to the general development of industrially relevant competence in the regional population (see Figure 12.1).

Some of the problems with the third mission in relation to the first and second missions (research and teaching, respectively) are:

- from an R&D-perspective, the problems involved are often cross-disciplinary in nature, embedded in the regional context, and difficult to address to a specific scientific discipline as an X-ological or Y-ological problem,

- from an educational perspective, the group of persons of relevance for further and continuous learning in the region is very heterogeneous and have a mixture of varying backgrounds, experiences and personal ambitions for the future. This makes it difficult to create suitable classes on a traditional campus and creates much more need for customisation and personification of the learning process than in the traditional educational framework,
- the competence needed to solve regional problems is a mixture of scientific disciplinary knowledge, industry-specific know-how and specific under-standing of the regional context to make the subject matter relevant. To make such blending and mixing of knowledge domains effective, new organisational models are needed,
- when such new kind of competencies are achieved they will differ from conventional academic degrees and credits, as they are related to new emerg-ing competences and new jobs and functions in the labour market. These competencies are perhaps much more region-specific than is traditional higher education itself. New ways to appreciate and accredit such competencies must be found to support serious lifelong learning efforts in the regional context.

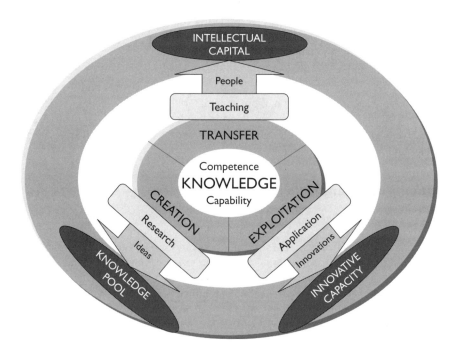

Figure 12.1 The three missions for universities, where the third mission is oriented to exploitation, application and creative use of the available knowledge to increase the innovative capacity of a region.

This background prompted general interest in experimenting with new models for learning processes to make possible a number of shifts and transformations of educational institutions. Our aim was to move away from older traditional educational frameworks to a new 'Technology Enhanced Learning' framework, allowing a more learner-centred architecture for the learning environment and a more situated and action-oriented approach to the learning process, combining concepts for both lifelong and lifewide learning (Skolverket 2000).

The CoLabs.eu project

The original project proposal summary was the following:

> A set of micro-clusters of Triple-Helix-alliances[2] related to eLearning and the digital knowledge industry will be set up in six selected regions across Europe. Each micro-cluster will contribute with regional knowledge and competences to the common and shared collaboratory for the accumulation, exchange and sharing of knowledge and competence related to eLearning and digital knowledge management in general and for the regional support of the universities' third mission in particular. Each partner will have the option to set up a regionally adopted collaboratory, a CoLab, based on a prototype and a set of templates for collaborative eLearning that will evolve in the common, shared collaboratory for all the partners. The network of CoLabs will experiment with a number of different learning scenarios, virtual fieldtrips and both physical and virtual workshops to exchange experiences and learn from each other. Each region will present their current regional capacity and bottlenecks for innovation and in what way the regional micro-cluster of partners can tackle and solve these issues by taking the problem on their third mission agenda with support from the other regions. CoLabs.eu, the acronym for the project, will be established as a formal organisation after the project period and proceed as a virtual organisation and/or a network of excellence centres in the field of collaborative eLearning to support the third mission of European universities and colleges.
>
> (From CoLabs.eu proposal 2002)

The envisioned learning environment was called a collaboratory or *CoLab* for short. A CoLab should contain most of the learning facilities that can support learning on different knowledge levels (see Figure 12.2).

The key issue was to find the best blended form of such facilities, where physical and virtual space could be used most effectively for a learning region. The CoLab model can be seen as an attempt to integrate the different facilities for learning that have evolved over time into a new kind of learning environment. Such new facilities must be more adapted to the new 'Habitorium' for the European citizen in the evolving knowledge society when ordinary citizens begin to live, work and learn in *mixed real–virtual environments*.

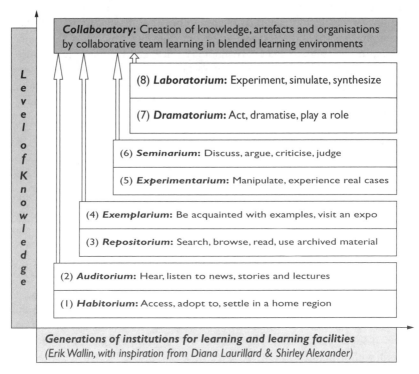

Figure 12.2 Facilities for learning on different knowledge levels, from learning by just living (in a 'Habitorium') to learning by creating the subject matter (in a 'Collaboratory').

The partners and the partner regions for the CoLabs.eu project had been selected to encompass a rich variety of areas of Europe in order to identify a true common and basic framework for learning regions in general and the third mission for universities in particular, irrespective of geographic location (north, south, centre, west, east), language (Swedish, Danish, German, Italian, Finnish or English), regional economic structure (urban, rural), industry and employment ('old', 'new' economy) and higher education institutions (faculty-rich, faculty-poor universities/ colleges). The partner regions and the initial distribution of CoLabs can be seen on the map shown on Figure 12.3.

The project partners and regions were:

- Lund University (co-ordinator): Sydsverige, Sweden (NUTS SE04)
- Ed-consult: West Jutland, Denmark (NUTS DK00A)
- Ed-lab Gmbh: Mecklenburg-Vorpommern, Germany (NUTS DE8)
- CSP: Piedmont, Italy (NUTS IT11)
- Levón Institute: Väli-Soumi, Finland (NUTS FI14)
- Knownet Ltd: West Wales, UK (NUTS UKL1).

Figure 12.3 The set of partner-regions for the establishment of the initial network of CoLabs.

Target groups for the project were primarily representatives for the three key stakeholder groups in the regions according to the Triple-Helix model, i.e.

* professors, researchers, teachers and students from academia,
* managers, business people and entrepreneurs from industry and business associations,
* politicians, members of local village associations and similar.

The project activities were also targeted to disabled people and others who had problems in accessing physical learning spaces. These groups should be given the opportunity to learn, communicate, work and collaborate in virtual communities. Also in most of the learning regions people in rural and remote areas were engaged, as many of these did not have easy access to physical knowledge centres. A number of small to medium-sized enterprises (SMEs) in rural areas were engaged in all partner regions.

Local learning initiatives

Following the general definition of the project, each partner had to define their own local or regional learning region initiative by establishing a Triple-Helix alliance in their home region, including universities or colleges of further education, industrial partners and local business partners, together with grassroot organisations and local authorities. Together these actors should be able to identify a common set of problems of relevance for the actual region and its citizens, and also be able to define actions to be performed as consequences of the local learning and innovation process initiated by the project partners.

It became clear that each partner already had some kind of ICT platform at hand which they were accustomed to and it was generally agreed that, within the resources and timeframe allocated to the project, each partner could use this platform for the regional CoLabs design, establishment and management. That meant that a number of different ICT platforms for collaborative learning and teamwork were used in the project. Among these were some *Open Source* platforms (used by Vaasa, Knownet and CSP), a *First Class* platform (used by ed-consult, ed-lab and (partly) Lund University) and the *Microsoft SharePoint* platform that was established by Lund University in late 2003 and made available for the project partners at the beginning of 2004. The *VCP system* (Virtual Community Platform) was used as a common toolset for project management and administration.[3]

Each regional learning process was coached by one of the partner's project actors and was followed by a collaborative demonstration phase. This started with an onsite meeting and workshop for the regional Triple-Helix alliance representatives at each partner site and continued in online workshops between the partners to discuss the regional learning cases and the first versions of the established CoLabs. In these inter-regional communication sessions, a video conferencing system from Marratech AB in Sweden was used as the primary common online live channel. The demonstrations were evaluated informally by local citizens in the participating regions, some experts within the partnership and some external experts that were invited to join some of the live meeting sessions.

A fuller description about the regions and their socio-economic characteristics is given in a report from the project (Wallin et al. 2004d), together with a detailed overview of how each project partner carried out experiments in their regions and how they promoted lifelong learning processes and local innovation. Each CoLab contributed to the best of its ability with regional knowledge and competencies to the common and shared collaboratory through documentation, exchange, and sharing of experiences of the partners in the regional context. A detailed presentation of these practical attempts to initiate and support learning regions is made in the report. In the following, only some short summaries of the local learning initiatives at the partner regions are given.

CoLab Flyinge in South Sweden

One of the key actions of the project was to create a sustainable local organisation for the long-term development of the selected micro-region in the South Sweden region, the Flyinge village. A formal organisation called *Flyinge Utveckling* was already in formation when the project started and an informal partnership was established between this organisation and Lund University on behalf of the CoLabs .eu project. In this way, a number of local development initiatives could be taken and supported by the project. The micro-region was given a very clear definition in geographical terms and was established as a socio-economic fact with geographical boundaries and signposts on all major roads passing the Flyinge village. It has evolved as a good example of a modern Swedish local village association and has become a *real living laboratory* for third-mission activities at Lund University.

Local inhabitants were initially mobilised to engage in the collaborative authoring of a basic *textbook* for the region, the so-called *Flyinge Book*[4] for the description of the region, its history, present and future opportunities by writing about local historic events, the life of local companies and the deeds of 'local heroes'. The authoring process was supported by different ICT tools for writing and collaboration, one of them being VCP and its Composer engine. A documented and shared common knowledge of the region in the form of a textbook as show in Figure 12.4 was considered a prerequisite for further collaborative activities in the local community.

The website for Flyinge Utveckling (see Note 4) is promoting local events and publishing news of relevance for the local inhabitants on a regular basis. The website has become very popular and is a vehicle for forming the identity of this micro-region as Flyinge Village ('Flyingebygden'). Evaluation indicates that people have learnt many things about their home region while engaging in the authoring of the book and their interest in their local surroundings has increased.

CoLab West Jutland, Denmark

The region involved in the learning project initiative taken by the partner *ed-consult* in Denmark is West Jutland (Ribe, Ringkjøbing and Viborg). The industry in this region is mainly based on tourism, agriculture and fishery, though it is worth mentioning that some innovative high technology industries, such as Bang & Olufsen and Vestas (the producer of windmills), are located in the region. The biggest problem in the region seems to be the *brain drain* of young people, who leave to be educated at large cities and seldom return, because the area doesn't

Figure 12.4 The Flyinge Village Book produced by local inhabitants as a virtual textbook to learn more about Flyinge as a local community.

offer opportunities for employment where higher academic degrees are of relevance. The region moreover is not very well served by education and citizens do not have many opportunities for lifelong learning.

Between 2003 and 2004, after an experimental period in summer 2003, Edconsult undertook the development of a lifelong learning centre in *Nymindegab*, a small tourist village (about 300 inhabitants), usually frequented during the summer time. The challenge was to use the old conference centre, located in the town centre, to experiment with some modern learning courses using ICT instruments. In this experiment, new technologies were used to teach traditional and local subjects such as Danish language and culture, with remarkable success, for German tourists who used to spend their summer holidays in Nymindegab. Also local inhabitants and enterprises took advantage of the centre and appreciated the initiative. The experience helped to create closer social relations between local inhabitants and German tourists. As a result of this process, the local bank financed the project totally and *Læringhuset* (a 'Learning House') was opened in September 2004.[5] This represents one of the most significant outcomes of CoLab West Jutland and has become an Open Learning Lab for West Jutland (see Figure 12.5).

Three complementary learning process initiatives were also undertaken in the region related to the CoLabs.eu project:

- *Kulturhus Bovbjerg Fyr.* A lighthouse that will be turned into a culture and lifelong learning centre. A Triple-Helix Association Foreningen Bovbjerg Fyr was founded to realise the project. The focus will be on creative courses and workshops. Through eLearning and cultural networking, the centre will build a bridge between tradition, cultural development and tourism. It is based within local premises to the benefit of the area and will contribute to a greater understanding of cultural diversities and ideas for rural development in Europe. The house has a social perspective by creating job opportunities for marginalised groups such as long-term unemployed women, immigrants/ refugees and the disabled.

• *Fjordnet* is another association organising cultural, sports and educational events for people who moved to the region and are isolated. A learning community for Fjordnet has been established at the CoLab West Jutland site.

• *Nymindegab Museumsforening* was founded in 2003 to support the construction of an art museum in the town. All the members are now networked on the CoLab West Jutland site. It is planned to set up a lifelong learning and learning resource centre at the new museum centre and co-operate in further educational and cultural projects.

Figure 12.5 The Open Learning Lab established at Nymindengab in West Jutland, Denmark.

CoLab Güstrow in Mecklenburg-Vorpommern, Germany

The region where most of the activities of Ed-lab were developed is located in Eastern Germany in Mecklenburg-Vorpommern, a federal state with a very high unemployment rate. Lifelong learning and innovative learning are really important opportunities for this area, which is trying to make radical and structural changes to restart its economy and stay competitive. Firstly, Ed-lab established a Triple-Helix alliance with the academic partners, the public institutions and private industry. The major target groups for the learning initiatives in Mecklenburg-Vorpommern were *multipliers* – the Chamber of Commerce, the German Institute of Adult Education, the Mecklenburg-Vorpommern Association for Adult Education (folk high schools), Rostock Universities and some additional public and private educational institutions in the region. Ed-lab managed to introduce a 'Media and Education' programme to Rostock University, integrated within a standard degree. The programme was a success, probably because it is a good combination of two elements: an innovative subject, and innovative learning methods and technologies. A pilot programme was carried out with 40 students, employed in the areas of education, training and the media, about innovative forms of learning, with a teacher-moderated and dialogue-based form of eLearning. This kind of online courses suits a region like Mecklenburg-Vorpommern, which is sparsely populated: using web-based courses allows those in the remote areas to have access to high-quality degree study programmes.

Ed-lab also established collaboration with the Association for Folk High Schools, which represents all such schools in the region. The association is actively delivering lifelong learning at low cost to all the towns and villages regionally. Ed-lab managed to convince the association of the possible outcome of a lifelong learning framework. All the teachers involved in the project learnt the skills to develop online courses and the project has enabled them to deliver flexible education and training across the region. Many courses were organised in the field of language learning, but some in natural science, and health and nutrition.

A significant success was also the collaboration with IFNM, the Institute of New Media in Rostock. Ed-lab was in charge of a course about eLearning potential and pedagogical coaching for unemployed graduates of this school. Last, but not least, *Gut Gremmelin*, a lifelong learning centre for public and private employees, has been extended as a state-of-the-art facility for blended and collaborative eLearning (see Figure 12.6). It has hosted a number of important events related to lifelong learning, not only at a regional level but also at a national and international level.

CoLab Map Dschola in Piedmont, Italy

The Italian project partner was CSP (Centre of Excellence for research, development and testing of ICT) in Turin, working with typical Triple-Helix alliances in their R&D projects.

'Dschola' is a community consisting of a selected group of primary and secondary schools, the Centres of Service, Animation and Experimentation (CSAS), with proven technical and didactical excellence at regional level, aiming at disseminating their experiences and expertise to all the schools in the Piedmont and Valle d'Aosta Region (North-West Italy). The network, involving more than 2,800 educational structures and about 50,000 teachers, was developed through a collaborative work

Figure 12.6 The website for Ed-lab's facilities for blended eLearning of adults at Gut Gremmelin, Mecklenburg-Vorpommern in Germany.

structure among different players, all working at distance in a shared, co-operative and interactive use of ICT and multimedia, sharing the aim of improving educational, training and experimental services through ICT. The project policy concern is moreover directed towards proposing a model for the implementation of ICT use in the educational field, founded on and highlighting best practice experiences, sustaining the creation of a virtual community of schools in a co-operative framework (as suggested by the slogan of the project: 'Schools for schools'). By customising the use of ICT knowledge and technical innovation, the project provides a training model in which teachers' skills are used and improved.

A specific initiative carried out in the CoLabs.eu project framework consisted of the setting up of a community of practice (Wenger 1997) on *concept mapping* in education (see Figure 12.7). From the very beginning, the community has worked up and shared some founding documents: the Manifesto and the Documentation Template. The Manifesto highlights that the community refers to a more comprehensive class of knowledge representation models – based on concept nodes – namely, 'Rappresentazioni della Conoscenza', RdC. These include Concept Maps, Mind Maps, Block Diagrams, Semantic Networks, and Schemes. The first purpose of the community is to differentiate the forms of knowledge representation from each other in order to recover the general function of knowledge representation connected with the learning environment.

Conceptual maps are above all an excellent mediation instrument in the educational framework, where the teacher can direct the pupil to a continuous

Figure 12.7 The website for the Dschola collaboratory at Turin, Piedmont in Italy.

process of 'revision' of the same map, and be informed on the pupil's conceptions. If we assume that concept mapping is a language, it is clear that it has a proper 'grammar'. In order to separate the pedagogical dialogue described above from interferences, it is necessary to concentrate on the concept mapping syntax. The community now expects that the members will grow in terms of people and institutions, providing know-how and warranties for good practice in applications of concept mapping. The community uses email and discussion threads, both public and private, testing CmapTools collaboration tools for closer interactive work among members in synchronous and asynchronous modalities.

CoLab eKylve in Väli-Soumi, Finland

The idea for the Finnish partner, Levón Institute, was to create virtual groups of different activities and interests in a number of selected rural villages. The project managed to mobilise the inhabitants in 20 selected rural villages to engage in a virtual collaborative experiment in the field of local education, village environment planning, and the use and further development of interactive local internet-based information services, all created by the inhabitants themselves using Open Source Marratech software (see Figure 12.8). The history of the experiment is that formerly in rural villages there was a tradition of meeting other people in the

Figure 12.8 The website for eKylve and the small villages' collaboration at Väli-Soumi in Finland.

centre of the village, in the village shop or in other public places. Due to a great decline in local services in the 1980s and 1990s, this behaviour had almost vanished. The media used in the effort, PC-based video-conferencing equipment, made the experiment within our project quite unusual, even when considered in world-wide terms. The outcome of this development means that the village meetings and local exchanges are completely virtual, including learning sessions and meetings of the village associations. The virtual community, in this project, replaced the lack of a physical space for citizens to meet and discuss their problems.

The project involved many local organisations, including local NGOs, vil-lage associations, sports associations, farmers' associations, fishing and hunting associations, and small corporations functioning in the rural villages. All were asso-ciated into an electronic, interactive internet-based network called 'South – Ostrobotnias electronic village network' (in Finish abbreviate *eKylve*) where they could meet online using text-based services or PC-based video-conferencing sites.[6] They can moreover discuss issues of common interest, such as local investments in broadband technology, and further development of electronic villages. The major result in the local learning process was a new virtual form to interact between the inhabitants, used in learning as well as in social events and meetings. The use of video-conference classrooms was successful in enforcing the traditional teaching procedure in many different kinds of learning contexts that were of relevance in these learning initiatives.

CoLab Tir Na Gog in West Wales, UK

The main aim of the project undertaken by the partner KnowNet within the CoLabs.eu project was to establish a Welsh CoLab based around the music industry. The objective was to provide a service for the music community through the establishment of a collaborative internet space facilitating communication and learning within the music community. The target community is based within a rural population with a poor transportation network and few employment opportunities. As a consequence the area suffers from high levels of academic and professional migration to the north western cities of England. The music industry is relatively strong in the region, partly as a result of the tourist trade, but is extremely dispersed, and not organised in any formal way, being largely based on informal contacts and networks of bands and individual musicians, record shops and retail outlets, promoters and venues, technicians and recording engineers and increasingly multi-media developers. Moreover, the music industry represents one of the few opportunities for interesting employment for young people in the region. The website, called 'Tir Na Gog',[7] has been developed on the basis of the Open Source Plone software (see Figure 12.9).

Plone is a growing product and is highly flexible, allowing extensive customisation, providing a Content Management System allowing individuals and groups

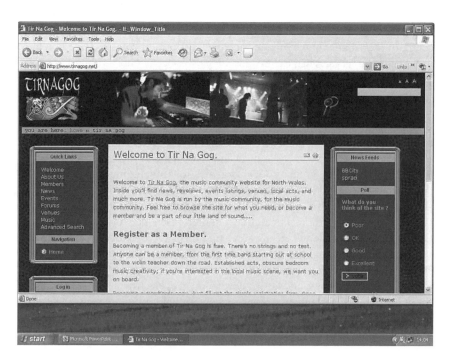

Figure 12.9 The website Tir Na Gog for collaboration in the music community set up at Bangor in West Wales, UK.

to contribute to developing a shared web space. The site aims to provide people from the music community – bands, retailers, DJs, – with a platform to publicise their own activities, and to provide links with others in the community. The general aim was to create a network of musicians, promoters, venues, studios, publishers and customers. Each member of the site has their own profile showing who they are and what they do. They can submit news, reviews, MP3s, pictures, and much more. The development of the platform has been carried on through an iterative process, with community panel meetings discussing and examining development work and guiding future stages. Communication has been moreover an important focus for the project. The project has been represented at music festivals and local events. A flyer has been extensively distributed through local networks and through music industry outlets. The project has been featured in the Welsh media, including on BBC radio. Regular newsletters have been distributed to a mailing list.

Making the village a virtual campus

The different CoLab versions presented above illustrate different approaches to the concept of a learning region. In all of them there is a strong *contextual binding* to the region and its people (Skolverket 2000). In some of the CoLabs the local inhabitants have been the producers of the learning material (CoLab Flyinge in Sweden) and/or the learning environment (CoLab eKylve in Finland). In most of the learning projects there are close relations between two other basic social activities: the art of *living* and the art of *working*. During the CoLabs.eu project, the concept of *lifewide* (Skolverket 2000) learning has evolved to capture and understand that kind of phenomena. But lifewide learning is indeed highly contextual and dependent on the local culture, language, infrastructure and people. This suggests additional arguments for trying to not only make the village a virtual campus but also to make the village and its future the *key* subject matter for both lifelong and lifewide learning so that people can integrate the art of learning, the art of working and the art of living in their everyday local life.

Manuel Castells (1966) has compared our current situation with the situation in Greece around 700 BC when the alphabet was invented. This made it possible to distinguish between spoken speech and written text, and made a more theoretical conceptual discourse possible as a number of readers could discuss the same text without talking to the speaker/author at the same time. In fact, the speaker/author could be far away and even dead without disturbing the evolving discussion based on what he had said (written down). The current integration of digital representations and expressions of many different pieces of reality can be considered as a similar 'step forward' in human civilization and our means of communication. We have learnt more about this in the CoLabs.eu project.

One aspect of the new communication era is the possibility to assemble people from all over the globe in virtual discussion rooms to discuss almost everything and with access to a very rich library of sources for discussion in real time. Virtual online communities are such things. But on the other hand, we have the 'normal' and 'real' places where communication also is based on local languages, 'secret codes', gestures, smells and other very sophisticated bits of information as our different CoLab experiments have shown. These two modes of communication must now be used more effectively together (see Figure 12.10).

Obviously the set of partners in the CoLabs.eu project have covered many different local cultures and learning traditions. This has given the project a true European dimension, where the difference between regions has also been taken into account in the creation of the digital architecture for collaboration. The inter-regional collaboration experiments opened up a number of Village-to-Village exchanges of people, services and products. One such example of a potential exchange within the network of CoLab regions is in the equine field, where Flyinge is world renowned for its horse breeding and horse riding. In almost all of the partner regions, it seems to be possible to develop further collaboration facilities to make such exchanges possible. Within the framework of the project, such exchanges were not only discussed and drafted, but could be further developed in the future.

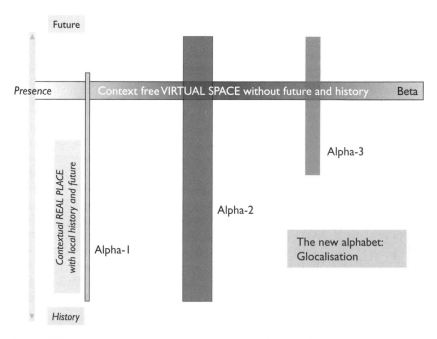

Figure 12.10 The new communication infrastructure for global–local collaboration and networking.

European conversity

The basic model for collaborative learning used and tested in the CoLabs.eu project was the *Conversity* model developed by this author over a number of years. Obviously, the model is close to what has been coined Mode-2 knowledge creation (Gibbons et al. 1994). The model is congruent with the Triple-Helix model but is based on a grounded metaphor other than the traditional Triple-Helix concept (evolving living matter), namely additive colour blending (RGB technology[8]). Using additive colour blending, most other colours – including white – can be constructed by different mixtures of the three components. In a similar vein, the partners of a Conversity alliance can generate a number of new colours or synergies by mixing their different base values and competencies. The colours represent different interests and learning traditions according to the descriptions made in Figure 12.11.

Conversity©	Gene	Organism	Environment	Composition
Perspective	A. Academic	B. Business	C. Civic	A×B×C=Triple Helix
Colour	Green	Blue	Red	White
Competence	Academic	Business	Civic	Intelligent creativity
Higher Value	The Truth	The Beauty	The Justice	The Sustainable
Orientation	Theoretic	Practical	Social	Innovative
Type of Art	Questioning	Design	Communication	Taking measures
Motivation	Honour	Wealth	Power	Welfare
Base Activity	Thinking/Reading	Doing/Making	Acting/Talking	Learning/Conversation
Occupation	Student	Worker	Politician	Professional Citizen
Site/Place	School	Factory	Meeting Room	Network
Task	Make a Course	Do a Job	Settle an Issue	Add a Value
Benefit/Output	Certificate/Credit	Money/Income	Support/Mandate	Trust/Shared Future
Extra ordinary	Discovery	Innovation	Revolution	Conversion
Knowledge Base	Public Literature	Private Experience	Common Sense	World Wide Web
Representation	University/College	Industry/Company	Public/Authority	Alliance/CoLab

Figure 12.11 The Conversity-model for the creation of new synergies between academia, industry, public authorities and civic communities by a network of CoLabs on the regional level.

The concept is an attempt to integrate three higher value dimensions or competence traditions prevalent in most European countries: the *academic*, the *business* and the *civic* tradition. To create synergy between these three value dimensions, the Conversity concept is manifested by two inter-related installations:

- *CoLabs*. A set of physical places where the stakeholders for the three value profiles can meet, interact and share resources with their shared regional context as a common ground in a dedicated CoLab.
- *The Conversity*. One common virtual space where participants from different regions can meet online or offline to share knowledge, work and ideas related to collaborative eLearning within the selected subject areas from an

inter-regional and global perspective and with local foresight management as a common and shared concern in a community of practice.

As a result of the CoLabs.eu project, a *European Conversity* is proposed to be set up as a European competence centre for university third-mission operations in the regional context of the third industrial epoch. This means actively trying to contribute to education process re-engineering, where learning processes can be situated more closely to the social context in which the learners have their physical homes, such as a village. It also means contributing to a higher degree of granulation of what today are called 'courses', so that learners will have the option to access learning resources on demand, just in time, just in place and just enough. This should be possible to achieve by contributing to the more general use and further development of industrial standards for eLearning object construction and exchange. European Conversity will therefore try to contribute to an industrialisation and commercialisation of education in general, and higher education in particular, in order to empower the ordinary citizen with learning capacity and relevant competencies to tackle issues of general and personal concern in the third industrial epoch, such as regional foresight for local village development in the global context with the help of modern technology. In short: *epoch making in the small.*

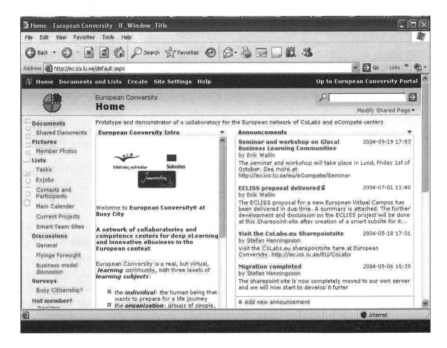

Figure 12.12 The prototype website for European Conversity as a network of local CoLabs for learning and collaboration in subject matters of relevance for the future.

A draft for a business model for European Conversity and the further investment in the Conversity model (the methodology, the collaborative instruments and the competences needed for efficient and effective third-mission operations) is currently in development (see Figure 12.12). This will build upon the results of the CoLabs.eu project through a more elaborated business model for the eLearning value chain (Wallin et al. 2004b).

Notes

1 See http://ec.europa.eu/education/policies/lll/life/regio/index_en.html for full details of the R3L programme.
2 Collaborating actors from the Academic, the Business and the Civic world corresponding to the Gene, the Organism and the Environment in biological evolution as discussed by Henry Etzkowitz and others (Etzkowitz 2002).
3 Some archived material from the project can be accessed through the project's old website at VCP (see weblink references at the end of the chapter).
4 The book has now been published and can be accessed at Flyinge Development website at http://www.flyinge.nu.
5 See weblink reference for CoLab Denmark at the end of this chapter.
6 See weblink reference for CoLab Finland at the end of this chapter.
7 See weblink reference for CoLab UK at the end of this chapter.
8 RGB stands for Red, Green and Blue used in the RGB colour model to create various types of other colours, including white. See weblink reference to a Wikipedia article at the end of this chapter.

References

Castells, M. (1966) *The Information Age: Economy, Society and Culture, Vol I: The Rise of the Network Society*, Oxford: Blackwell.
Etzkowitz, H. (2002) *The Triple Helix of University–Industry–Government Implications for Policy and Evaluation*, working paper 2002–11, Stockholm: SISTER.
European Commission (2002) *Call for Proposals (EAC/41/02): European Networks to Promote the Local and Regional Dimension of Lifelong Learning (The 'R3L' Initiative)*, Brussels: Commission of the European Communities.
Gibbons, M., Limoges, C., Nowotny, H., Schwartzman, S., Scott, P. and Trow, M. (1994) *The New Production of Knowledge: The Dynamics of Science and Research in Contemporary Societies*, London: Sage.
Skolverket, E.W. (2000) *Lifelong Learning and Lifewide Learning*, Stockholm: Liber.
Wallin, E., Hausman, B. and Möller, M. (2004a) *Business Models to Support Learning Regions – Commercialisation Strategies Evolved from the CoLabs.eu Project*, Lund: Lund University FoV Rapport No. 7.
Wallin, E., Henningsson, S. and Möller, M. (2004b) 'The higher value chain of eLearning', in M. H. Breitner and G. Hoppe (2004) *E-Learning – Einsatzkonzepte und Geschäftsmodelle*, Heidelberg: Physica-Verlag, pp. 211–218.
Wallin, E., Leinenbach, J. and Eagan, J. (2004d) *Making the Village a Virtual Campus – Best Practice Examples of Learning Regions in the CoLabs.eu Project*, Lund: Lund University FoV Rapport No. 6.
Wedgewood, M. (2002) 'Knowledge exploitation and regional development', paper

presented at the 'Tillväxt 2002' conference arranged by ITPS, NUTEK and VINNOVA, April, Piteå (handout).

Wenger, E. (1997) *Communities of Practice – Learning, Meaning, and Identity*, Cambridge: Cambridge University Press.

Weblinks

CoLabs.eu project: http://r3l.euproject.net/go.cfm?PageId=3030
CoLab Flyinge, Sweden: http://www.flyinge.nu/boken/smakprov.html
CoLab Nymindengab, Denmark: http://www.ed-consult.dk/en_projects.htm
CoLab Gut Gremmelin, Germany: http://www.ed-lab.net/elearning_consulting.html
CoLab Turin, Italy: http://www.csp.it/eng/prog.php?IDprog=107
CoLab eKylve, Finland: http://www.ekylve.fi/
CoLab Tir Na Gog, United Kingdom: http://www.o4l.org/communities/tirnagog/
Wikipedia *RGB color model*: http://en.wikipedia.org/wiki/RGB_color_model

Chapter 13

Cities as engines of growth

Patricia Inman and Larry Swanson

It is a common misconception that communities must choose between economic prosperity and individual opportunity. Equitable employment and fair trade need bases in successful economic enterprise. Providing quality of life for all includes a generous dose of social capital tempered by economic development within thoughtful institutions.

This chapter suggests that developing an infrastructure for connected communities would find cities as the economic growth engines around which clusters of enterprise would organise. The Regional Economies Assessment Database (READ) provides appropriate documentation for such an organic view of economic development and sets the table for dialogue among diverse stakeholders.

Why regional policy?

Economies have a physical sense (Kemmis 1990). The strength of an economy is the result of a market for a resource found in a particular place and the cluster of services that support its market. While cities provide a business hub, rural activities extend and are connected to these. Cities start as settlements of individuals who gather near a resource. Jane Jacobs explains that these resources are an inheritance from the earth's past expansion that initiated the first clusters of economic development (2000: 54). Commerce and its related activities cluster around these centres and grow into cities that experience repeated bursts of importance, replacing and shifting in an effort to sustain themselves. These bursts result in powerful economic forces. Economies follow natural centres rather than political ones.

Regionalism is an integrative approach to policy that follows this geographical focus, looking beyond political and jurisdictional boundaries. This allows for the study of social, economic, and environmental issues through the creation and sustaining of organisations that do not comfortably fit into the established framework of local, state and federal governments. The institutional framework for regional initiatives varies according to the objectives, scale, participants and timeframe of each initiative. Regional development honours place and its resources, both physical and human.

This complexity leads to one of the most serious obstacles mentioned – lack of a common vision. Regional issues in the Chicago metropolitan area have been studied by Northern Illinois University's Center for Governmental Studies for the past two decades (www.cgsniu.org). While Chicago's urban population density is greater, the metropolitan area has experienced much the same intensity of growth around its urban hub. Declining rural economies stand in stark contrast to areas of tremendous growth. Both agriculture and manufacturing were sectors needing revised economic strategies. Any type of long-range planning would require a regional approach to the promotion of sustainable communities that provide living-wage job opportunities for all. While some regional strategies had been proposed in the past, they had not always succeeded in effective collaboration (Dahlstrom 2002). One of the most significant reasons that collaboration has not been successful is the lack of effective data that moves beyond political boundaries and incorporates the life patterns of citizens. Regional solutions are only as good as the data input allows.

One exception to this in the Chicago area is the leadership provided by *Metropolis 2020*. The commercial Club of Chicago began the 'Metropolis Project' in 1996 and after a two-year research and learning process issued a report entitled: *Chicago Metropolis 2020: Preparing Metropolitan Chicago for the 21st Century*. A public–private leadership organisation was formed (www.chicagometropolis. org) and its members have been busy working in areas most crucial to the future economic success of Chicago and its region. *Metropolis 2020* allows business leaders and elected officials to join together to focus on regional matters.

Like the Chicago area, the strength of the Montana economy springs from the interaction of people with a powerful history of agricultural production complementing a thriving arena of commerce. Previously, concentrated urban issues were viewed separately from rural activities. Montana, Big Sky Country, has been romanticised as the land of open spaces. While it is true that Montana is a land of vast spaces with enormous beauty, the fact is that most of the development has occurred in the cities. Rural development has been driven by activity in the cities. It is the synergy of urban and rural activity that structures the economy. Regional analysis, addressing the relationship of rural and urban development, is essential to providing guidance in thoughtful economic development for such scenarios. Data analysis in the past has been structured around political boundaries – city, county, state. Regional data analysis differs in that it looks to urban hubs and related rural activities regardless of these borders.

The University of Montana Law School studied regional initiatives in the West in an effort to determine how best to promote regional thinking and action (McKinney et al. 2002). This research looked at why regionalism works, various regional initiatives, types of institutional frameworks that support regionalism, accomplishments of regionalism, key ingredients to success, and obstacles and challenges that emerge. The methodology included the identification of 72 regional initiatives, identifying a list of participants, the objectives of the initiative, a description of the institutional framework, and the scale or region of the initiative. A survey asked regional practitioners to explain why the initiative was started, what it produced, the key ingredients to success, and the obstacles and challenges they experienced in sustaining the initiative. One of the most striking findings was the fact that regional initiatives are initiated by a diversity of actors (citizens, various levels of government, public–private partnerships) espousing different objectives (knowledge building, community building, resource sharing, advisory, advocacy and governance) and embracing a variety of institutional frameworks (ad hoc partnerships, non-governmental organisations, research organisations, government-sponsored initiatives and hybrid initiatives).

The Chicago metropolitan area and the seven largest population centres in Montana would seem to have little in common. The opposite is true. Montana's cities, once too small to participate in many facets of a more urban-based economy, are seeing increased income growth. They have become 'economic engines' – places where economic growth, diversification and advancement are centring and spreading into surrounding communities. But the needs of cities have not been considered in economic development deliberations in Montana. A refocused study of economic change in the region and what this change requires for greater economic prosperity is needed. The O'Connor Center for the Rocky Mountain West has proposed a new framework for economic development in Montana. This initiative, modeled after Chicago's *Metropolis 2020*, is constructed from the bottom-up, region by region, not top down. New thinking and approaches would take advantage of emerging growth patterns and better position regions for future economic prosperity.

While Montana's proposed project is parallel to Chicago's *Metropolis 2020*, it has a data collection tool not available in Illinois. The O'Connor Center for Rocky Mountain West at the University of Montana has developed a programme of data collection that incorporates commonly used data with social indicators not often included in economic assessment. (Swanson 2000). This programme, the Regional Economies Assessment Database (READ), identifies regions of local economic interdependence and examines key trends in their development and change. Demographic analysis provides a more accurate picture of social and economic activity. Data can be viewed across time, space and, most importantly, in the context of a peer analysis. Regions with similar characteristics can compare growth patterns and look to others for 'best practices'. Currently this database has been developed only for the western United States.

Economic regions – regions of economic interdependence

Fundamentally, the READ system represents a comprehensive effort to better understand how the economy actually organises itself in space, region by region. Considerable effort has gone into the identification of sub-state economic regions. While there is no single way to determine the size and reach of an area economy, it is clear regional economies at the sub-state level are largely organised around major population centres and their surrounding trade and service centres.

Regional economies are organic, dynamic systems constructed of relationships between people, businesses and organisations occupying communities within common regions of interaction. These relationships can be firsthand, secondhand, indirect or incidental. But they are real and largely determine the character and quality of economic life at the community level. 'Regional communities' tend to be nuclear in structure, and centred around the dominant population centre of a region. Surrounding cities and towns within the sphere of these centres are economically independent. While small towns and large centres within common regions have different economic roles and potentialities, their economic fates are closely interconnected. Likewise, the economic fortunes of the diverse people living within common regions – urban and rural, rich and poor, white and black, educated and uneducated, old and young – are inextricably interconnected.

There are many different types of region. A region classification system has been devised in READ based on key differences that heavily influence both the types and levels of economic activity found within them. A 'hierarchy' of regional centres and region types is visualised, reflecting an 'urban–rural' continuum, ranging from regions centred around major metro centres to regions centred around progressively smaller centres to sparsely-populated isolated areas that are not closely linked to particular population centres. This scheme helps in identifying where particular regions 'fit' within the larger economy and helps account for regional variations in different types of activities according to varying market area population and income 'thresholds'. This is extremely important in gauging economic development potentials for a particular area or region.

This system differs markedly from others in the past. Most economic data are compiled for units of political geography, including counties, states and the nation. However, most of the economy does not operate according to political jurisdictions and examining its change using such units will not accurately reveal important regional variations in the economy's structure and change. The research on regional policy development has shown that there can be no shared vision without a common understanding. This technology provides the ground for democratic decision making in a contextual analysis. READ provides the framework upon which to structure more customised area analysis. Communities can see how they fit into a larger economic picture and so can connect the dots in building economic capacity that allows, among other things, sustainable employment. Housing, land use, transportation, educational and workforce needs are addressed in an appropriate context.

READ is designed to allow complex structures and functioning economies to be systematically examined and assessed at many different levels. This includes the level of more meaningful sub-state regional economies. It is at this sub-state level that decision makers are being increasingly asked to address emerging problems and needs tied to the workings of the economy. READ provides leaders with a better understanding of conditions and trends in the larger economy, in their region and in other similar sub-state regions. It is in these regions where much of community and family life is played out and economic change is experienced directly.

The goal of READ – to better organise economic and social data around sub-state economies – is challenging. However, for the past ten years the O'Connor Center for the Rocky Mountain West has field-tested this programme in areas west of the Mississippi River in the US. Regional positioning, supported by localised data, becomes the framework for an ongoing analysis. READ establishes the broad strokes for more customised study as areas focus additional resources filling in information gaps. While the initial intent was to provide a basis for economic development and workforce development policy, this data structure provides the base for diverse policy development.

While other types of regional data analysis have been done in the past, several advantages of READ emerge. The limitation of data systems in the past, besides the lack of appropriate data input, has been the need for *consistent* data outside of a subject city. There have been various strategies in assessing regional capacity, but few aligned so that regional comparisons could take place. READ allows for regional data analysis with consistent data input. Additionally, it would provide the common ground upon which leaders could collaborate and effectively use regional resources. READ would allow individuals guidance in workplace needs, providing career and educational guidance. Social programmes would be able to co-ordinate resources. Transportation opportunities would reflect regional needs. Thoughtful economic development would take place in the context of informed regional analysis.

Providing common vision

The reality of place-centred economic development is complex. While cities and rural areas often face different social issues, the fabric of a local economy ties them together. The hub of such an economy is situated in the largest centres of population, the cities. A regional analysis assumes dynamic patterns of social interaction encompassing diverse populations. Once we have analysed the data and completed a peer review, how do we sustain communities of learners who will move forward in a thoughtful manner?

Research indicates that diverse partnerships, such as those described in regional initiatives, are best served by highly flexible frameworks of diverse learning communities incorporating systems thinking and holistic education (Hollander and Hartley 1999). A process model developed by Guba and Lincoln (1989) allows for constituency input through cyclical interviews. This is the raw data from which regional issues, concerns and action plans are formulated.

This methodology is based on the assumption that various stakeholders construct reality differently (Inman 2004). Qualitative interviews are validated by the use of quantitative data such as labour market statistics or regional literacy rates. This stands in marked contrast to the usual quantitative focus, with qualitative data providing numerical interpretation. READ and its peer evaluation provide another dimension to such a discussion. Stakeholders are educated to perceptions. The difficulty of finding a common vision, mentioned earlier in the chapter, is addressed in such a fashion. While peer review initiates discussion between diverse populations, learning communities carry the action forward. This scenario places the focus on the lifelong learning options as regions teach and educate each other.

Lessons to learn from emerging economic patterns

Montana on the Move (www.crmw.org/MontanaOnTheMove), using the data provided by READ, initiated such a discussion and provided a statewide network to help Montana's regional communities strengthen and unify local economic development efforts providing professional support to community leaders by:

- analyzing national, regional and local economic trends,
- organising public and private interests to create a community development strategy,
- networking with other communities to examine issues of mutual concern,
- creating unity of purpose among communities to solve common problems.

Organising conversation around urban hubs, this collaborative initiative provides a statewide network for cities to work together to identify and solve common problems. READ plays a strong role in supporting informed dialogue. The following lessons were suggested in recent documentation:

Look Forward. Promising strategies for economic improvement must reflect where the economy is going, not where it has been.

Customise Strategies. Needs and opportunities vary widely from place to place. Goals and strategies must likewise vary.

Cities Matter. Recognising that most growth is focusing in and around 'city regions', more attention needs to be focused on the needs of cities as the 'settings' if not the 'engines' of economic growth, diversification and advancement.

Urban–Rural Relations Matter. Pursuing economic development town by town or county by county is difficult. Influencing local economies sub-region by sub-region with healthy urban–rural partnerships has potential.

Becoming 'Learning Regions'. Successful businesses are adaptive businesses. Successful communities are adaptive communities. Adaptive communities must be 'learning communities' keeping abreast of change.

Think about 'Regional Positioning'. Local economies can't be remade by local leaders. What they can do is find ways of better positioning themselves – businesses, schools, workforces, governments, families – for future change. Anticipate future change and position yourself for it.

Human Resource-Based Economy. The economy is less and less 'natural resource based' and more and more 'human resource based'. Do we know how to invest in human resource development? Well-designed, well-funded, adaptive systems for education and workforce development are essential for economic prosperity.

Environment as 'Key Economic Asset'. In the new economy, a quality environment is a key economic asset. Protecting and enhancing environmental qualities is not the enemy of economic development. It is essential for economic development.

(www.crmw.org/MontanaOnTheMove)

The topic most frequently brought forward in these civic discussions is the importance of systemic workforce development. The unique profile presented by regional data analysis reflects a new urban–rural integration for cluster-based enterprise. Stuart Rosenfeld has worked with policy makers in Montana to articulate this organic form of economic development. Rosenfeld defines a cluster as a 'geographical bounded concentration of similar, related or complementary business, with active channels for business transactions, communications, and dialogue, that share specialized infrastructure, labor markets and services, and are faced with common opportunities and threats' (2002: 9) A cluster consists of groups of companies or services and all of the public/private entities on which they in some way depend. These include suppliers, consultants, bankers, lawyers, education and training providers, business and professional associations and government agencies. Clusters grow through the documentation and facilitation of social connection, which allows for exchange of information and resulting innovation. This connection of small to medium-sized enterprises allows for flexible adaptation to changing local needs and Rosenfeld, of Regional Technology Strategies, has done extensive work on the development of cluster-based economic strategies.

Clusters of enterprise are defined through an ongoing assessment of existing regional skills in the incumbent workforce, as well as those who are un- and under-employed. Analysis of skills needed to support and expand existing clusters provides guidance for regional educational opportunities. Such an analysis allows for increasing the skill breadth and depth needed for incumbent promotion of those currently employed. In turn this provides entry-level, sustainable employment for those at lower skill levels.

Entrepreneurial initiatives expand the cache of jobs. Data indicating potential cluster support would provide a basis for business incubators. Assessing cluster activity and existing skill levels within a regional workforce is different from the usual workforce education that generically prepares individuals for work. A cluster analysis and description of needed skills allows for demand-driven workforce development. Individuals develop skills reflecting local need. Definition and development of such viable employment opportunities and the provision of appropriate education at both the recruitment and incumbent level provide flexible support for business clusters. While most research has focused on the skill deficits in politically defined areas, this concept forges links between clusters in geographic regions – the distance people are willing to travel for work or the distance local resources are easily accessed. Cities form the hub of such an integrated urban–rural initiative. Using ongoing cluster and skill assessment, learning regions can be developed to support both individual and organisational success.

Cluster-based policy differs from traditional workforce development in at least two areas: organisation of intermediaries and educational programme focus. As intra-cluster communication is essential for growth, connection is of the utmost importance. Organising by cluster provides the common ground needed for discussion. 'Government services typically are organized by function. Small business services, training, technology extension, marketing, and recruiting are separate programs staffed by specialists in a particular industry. Clusters provide a better organization framework for delivering services that are more problem-oriented, not program-oriented; address needs interdependently; and work with customers collectively, not individually' (Rosenfeld 2002: 12). Urban hubs organise regional programmes. Collaborative programme development connects individuals and businesses to resources otherwise not available. Once clusters have been defined and educational resources inventoried, learning regions effectively use scarce programme funding.

However, it is not enough to organise and focus programmes appropriately. Services offered and programme access must be clear. Service barriers must be removed and institutional supports made transparent. Individuals use their community and regional context as guides for meaningful life options. This demand-based approach not only incorporates individual aspirations, but also community and regional labour needs. Skill development then supports individual potential, but also community prosperity. This model requires the following:

- defining regions that organise around urban centres,
- identifying clusters of economic opportunity within these regions,
- documenting the links between these clusters,
- taking inventory of institutional resources to support and expand pathways to increased career opportunities and stronger regional economies,
- modifying programmes that support and expand economic clusters, including entrepreneurial initiatives.

Conclusion

While policy for regional development has been considered in the past, READ is a new tool for assisting local decision makers in devising strategies for local economic improvement. Cities provide the focus for decision making and organic economic development. We live in a time when local communities are being looked to more for policy input but are actually capable of controlling less. Many forces affecting the community are embedded in the 'supra' community being influenced by national and global forces. These forces, while impacting locally, are not always obvious. Although difficult to comprehend, they must be considered in local planning. READ and other regional data assessment help chart such influences.

The face of the new economy that emerges from such a creative data analysis reflects the continuing developments in information technology, growing internationalisation, massive restructuring within traditional industries and changing patterns of population growth and migration. By focusing on the specifically regional character of these and other issues, we embrace a broader set of solutions.

References

Dahlstrom, R. (2002) *Census Data Analysis of Mobility Patterns of Northern Illinois Residents*, DeKalb, IL: Center for Governmental Studies.

Guba, E.G. and Lincoln, Y.S. (1989) *Fourth Generation Evaluation*, Newbury Park, CA: Sage.

Hollander, E. and Hartley, M. (1999) 'Civic renewal in higher education: the state of the movement and the need for a national network', in T. Ehrlich (ed.) *Higher Education and Civic Responsibility*, Phoenix, AZ: Oryx Press.

Inman, P. (2004) 'The engaged institution', *Journal of Adult and Continuing Education*, 10(2): 135–148.

Jacobs, J. (2000) *The Nature of Economies*, New York: Random House.

Kemmis, D. (1990) *Community and the Politics of Place*, Norman and London: University of Oklahoma Press.

McKinney, M., Fitch, C. and Harmon, W. (2002) 'Regionalism in the West: an inventory and assessment', draft prepared for the Public Land and Resources Law Review (University of Montana School of Law), draft of 2 May.

Rosenfeld, S. (2002) *A Governor's Guide to Cluster-based Economic Development*, a report prepared for the National Governor's Association, Carrboro, North Carolina: Regional Technology Strategies, Inc.

Swanson, L. (2000) *User's Guide to READ: Using the Regional Economies Assessment Database System*, Missoula, MT: O'Connor Center for the Rocky Mountain West.

Chapter 14

Rationalising public place commodification and the ramifications of this choice in Alberta, Canada

Theresia Williams

This chapter considers the ramifications of policy supporting the commodification of public places. While commodifying public place is often heralded as a tremendous economic boon to communities and cash strapped governments in Canada, there are also serious consequences within the social commons when public place is commodified. I begin this chapter by outlining and describing the concept of place and the issues of public place commodification. I specify the social problem and policy problem from my own perspective as a critical researcher concerned with issues of power, declining social capital within communities and democratic responsibilities of government to address the needs of all society members.

In the second section, I consider a specific policy adopted by the provincial government of Alberta; the Public Private Partnership approach, or P3s as they are fondly identified by the Alberta government. I examine this policy approach from a rational choice model and a democratic approach to policy. After evaluating these two approaches in policy, I consider the potential of adopting a more comprehensive approach; the use of the precautionary principle combined with an evaluation/monitoring approach to address this public place debate.

Place, public place, social capital in place

Place is often associated with the physical locale of a particular location. Place however exists within a broader context of significance. Relph noted that:

> A place is above all a territory of meanings. These meanings are created both by what one receives from and by what one gives to a particular environmental context . . . what is received from a place includes pleasure or displeasure, loneliness or companionship, a sense of security or danger.
>
> (1993: 36)

Place is constructed socially as well as physically. Place exists in the abstract and the concrete. Place has the capacity to impact individuals on both a personal and societal level. It can frame our own identities as well as the identities we construct for others.

I subscribe to a definition of place as encompassing the physical but broadening as well to the personal and the social interactions that create sustainable and livable communities for all citizenry. Place, then, defines itself within many contexts: the social, the physical and the personal.

Access and use of public places such as parks, town squares, libraries and others serve practical and affective purposes for citizenry. Public places allow for millions of interactions on any day between citizens of all ethnicities, social classes, income levels, ages and genders. The social interactions of individuals in a variety of public activities within public places create opportunities for social bonding. Illich (1973: 11) noted the need for conviviality between individuals in place as 'autonomous and creative intercourse among persons and intercourse of persons with their environment'.

Our public places serve as structures within our society that afford the opportunity for integration, social interaction and negotiations between various sectors within society. These negotiations that can occur within public places are what provide for the humanity in our societies.

When we remove connection within a society between all members of a population we influence our comprehension of humanity. Within the public social commons, Kuttner notes that:

> [P]eople of all social classes actually meet and interact with each other . . . they wait together, flirt, swap stories and advice, save each other's place in line, keep an eye on each other's kids. . . . The middle class is reminded that poor people are human and a common bond is built. . . . Although the bond may not be deep, it is and has been sufficient that through such social contact we see others as people with similarities, rather than marking them as the other.
>
> (1984: 231)

This normalcy for the middle and upper class to have contact with lower income classes is what ensures that public place continues to be viable within communities. Embeddedness within a community is heavily shaped through social networks and relations within communities. Flora noted that social capital within a community thrives 'when individuals within a social system interact with one another in multiple roles over a period of time' (1998: 488). Without the continued provision of public places within community, society and citizenry become demarcated. Critical components of civility, democracy and humanity within community become significantly weaker. Legitimacy and trust within communities is established through a variety of networks. 'Networks are most effective for the community as a whole when they are diverse, inclusive, flexible, horizontal (linking to those of similar class) and vertical (linking to those of different class)' (ibid.: 492). Public place matters as a sphere within the social commons for individual and community connection and integration.

Issues of public place commodification

Globalisation and advanced capitalism have accelerated much of the developed world into a state of high competitiveness. The value of land and the corresponding implications of increased urbanisation in urban centres have created a tremendous challenge for urbanised and rural areas. Chawla (2002) notes that within North America some 75 per cent of the population now live in urban centres.

Along with this increased move towards urbanisation have come also the throes of neoliberalism. In a neoliberalist era, cost cutting and the reduction of civic services in favour of privatisation of services is a necessity within the ideology. Senior governments download responsibilities for services to private individuals as well as to more junior levels of government. The consequence of decreased funding resources for local governments has resulted in difficulties with maintaining existing public places, and the further challenge of finding funding to develop future public places or to maintain existing public amenities in a state of reasonable repair. 'Provincial downloading of responsibilities without providing adequate fiscal resources for local governments has made local government vulnerable to cost saving strategies' (Grant 2003: 9).

Local governments themselves may not fully ascertain how their own actions continue to erode public place and create issues of lack of place and social connection within communities. Unable to keep up with the demand for public amenities, governments often resort to private ventures for the development of public amenities. The corporate community offers a vast array of financial and material resources that have tapped into all sectors of the public domain. Public place is 'for sale' and anxious governments seek out private capitalists as a solution to public place development. This development of private public place however comes at more than a financial cost.

The communal commons of public place becomes altered when we commodify it. 'Civitas'-organised community life takes on a different context for members of different classes with commodification. Those who can afford private spaces are segregated from those who cannot. The privatisation trend in North American societies to gated communities, privatised recreational amenities and 'public places' geared for only select members of the public, changes our dynamics of interaction within society and our capacity to be inclusive, tolerant, appreciative and cognisant of all segments of a society. The importance of interface and connection between all citizens of a community cannot be overstated (Blakely and Snyder 1997).

Public place commodification and policy responses

The rational choice model

Rational choice policy decisions are finding their way into rationalising the need for commodification of public places. The rational choice approach to policy making begins with an assumption that there is a set of truths and facts that are indisputable. This form of policy analysis was developed as an approach to ensure that public administrators would make decisions based on sound environmental scans, science and thorough analysis of situations that would impact government and the citizenry. Facts are presented as neutral and as having no values or biases within them. Clemons and McBeth (2001: 49) note that: 'presumably an objective expert would have studied the problem and gathered facts to analyze . . . goals would have been carefully thought through, articulated and operationalized, so that the costs and benefits of the alternative means evaluated are relevant to the desired ends.' Rational choice policy approaches generally have economic costs as the basis for analysis and are founded on a positivist approach of *a truth* or *a correct answer*. Science is used as a methodical foundation of conducting what is presented as a neutral and impartial review of the problem. Administrators present this impartial review and politicians are then, if the policy is true to form, supposed to make sound and focused decisions from this neutral base of information. Clemons and McBeth (ibid.: 46) observe that rational choice policy analysis is 'still the king of the hill' and is the most frequently employed method of policy development in bureaucracies.

The rational choice approach does not come without problems. Neustadt and May (1986) note that while rational choice appears to be a neutral policy approach, it is often plagued by decisions made through stereotypical assumptions, lack of examination, past emphasis of the issue and little or no effort to seriously consider a variety of choices. It is an expedient policy approach and may appear to be a democratic and financially viable approach to addressing the development of public places. Rational choice approaches however struggle with a lack of understanding or explanation of the real situation or problem; a lack of comprehending how this application or choice would really sit within the world; and a lack of predictability (Clemons and McBeth 2001). While these are significant issues of concern, they do not appear to have impacted the popularity of this approach and its application to rationalising commodification of public amenities particularly in Alberta, Canada.

Alberta and the Public Private Partnership policy (P3s)

The Canadian neoliberal government's infatuation with private partnerships is succinctly articulated in an article by one of Canada's former federal finance ministers. In Canada's *Globe and Mail* newspaper, Wilson (2004) articulates the government/private industry argument for the development of P3 policies. Former federal finance minister, Michael Wilson, discusses the tremendous decay and crumbling of public infrastructure and services, and points to the potential in the development of public private partnerships to 'save our services'. To Wilson, billions of dollars pouring into P3 projects in other countries has had impressive results in the construction and upgrading of infrastructure such as roads, schools, hospitals, police stations and housing. The economic benefit of such partnerships in the short term is strongly expounded. In the province of Alberta, the provincial conservative government expresses the benefits of the private development of infrastructure needs, including hospitals, schools, and colleges, to meet the needs for Albertans to build 'better lives for themselves and their families. We are investing in Alberta's future' (Province of Alberta 2003a). The government's literature builds on the economic values of the public private partnership model and comes from an argument of 'concerns about public debt and fiscal responsibility' (Province of Alberta 2005b). It is an interesting argument to make when the province of Alberta basks in a staggering amount of financial surpluses year after year (Province of Alberta 2005a). Perhaps by building on the perceived public fear of debt, the government of Alberta hopes to reinforce the apparent benefits of public–private partnership arrangements: lower lease rates as long as the government maintains itself as the anchor tenant in privately-funded facilities; projects are built earlier which result in lower cost facilities; there is immediate access to the facility for the citizenry; and financial risk is eliminated or reduced for the provincial government because it would neither own nor maintain the amenity. Longer-term data on full public access to facilities, employment loss and other social considerations are not presented nor discussed in any of the provincial literature reviewed on public private partnerships in Alberta.

Critical perspective of the rational choice approach in examining the use of P3s

Employing a rational choice approach of cost–benefit analyses where economic considerations are the prime and sometimes only consideration of P3 projects, the immediate cost reduction of the P3 option may indeed look very attractive. However, as the rational choice model points out, there are flaws within this system and its application to policy approaches. In the case of the P3s some issues that should be considered are:

1   *Group theory perspectives*. The access to government and policy makers largely determines within any society whose needs are best met. Adopting the P3 model benefits private businesses significantly in terms of their access to projects that were exclusively public domain. It also increases private business opportunities and private access to involvement in issues of public determination and need. Equitable access to financial means and or resources for public place investment does not however exist for non-profit organisations.

2   *Elite theory* would suggest that in a neoliberal government climate those individuals with the most power would be the ones who not only make the decisions, but benefit most strongly from those decisions. Blakely and Snyder (1997) provide a case in point in the United States, where the increase in gated and walled communities has sparked tremendous concern among academics

on the social segregation of the poor. Not only are housing options altered for those of lower income but so is the access to public facilities and amenities. Public services decline as those with income can afford to access enhanced or necessary services and those without can only access whatever public services still exist. As private investment increases, this is a serious concern for those who do not have the economic means to access private services and resources that were previously accessible to all sectors of the population. In turn, the structure and integration of society is altered without understanding the long-term consequences of this altered approach.

3   *Incrementalism*, another rational policy critique, suggests that decisions regarding public services are made from the starting points of current situations. The need for services for residents is clearly articulated by the Alberta provincial government in its public–private partnership policy statement; however, the need to address rising costs and deficits is also strongly articulated. Which takes most priority? And equally important: why are private partnerships considered one of the better economic choices to make? It is ironic that deficit issues are considered the most pressing priority in a province recording ongoing record surpluses (Province of Alberta 2003c). The provincial ideological stance suggests that sole government investment in public services is a non-preferred approach. This would support the basis of elite theory, which suggests that those with power develop, support and encourage policy approaches that best meet their own needs. Private business stands to gain financially from the sale of public institution responsibility to the private sector. Those without power – the poor, the disabled, children and others – rarely have voice in society decision making when governments operate from a neoliberal philosophy.

A democratic approach

Democracy according to Clemons and McBeth 'is not about voting and polling, but an ongoing inclusive participation that leads to real outcomes' (Clemons and McBeth 2001: 244). Sincere democracy requires a commitment to meaningful empowerment and participation of all members of a society in decision making. Democratic participation in policy decisions recognises that there are members of societies who have not been a part of the structures that make decisions affecting the social commons. Democratic policy analysis invites a postmodernist perspective of civic mindedness, active listening, active promotion of community discourse, inclusive participation and empowerment and education (Clemons and McBeth 2001). These are substantial goals that suggest the heart of any democratic process involves restructuring some of the existing approaches currently in practice in policy decision making.

Dialogue, a key concept of Freire's (1970) adult education and emancipation philosophy, sits as a central feature in all democratic policy approaches. Inclusive dialogue is a key to democratic policy building. Opening dialogue with all sectors of society requires time, creativity and a sincere approach to moving beyond elite or limited input. Democratic policy proponents recognise that within dialogue, choices must also be made in all policy decisions. They do stress, however, that the process of inclusion and involvement is key to choices and decisions. There is a recognition that ultimately some decisions must be made in the end that do not involve complete consensus, but the process of involving society members in a sincere way is critical if we are intent on democracy and democratic policy. Questions must be asked regarding *democratic* public place development that does not benefit all sectors of society.

Alberta perspective regarding P3s and democratic policy approaches

The Alberta provincial government details in its information on the public private partnerships, that tremendous growth in the province of Alberta is requiring creative alternatives to address population demands (Province of Alberta 2003a, 2005b). Embarking on public private partnerships has provided the government with the opportunity to develop several new continuing care projects, a research council facility, several new college and university buildings, bridges and roadway projects. From an economic perspective, costs appear to be beneficial in the imme-diate term and risks and management facility costs appear substantially lower. The province provides a detailed guidance document for all private businesses interested in partnering in P3s (Province of Alberta 2003a). The document reviews cost–benefit analysis in detail; qualitative analysis is a very minimal portion of this document and does not address any long-term assessment of potential social implications of these partnerships.

The Provincial P3 documents do specify that utilising the P3 policy also ensures that fewer employees are needed to maintain facilities or provide management services for facilities. In addition, the policy guidelines note further benefits, such as business opportunities are opened up for the private sector, and the government resists incurring debt to provide needed infrastructures and public places for citizens. Allowing the private sector to become heavily involved in private place developments that utilise public space also allows governments to avoid costs such as extra policing needs, providing schools, providing fire services, road services, and so on. Private developers that develop these places pass these costs on to those citizens who choose to use privately-based community amenities. For the government, the democratic approach is maintained in that choice is available. Individuals who wish to access services such as swimming pools, parks, healthcare facilities, schools in particular neighborhoods and so on can do so, provided they can pay for these services.

The conservative government of Alberta has been elected to majority govern-ments for over 15 years so can justifiably claim that democratic choice in Alberta has produced a government that the people have voted for based on conservative government policies and ideology. In the current affluent provincial economy there appears to be little desire for change in government approach or policy by those citizens who are prospering in an affluent economy. Perhaps those enjoying affluence are less likely to question whether true democracy is at the heart of rational choice policy.

Critical perspective

In 1979, the United Nations Research Institute for Social Development (UNRISD) (Pearse and Stiefel 1979) characterised citizen participation in decision making as either systems maintaining or systems transforming. Systems maintaining processes invoked an approach of making citizens more receptive to decisions made by experts or authorities with limited questioning or objection. Systems transforming policies sought to involve citizens directly in decision making even when doing so would challenge existing structures of power and authority.

The democratic policy approach articulated by Clemons and McBeth (2001) approaches decision making in a systems transforming similar fashion. There is a significant difference in conveying democratic approaches and actually embarking on democratic approaches. To pretend to liberate by further indoctrinating only adds to the oppression of individuals.

Embarking on a democratic approach to consider the implications of P3 proposals would require active and informative dialogue with all members of the Alberta populace. It would also require the provision and understanding of the implications of enlisting in private–public place development. A frequent complaint of utilisation of the rational choice policy approach is that little time is available or invested in considering long-term implications of policy decisions (ibid.). In a booming economy such as the one Alberta has, arguments for speed and time fit within the rational choice policy approach yet questions must still arise on this approach. Who sets a timetable on reasonable time for policy development? What happens to the social integration of community residents when segregation occurs based on economics, age and cultural background? How is society demarcated because of this very real isolation?

Case studies and longitudinal studies of urban centres in the United States might prove useful to considering whether or not the 'advantages' of P3s remain advantageous in the long term. The city of Baltimore (Levine 2000) is a case in point. The city consists of three Baltimore's: a 'renaissance city' with a revived urban infrastructure of upper income condominiums, luxury hotels, high rise offices and tourist attractions; an underclass city of dilapidated neighbourhoods characterised by social exclusion, crime, poverty and rundown or abandoned housing; and a 'prosperous suburb' that consists of middle-class citizenry, jobs and businesses. In 1994, Baltimore received the designation of need for assistance by the US agency for International Development. The agency identified Baltimore as needing 'third world development techniques' (ibid.: 124) to address its many social issues. Levine concludes this case study by noting that unless a comprehensive approach of addressing equitable and balanced development is adopted, the future of

Baltimore appears dismal. Clearly, public place development by the private sector must be limited if we are attempting to achieve any balance in society.

Towards a comprehensive approach: the precautionary principle and other approaches addressing public place issues

The precautionary principle approach requires extensive consultation in matters of policy, careful and limited implementation of development in areas of uncertainty as well as ongoing monitoring of policy or development prior to full-scale development. Countries such as France and Australia utilise the precautionary principle in assessing environmental concerns but the policy in France has also recently made its way into issues of public consultation in food safety and government practices (Weill 2003). Weill suggests that the state, experts and the public become more integrated and open to consultation within the public realm. The acknowledgement of the role of the public in policy decisions is in response to a changing citizenry seeking input on matters that affect their lives. Policy could be developed that requires in-depth public consultation on the development of any private–public venue. It would be of critical importance to insure that the public as well as governing bodies are informed of cumulative loss of public places and the implications of this loss. This would require a concentrated effort to engage a more informed and more responsive populace in civic involvement. This would necessitate concerted effort on the part of public institutions and the public to inform all members of the populace on the responsibilities of citizenry. It would also entail substantial change in the way governing is done in Canada.

It is easy to turn to the private sector to address public place issues that were previously the domain of governments. However, the role of democratic government needs to consider seriously the challenges of globalisation and an advanced state of capitalism. Democracy suggests that to govern by democracy means rule by the people (Held 1996). In this context, rule by the people would mean that all members of the public have opportunities for sincere participation in policy decisions within a democratic society. Democracy, according to Held,

> comes closest among the alternatives to achieving one or more of the following fundamental values or goods: political equality, liberty, moral self development, the common interest, a fair moral compromise, binding decisions that take everyone's interest into account, social utility, the satisfaction of wants and efficient decisions.
>
> (1996: 3)

Embarking on true democratic policy approaches would ensure the public is well informed of the implications of loss of public place. It would also require a conscientious plan for development of socially integrated communities that mix a variety of income levels, housing and public facility forms within public place.

It would also clearly identify the role of public place development by government and the role private developers could have within the public sphere. This clear delineation of roles would recognise and address the responsibility of government to ensure that public place is provided and accessible for all citizenry.

Summary and conclusion

This chapter has discussed the context of public place development and maintenance as necessary to sustain social integration and social capital within Canadian communities. It has considered the role of private partnerships in the development of public places and amenities within the Alberta context. A review of the Public Private Partnership policy in Alberta has been undertaken from both a rational choice and democratic policy choice perspective within a personal critical context.

Ultimately, review of any policy issue is fraught with the difficulty of determining whether or not approaches to policy within a specific context are possible. Not only is such a change possible within Alberta, but it is critical. The sustainability of any community faces many challenges in a globalised economy, but the sustainability of a community developed on a resource-based economy is especially more critical. Resource economies provide an abundance of riches within a short period of time; this also provides a window of opportunity for governments to consider the long-term implications of developing a sustainable and viable community for all residents.

> Communities are constantly changing and expanding. Once the wrong policy choices have been made (often unintentionally), their effects are often almost impossible to reverse . . . building socially sustainable cities is not a utopian dream, provided citizens and decision makers are well informed and the political will exists.
>
> (Polese 2000: 332)

References

Blakely, E.J. and Snyder, M.G. (1997) *Fortress America: Gated Communities in the United States*, Washington, DC: Brookings Institution Press and Lincoln Institute of Land Policy.

Chawla, L. (2002) 'Cities for human development', in L. Chawla (ed.) *Growing up in an Urbanising World*, Glasgow: Bell & Bain.

Clemons, R. and McBeth, M. (2001) *Public Policy Praxis: Theory and Pragmatism, a Case Approach*, Upper Saddle River, NJ: Prentice Hall.

Flora, J. (1998) 'Social capital and communities of place', *Rural Sociology*, 63(4): 482–506.

Freire, P. (1970) *Pedagogy of the Oppressed*, New York: Continuum Publishing.

Grant, J. (2003) 'Planning responses to gated communities in Canada', conference proceedings from 'Gated communities: building social division or safer communities' September, at: www.bris.ac.uk/sps/cnrpapersword.

Held, D. (1996) *Models of Democracy*, Stanford, CA: Stanford University Press.

Illich, I. (1973) *Tools for Conviviality*, New York: Harper & Row.

Kuttner, R. (1984) *The Economic Illusion*, Boston, MA: Houghton Mifflin.

Levine, M. (2000) 'A third world city in the first world: social exclusion, racial inequality, and sustainable development in Baltimore, Maryland', in M. Polese and R. Stren (eds) *The Social Sustainability of Cities*, Toronto: University of Toronto Press.

Neustadt, R. and May, E. (1986) *Thinking in Time*, New York: Free Press.

Pearse, A. and Stiefel, M. (1979) *Enquiry into Participation – A Research Approach*, Geneva: United Nations Research Institute for Social Development.

Polese, M. (2000) 'Learning from each other', in M. Polese and R. Stren (eds) *The Social Sustainability of Cities*, Toronto: University of Toronto Press.

Province of Alberta (2003a) *Public Private Partnerships: Alberta Infrastructure Guidance Document* at: www.infratrans.gov.ab.ca/policies_%26_Legistaltion/policies/index.htm.

Province of Alberta (2003b) *Alberta Finance News Release*, at: www.finance.gov. ab.ca/whatsnew/newsrel/2003/0226.html.

Province of Alberta (2005a) *Annual Report to Albertans on Budget 2005*, at: http://www. finance.gov.ab.ca/publications/annual_repts/govt/gansrepo06/highlights.pdf

Province of Alberta (2005b) *Managing Contracts under the FOIP Act: A Guide for Government of Alberta Contract Managers and FOIP Coordinators*, at: http://foip.gov. ab.ca/resources/publictions/pdf/contractmanager.pdf.

Relph, E. (1993) 'Modernity and the reclamation of place', in D. Seamon (ed.) *Dwelling, Seeing, and Designing Toward a Phenomenological Ecology*, Albany: State University of New York Press.

Weill, C. (2003) 'Can consultation of both experts and the public help developing public policy? Some aspects of the debate in France', *Science and Public Policy*, 30(3): 199–203.

Wilson, M. (2004) 'The road to saving our services', *Globe and Mail*, 8 March p. A13.

Chapter 15

'Cultural presence' and disadvantaged groups

Do HEIs make a difference?

Lesley Doyle

Introduction

In a focus on social cohesion and learning regions, it seems inevitable that some consideration should be given to the role of universities. Higher education institutions (HEIs) are ideally placed, geographically speaking, to offer to the lives of the people around them cultural experiences to which they may not normally have access via their own social networks – and the communities living and working in and around the HEIs are also well positioned to reciprocate. But it would seem that for HEIs, research – central though it is to their function – does not begin at home. It is not easy to locate findings on the outcomes of their interactions with the communities in their immediate vicinity, and even more difficult at a regional level. Add to this the nebulous nature of the impact of cultural presence, and the all-pervading policy drivers of social inclusion, regeneration and regional development, and it soon becomes evident that to come to any conclusions on the evidence available relating to the impact of HEIs' 'cultural presence' on disadvantaged communities, requires some investigation.

The principal objective of this chapter is to consider the available evidence on the impact of HEIs' 'cultural presence' in disadvantaged communities by drawing on stakeholder interviews, policy and documentary analysis and academic literature. Strengths, gaps and weaknesses in the literature are identified and some existing theoretical frameworks are explored for their contextualising utility for understanding the cultural role of HEIs locally and regionally. Finally, some suggestions are made for future research in the field.

The report[1] from which this chapter is drawn began by noting that, although there is a growing emphasis on the importance of investment in education as a cure for social and economic ills, an earlier international comparative study on 'The role of universities in the transformation of societies' (Brennan et al. 2004) found that the evidence to support such beliefs can be difficult to come by: 'It is necessary, at the very least, to distinguish between the "intended effects" of higher education's engagement with its communities – the goals of the mission statements and the initiatives of its policy makers – and the actual and even unintended consequences of a university's activities for its various local communities and groups.'

Definitions

It is useful to begin with an attempt to provide some parameters for the rather nebulous terms 'culture' (sport and leisure are largely excluded here, though some references are made to them) and 'cultural presence' and what 'disadvantaged' might mean in these contexts. Raymond Williams (1958), an early pioneer in the field of 'cultural studies', wrote: 'I use the word culture in these two senses: to mean a whole way of life – the common meanings; to mean the arts and learning – the special processes of discovery and creative effort.' Whilst the focus in this chapter will be mainly on the second of these, there is a sense in which the cultural presence of universities can enhance and invigorate the former (Duke et al. 2006), what Hamilton and Sneddon (2004) refer to as a 'buzz'. The latter also give some examples of cultural activities taking place at or with the involvement of universities. These fall into four main categories: public provision (museums and gallery provision and activity, university music and theatre, literature events, public lectures); student-centred (student work placements and projects, student /graduate exhibitions and shows); continuing professional development (CPD courses and continuing education including Easter/summer schools); and cultural collaborations (with the cultural sector and with cultural industries and work with the wider community and schools (Hamilton and Sneddon 2004: 9).

In an extensive report for the OECD on the role of universities in regional development (Duke et al. 2006), the North East of England team identified direct and indirect benefits of culture – investment being an example of the former and the attracting of the 'creative classes' of the latter (Florida 2002). But a third form is 'culture as an end in itself, enhancing the quality of life and richness in living to which economic development might be thought to be a means . . . the universities play a role in reflecting the [North East] region's history, culture and identity back to itself and to newcomers, as a place of interest and a place to be', thereby recognising the interdependence of the university and its cultural setting.

The definition of 'disadvantage' is taken in this chapter from the UK Department of Social Security's (DSS)[2] Poverty and Social Exclusion report (1999), which states, albeit somewhat vaguely, that there is 'no one single measure of poverty or of social exclusion which can capture the complex problems which need to be overcome . . . there are complex, multi-dimensional problems that create a cycle of disadvantage', for example lack of work and of opportunities to acquire education and skills.

Stakeholder interviews

To access several possible sources of data on HEIs' cultural impact on disadvantaged communities, and to provide a practitioner's perspective, short telephone interviews were carried out with staff identified as responsible for holding data on activities in one regional and two local (city) councils, four cultural organisations (e.g. dance, art), one urban regeneration company (URC) and three universities. The location was Scotland (which for the purposes of the UK-wide report constitutes a region). The respondents were all asked the same question: Are you involved in any cultural activities (with an HEI) focused on a disadvantaged group or community? If so, what documents, evidence, information or research are available on the *outcomes*? Table 15.1 gives a clear picture of the findings. In short, none of the telephone interviews resulted in the information requested, though every one of the respondents could provide at least some information or access to documents, reports or research on different aspects of their cultural activities and/or HEI involvement and/or work with disadvantaged communities. Only the URC was required to produce evidence of outcomes (to the funders, the Scottish Executive), but at the time it was not involved in any cultural activity with an HEI. The university strategy documents all referred to cultural activities as part of their mission at one point or another, but none collected data on the outcomes of their activities nor did they have measures available by which this was possible. The data does also appear to highlight a lack of activity which is specifically targeted at disadvantaged communities, though that is not to say that the activities which are in place, and recorded, are not also taken advantage of by these communities.

Table 15.1 Results of telephone interviews with practitioners in HEIs, cultural organisations, urban regeneration and local and regional authorities

	Cultural activities?	Cultural activities with HEI?	Focus of cultural activities on disadvantaged communities?	Documents, evidence, information or research on outcomes?	Offered documents, evidence, information or research on outputs
CO 1	Yes	Yes	No	No	Yes
CO 2	Yes	No	No	No	Yes
CO 3	Yes	No	No	No	Yes
CO 4	Yes	No	Yes	No	Yes
RA	Yes	Yes	No	No	Yes
LA 1	Yes	Yes	No	No	Yes
LA 2	Yes	Yes	No	No	Yes
HEI 1	Yes	n/a	No	No	Yes
HEI 2	Yes	n/a	No	No	Yes
HEI 3	Yes	n/a	No	No	Yes
URC	Yes	No	Yes	Yes	Yes

Notes: CO: cultural organisation (separate from HEI); LA: local authority; RA: regional authority; FB: funding body; HEI: higher education institute; URC: urban regeneration company.

Policy drivers

The results of the telephone interviews are somewhat surprising given the policy drivers for HEIs to develop their cultural presence with disadvantaged communities, at national and regional and local levels. To be fair, however, the drivers are to be found somewhat tangentially in a number of areas, including social inclusion, community development, regeneration and economic development, as well as culture policy. So, for example, in 1999 the DSS Poverty and Social Exclusion Team produced *Opportunity For All – Tackling Poverty and Social Exclusion* and stated: 'In every part of the UK, we are determined to deal with the problems of social exclusion and its causes.' One of its key initiatives was: 'Action to improve access to cultural and leisure services such as libraries, free access to museums and galleries and to extend opportunities for voluntary work' (DSS 1999) and in England, Scotland, Wales and Northern Ireland various regional social inclusion strategies set out programmes of work for action teams, including the development of indicators. Whilst this provides opportunities for HEIs to develop their cultural/community links at regional and local levels, their role is not highlighted. Similarly, other potential for HEIs at local level lies with Local Strategic Partnerships (ODPM[3] 2001) designed to encourage public, private, community and voluntary sectors to work together in a more integrated way. In 2004, the DCMS[4] (2004b) published *Bringing Communities Together Through Sport and Culture*, with the promise that as the lead department for sport and culture, it would build on the work with its agencies and key departments to support grass roots initiatives and local needs more flexibly. Better was the department's *Leading the Good Life* (DCMS 2004a), which argued that integrating cultural and community planning can strengthen the ability of local authorities and their partners to respond to community needs. Edinburgh is one city, among a number, which provides an example of an integrated cultural policy, in *Towards the New Enlightenment* (Edinburgh City Council 2005), which aims to enable all of Edinburgh's citizens and visitors 'to participate in, and enjoy, the widest cultural experience, including targeting initiatives to combat social exclusion; to foster partnership working with organisations throughout the city which are involved in working within, or supporting, cultural activities' and specifically mentions higher and further educational establishments.

HEIs' cultural presence is also associated in recent developments with their contribution to urban regeneration and economic development at both city and regional level. A UK government report by a consortium of research organisations, *The State of the English Cities* (ODPM 2006a), concluded that cities are becoming again 'the wealth of nations' (Boddy and Parkinson 2004; Buck et al. 2005), and that as part of the cities' capacity to promote community development, social cohesion, and civic and cultural identity they should 'encourage university and city links in which universities see the importance of their economic contribution to the local economy and to develop their cultural infrastructure and improve their quality of life'. Robson et al. (2006), for the ODPM in *A Framework for City-Regions*, write about 'enlarged territories, [which reflect the] . . . geography of everyday life rather than administrative boundaries' and note that in particular, 'the "cultural" catchment area of major cities can be very extensive'. Despite this, in the Greater Manchester City-Region, 'the creative industries' sector[5] has fewer linkages with universities and other educational institutions than other businesses – only 25 per cent (of the 400 surveyed), mainly through teaching and placements.

Literature

Turning now to the literature, it is the 'grey' literature such as reports produced by the HEI sector organisations where both the cultural presence of HEIs and their involvement with disadvantaged communities do receive attention, but not necessarily in relation to each other. Nor is there evidence on the impact of that involvement, the last of which is acknowledged as an object of concern. Reflecting government policy documents, Universities UK (2006) have produced a short report on the impact of universities in their localities and the need to reach wider communities. In HEFCE's[6] (2002) publication *Evaluating the Regional Contribution of HEIs*, a benchmarking tool is developed 'designed to help HEIs assess the contribution they make to their region using indicators, a combination of outcome statistics and more qualitative assessments of inputs and developmental potentials'. The indicators for cultural presence include, for example, 'Levels of participation by the community' and 'Fostering regional cultural identities', but the highest measure of success is 'Existence of formal strategy and evidence of implementation of recommendations'.

Universities Scotland's (2002) leaflet, *A Space to Create: The Cultural Role of Higher Education in Scotland*, highlighted the lack of data collection on universities' cultural links with the community and suggested that statements on the worthiness of the cultural presence of universities generally, and for disadvantaged groups and communities in particular, may not be as rooted in research findings as would be beneficial – an issue which exercises the authors of a number of reports.

The driver for Cultural Engagement and Knowledge Transfer (Hamilton and Sneddon 2004), commissioned by SHEFC's[7] newly established Knowledge Transfer Taskforce, was the need for output measures of cultural engagement for the purposes of grant allocation from their Knowledge Transfer funding stream, rather than directly the need to understand the impacts of cultural activities on communities. Nonetheless, the definition of knowledge transfer for the purposes of the study was 'activity which takes place within higher education in Scotland, in teaching, research or as outreach/community activity, and which has a benefit externally'. The data was collected from a survey of HEIs, interviews with key individuals and a more in-depth study of three institutions. The authors of the study issue a 'health warning' that: 'While our approach has uncovered the range of activity taking place in HEIs, we have not verified the size or significance of any individual project or range of activities. This report reflects the view of the HEIs themselves on what they do. We have not audited or externally validated any of this activity.' Most notably, the scoping study could not be specific on the 'huge role [of HEIs] in the cultural life of the community' because 'in early interviews . . . it was made clear that this data was not easily available and was not part of the management information collected by HEIs'. Thus, the report cannot provide data or analysis on the transformative impact on disadvantaged groups and communities. The authors commented that Scottish Enterprise's (Regional Development Agency) view is that: 'HEIs across the board make a huge contribution to the "buzz" of a place – both in what they do in the way of public access and also in the role their staff and students play in the cultural life of a place . . . [e.g.] task-forces or working groups in culture.' However, there was no data available to substantiate these views.

Following this, *Cultural Engagement: An Imperative for Scotland's Higher Education Institutions* (2005) was produced jointly by the universities' national organisation, Universities UK with the SFC and the involvement of the Arts and Humanities Research Council. It instigated a consultation process and set up a working group to develop metrics (specific indicators that can be measured in order to assess a university's impact on the physical or social environment) for types and levels of cultural engagement.

But these metrics themselves have their limitations, according to a senior Research Policy Officer for Universities Scotland: 'The measures of outputs will not address outcomes, e.g. performance art: they can count bums on seats but it is more difficult to come up with measurements of the quality and even more difficult of the impact on the general community. That doesn't mean we should let the perfect chase out the good so we will use what data is available.' To further identify the impact on different sectors of the community clearly presents further challenges.

Blake Stevenson's (2000) report, this time commissioned by the Scottish Executive on the role of the arts in regeneration, found the challenge not in the available data but rather in prevailing attitudes towards them, in particular the utility of 'soft data'. They write: 'There is a need for arts projects to have the confidence to present the soft data alongside the hard data, but also there is a need for funders and policy makers to understand more fully the importance of soft data. There are links between hard and soft data but these need to be made more apparent.' Similarly in the evaluation of projects: 'There is room for improvement both in the approach arts projects take in evaluating their own activities and in the way in which the arts are included in wider regeneration evaluations.' They also note that the arts are not separated from sports and leisure, with the result that the contribution of the arts to the regeneration of an area is often not visible in the data.

Similarly, there are many policy and strategy documents available from relevant organisations on the creative and cultural industries, public health (leisure and sport) and civic engagement. For example, the Regional Mission of Universities, through a series of examples, seeks to describe examples of HEIs' involvement in the provision of cultural activity including arts projects and involvement with 'disadvantaged' groups within the community but the emphasis here, too, is on description of 'outputs' rather than evaluation of 'outcomes'.

As already noted, the majority of publications directly relevant to culture in the context of HEIs or disadvantaged communities tended to be 'grey' in the form of policy and strategy documentation and publicity-style materials. Although a number of the former are produced with the aid of academics, in the academic literature the HEIs' role is not usually in evidence. Much of it is keen to justify the existence of the arts on social grounds. So, for example, Matarasso (1997) offers a comprehensive account of the social impacts arising from participation in the arts because this is where social benefits are most commonly attributed in policy discussion. Although the economic benefits of the arts had been researched in the UK, this was the first large-scale study of their social benefits. Matarasso offers a wealth of understanding from a large research project, with sound methodology on the value of social participation in the arts and a wealth of data on how this can be made effective. But he does not consider the role universities might have to play. Delanty (2001) views the university as a key institution of modernity and as the site where knowledge, culture and society interconnect and assesses the question of the crisis of the university with respect to issues that include cultural politics and the changing relationships between research and teaching. Not only has his work been criticised as containing 'too much abstract social theory and not enough political analysis' (Taylor 2001), but also he does not discuss HEIs' 'cultural presence' in their communities. At Manchester University, CRESC,[8] a £3.7 million Economic and Social Research Council (ESRC), is just one example of a number of funded major international research centres analysing socio-cultural change and it is the first in the UK 'to develop a broad, empirically focused account of cultural change and its economic, social and political implications' but typically, it would seem, does not include the 'cultural presence' of its own kind as a subject for research. In fact, no literature was found which linked specifically culture, HEIs and their impact on disadvantaged communities, so it was a question of identifying studies which tangentially cover different parts of the theme.

There is a large literature on the economics of culture, with the *Journal of Cultural Economics* particularly fruitful, and Riaz (2004) has produced a useful literature review of the evidence base for culture, the arts and sports policy. Generally, it is necessary to return to the 'grey' literature. On the role of the arts in regeneration, Evans and Shaw (2004) write on the *Contribution of Culture to Regeneration in the UK: A Review of Evidence*, for a report to the DCMS. On the arts and social inclusion, there is Jermyn's *The Art of Inclusion* (2004) and *The Arts and Social Exclusion: A Review Prepared for the Arts Council of England* (2001), and Reeves' (2002), also for the Arts Council England, *Measuring the Economic and Social Impact of the Arts*. Whilst Belfiore (2002) questions the strength of the connection between the arts and social inclusion, Jermyn (2001) concludes: 'Many claims are made about the impact of the arts and, on a wider level, of culture. Some of these are well supported by evidence, others are less well-supported. This does not mean that these impacts do not occur, but that some have been more rigorously researched or evidenced than others. There are still many gaps, particularly in the area of social impacts.'

Jermyn's (2001) review is extremely helpful, providing a wealth of definitions and relevant data and a good basis for looking at social exclusion in the context of

HEIs' cultural presence. However, Blake Stevenson (2000), already identified above as useful for the critique of hard and soft data for understanding how the arts are enjoyed, does not seem to identify HEIs as having a particular role to play with the arts in regeneration, though 'local people, regeneration specialists, arts practitioners and policy makers' all get a mention in plans.

Bennett and Belfiore (2007) of the University of Warwick's Centre for Cultural Policy Studies, suggest that: 'The notion that engagement in the arts can produce deeply transformative effects for the individual and society has a long and complex intellectual history.' Awarded a three-year Research Fellowship in Arts Impact Assessment by the Arts and Humanities Research Council and Arts Council England on the 'Social Impact of the Arts' (ongoing), they further note that: 'The socio-economic impact of the arts has become an increasingly important rationale for public investment in the cultural sector over the last two decades. However, current literature shows that neither the funding bodies and their clients nor academics have managed to establish a methodology robust enough to be accepted and consistently applied across a wide range of publicly-funded arts organisations.'

So far, the assumption has been that HEIs have an enriching effect on communities but this does not take into account the well-documented, if little researched, so-called 'town–gown divide'. In this divide there is evidence that far from being seen by local communities as a source of enrichment, HEIs can be alienated from them and even a source of antagonism. In particular with reference to the US, there are a number of evaluative and academic research projects and publications looking at the 'town–gown' divide. MacLeod et al. (1997) describe an experiment to discover processes by which marginalised, economically distressed communities can use institutions of the 'knowledge economy' to foster the social and technological innovation necessary for their survival. In the UK, Chatterton (2000) outlines the historical development of the cultural role of the university through a shift from the high-cultural role of the elite university to a broader cultural role for the contemporary mass university and, in Ireland, Boucher (2000) looks at the regional impact of the University of Limerick, including a section on the 'cultural impact' of some of the university's initiatives, precisely for linking the university with the local community.

The fields of 'community music', 'community media' and non-formal music production are also of interest and relevance as they show some of the educative cultural movements of recent decades that have developed (largely) outside HEIs, often originating outside official funding and formal education systems too (though in both the case of community music and community media formally funded today). There are both arts/media advocate-style publications and a relatively small number of academic research projects and materials. Everitt's (1997) well-regarded report on music-making in the community, UK and wider, includes non-formal music education. In Moser and McKay (2005), McKay's chapter on the development of community music in the UK, with a north-west regional focus, emphasises its countercultural and free jazz origins, non-formal education practices, and reluctance – perhaps occasionally refusal – to work with formal education networks and organisations.

Theoretical frameworks

Apart from the evident lack of data on the cultural activities of HEIs, there would seem also to be a lack of theoretical work to locate their cultural presence, their relations with local communities and their regional activities. This is despite the research being carried out, by HEI research centres and others, on cultural activities in the (rest of the) local community. It is suggested here that the concept of social capital would be a useful aid to unpicking the drivers and barriers to both HEIs' contribution to cultural lifelong learning in disadvantaged communities, and the level of engagement to and from those communities. In particular, what social networks are there between academics and local people and how far do they extend? Are they a factor in HEI/community cultural engagement? How can people identify with, and make part of their social network, people and institutions at regional level when they may be too far away to maintain sufficient contact for a social network to be formed and sustained? Field (2005) writes, 'social capital . . . asks us to view a whole range of social connections and networks as a resource, which helps people to advance their interests by co-operating with others', but whilst for HEIs it may be beneficial to engage culturally speaking at a local and regional level, why would anybody in a disadvantaged community take the trouble to reciprocate?

Still on the theme of learning, the concept of the 'learning region' may also be helpful in pursuing 'involvement' strategies at both a local and regional level. Goddard (2005), pursuing his notion of the 'third role' of the university at a regional level, uses it to explain that the process of finding a regional identity for HEIs is a controversial one and can be seen as both parochial (in the context of international research) or over extensive (for example, where cities have a long history with their town of origin). Goddard's interest is in the learning economy, but the term 'learning culture' might be substituted instead when he writes: 'Lundvall (1992) defines the learning economy as an economy where the success of individuals, firms and regions' – or local and regionally based cultural organisations – 'reflects the capability to learn (and forget old practices) . . . The learning region depends upon network knowledge which refers not only to the skills of individuals but the transfer of knowledge from one group to another to form learning systems.' Goddard creates a model to demonstrate what he calls the 'university/region value-added management process' (Figure 15.1), though it can be argued that the university/regional separation does not meet his desire to see the regional perspective wholly integrated within the university management mindset and that it fits rather better with the view that the HEIs' three roles are teaching, research and cultural and civic activity at a local and regional level.

Landry et al. (1993) provide further theoretical perspective, where they put forward a practical way of understanding the concept of 'impact' as it relates to

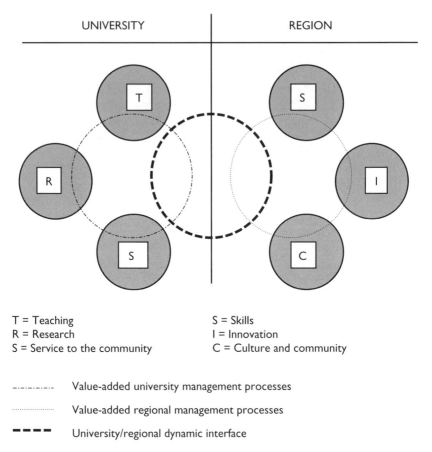

Figure 15.1 The university/region value-added management process (Goddard 2005).

arts processes and projects. They identify inputs, outputs and outcomes as the three basic components of performance used to measure the '3Es' of economy, efficiency and effectiveness, respectively. According to Lingayah et al. (1996), the differences in measurement of inputs, outputs and outcomes can be viewed in terms of a spectrum, where measurements at one end are relatively easy and 'objective' and move gradually to the other end, where they are much more difficult and subjective. It is the measures concerned with outcomes, with their notions of quality and quantity, which concern us here in relation to impact. Lingayah et al. suggest that the starting point for measuring outcomes must begin with an acknowledgement of the purpose of cultural activities, against which their effectiveness can be judged. They therefore have developed a 'measurement spectrum' for the measurement of inputs, outputs and outcomes. This approach could be useful for considering the differential impact of HEIs at regional level.

The strengths, gaps and weaknesses in the literature

There are some theoretical and policy literatures relating to 'culture' that can be referred to on the cultural presence of HEIs in disadvantaged communities, which relate to regeneration, social inclusion and so on, but it is not always easy to link these to specific empirical studies of HEIs' activities. For example, policy documents emanating from the DCMS argue for an integration of cultural and community planning as one way of strengthening local authorities' (and their partners') abilities to respond to community needs; and look to using culture and sport at local levels to create a sense of pride and belonging. In these contexts, sometimes HEIs are privileged with a specific mention, other times they are not.

The focus of this chapter has been mainly on the sense of culture as 'arts and learning', although it has to be said that although HEIs, in their own publicity documents and those of their organisations (such as Universities UK), claim cultural centrality as places of learning and debate, of outreach and community involvement, there are remarkably few academic studies which provide and interrogate evidence for these kinds of claims. As Brennan et al. (2006) point out, the existence of HEIs within 'multicultural' settings can even suggest a more confrontational notion of 'cultural presence'. This is in terms of class and it may well be the case with race as well but no studies on this were located. The cultural presence of students and their effects upon communities is one aspect of this, but it is necessary to cross-reference to some of the widening participation literature as cultural factors may be among the reasons for non-participation in higher education. The issues raised in the context of the cultural presence of HEIs may be an example of how the university itself needs to be 'transformed' before a wider social transformation can be attempted.

There is a wide range of strategy/policy literature, publicity documentation and also in the academic literature on outputs, but research on outcomes is more difficult to locate. The nebulous 'buzz' that higher education institutions can add to a city/town is referred to in the literature but not analysed in any systematic way. For example, there is no consideration of aspects of cultural enrichment and cultural exchange engendered by the presence of HEIs. Further, although HEIs have been commissioned by particular agencies to undertake evaluations of aspects of arts and regeneration, social inclusion in their own localities, they tend not to research their own impact on disadvantaged communities and do not collect data on their own cultural connections within the locality or region.

There is research on elements of the community who do not get involved in, or actively reject, cultural channels via the HEIs – for example, popular music. Indeed, the term 'community' itself, especially when used in phrases like 'community music' or 'community media', may be signifying that which takes place *outside* of formal education systems and institutions – in which case 'community'-based culture is explicitly 'that which does not happen with/in universities', although there are examples where it has been embraced by higher education with no evidence of resistance.

Much of the research seems to be about universities justifying what they do, individually and collectively. Despite this, it is difficult to get a full picture of HEIs' cultural activities and influence, still less of what the effects are upon disadvantaged groups/communities, the processes through which these effects are achieved and how they differ between regional and sub-regional settings.

Much research is driven by policy interests – e.g. metrics to justify funding – or practitioner interests – e.g. softer data to help development/enhancement of activities. And these may be relatively short term, reflecting particular funding initiatives which may not be sustained when the funding source has been removed. Measures of HEIs' cultural 'outcomes', as distinct from 'outputs', cannot provide insights into the impact of their activities on any parts of the community.

No research was located on how disadvantaged communities view or use HEIs as a cultural resource. There also seems little existing research on attempts to target initiatives and services to particular groups or on their take-up by particular groups. There is, though, some research in the widening participation literature which suggests that students from some groups and communities are regarded as presenting something of a 'cultural challenge' to institutions in certain locations (Brennan et al. 2006).

The gaps in literature are reflected in the lack of theorising on the cultural role of HEIs at local and at regional level. HEIs' activities on the cultural front are subsumed within other policies and strategies and areas of enquiry. Goddard's (2005) model of the two dimensions of HEI management is valuable – if controversial as far as this author is concerned – not least because it provides a context for cultural activity. Field (2005) and others on social capital and lifelong learning provide a means of unpicking the attitudes and networks of both communities and HEI staff at all levels, where, of course, there will also be a cross-over – itself a rich seam of data about their social capital and its impact upon their relationship. The most important gap this chapter has identified is that HEIs do not research themselves as often or as effectively as they do everyone else, particularly the 'third role' they have as a cultural presence and cultural resource, locally and regionally, alongside their teaching and research. At the same time, HEIs may need to look at their own data-gathering techniques more closely if they are to conduct meaningful empirical enquiry, particularly as the stakeholder interviews seemed to suggest a lack of activity. In any event, at present the answer to the question: 'Cultural presence' and disadvantaged groups – do HEIs make a difference?' is – we don't know yet.

Acknowledgements

The author would like to acknowledge the input and support of George McKay and Danijela Bogdanovic (University of Salford) in the preparatory work for this chapter.

Notes

1 An ESRC initiative on 'The impact of higher education institutions on regional economies' was the result of a study (Brennan et al. 2006) on cross-regional perspectives, including the cultural presence of HEIs.
2 Now the Department of Work and Pensions.
3 UK Office of the Deputy Prime Minister.
4 UK Department of Culture, Media and Sport.
5 The official definition of the creative industries is provided by the ODPM as 'those activities which have their origin in individual creativity, skill and talent and which have the opportunity for wealth and job creation through the generation of intellectual property' (State of the English Cities 2006), but it is not clear whether HEIs would be included.
6 Higher Education Funding Council for England.
7 Formerly the Scottish Higher Education Funding Council; now the Scottish Funding Council (SFC) (2005).
8 The Centre for Research on Socio-Cultural Change.

References

Belfiore, E. (2002) 'Art as a means of alleviating social exclusion: does it really work? A critique of instrumental cultural policies and social impact studies in the UK', *International Journal of Cultural Policy*, 8(1): 91–106.

Bennett, O. and Belfiore, E. (2007) *University of Warwick, Centre for Policy Studies, Fellowship and Arts Impact Assessment*, at: http://www.ahrc.ac.uk/evaluation/activities/summaries/fellowship_in_social_impact_of_the_arts.asp.

Blake Stevenson (2000) *The Role of the Arts in Regeneration*, Edinburgh: Scottish Executive Central Research Unit.

Boddy, M. and Parkinson, M. (eds) (2004) *City Matters: Competitiveness, Cohesion and Urban Governance*, Bristol: Policy Press.

Boucher, G.W. (2000) *Unireg Regional Case Study Report: The Shannon Region*, at: http://www.tcd.ie/ERC/pastprojects/uniregdownloads/Shannon%20Regional%20Report.pdf.

Brennan, J., King, R. and Lebeau, Y. (2004) *The Role of Universities in the Transformation of Societies: An International Research Project*, synthesis report, London: CHERI/ACU.

Brennan, J., Little, B. and Locke, W. (2006) *Higher Education's Effects on Disadvantaged Groups and Communities*, report of an ESRC Network on cross-regional perspectives on the transformative impact of higher education on disadvantaged groups and communities, at: http://www.esrcsocietytoday.ac.uk/ESRCInfoCentre/Forums/attach.aspx?a=269.

Buck, N., Gordon, I., Harding, A. and Turok, I. (eds) (2005) *Changing Cities: Rethinking Urban Competitiveness, Cohesion and Governance*, London: Palgrave.

Chatterton P. (2000) 'The cultural role of universities in the community: revisiting the university–community debate', *Environment and Planning*, 32(1): 165–181.

DCMS (1999) *Policy Action Team 10. Research Report: Arts and Neighbourhood Renewal*, at: http://www.sportdevelopment.org.uk/html/pat10.html.

DCMS (2004a) *Leading the Good Life: Guidance on Integrating Cultural and Community Strategies*, at: http://www.culture.gov.uk/global/publications/archive_2004/lgf_guidance_ ICCS.htm?properties=%2C%2C&month.

DCMS (2004b) *Bringing Communities Together Through Sport and Culture*, at:

http://www.culture.gov.uk/global/publications/archive_2004/bringing_communities_tog
ether_booklet.htm.

Delanty, G. (2001) *Challenging Knowledge: The University in the Knowledge Society*,
Buckingham: Open University Press.

Department for Social Security (DSS) (1999) *Opportunity For All: Tackling Poverty and
Social Exclusion*, London: Department for Social Security.

Duke, C., Hassink, R., Powell, J. and Puukka, J. (2006) *Supporting the Contribution
of Higher Education Institutions to Regional Development. Peer Review Report: North
East of England*, Paris: OECD.

Edinburgh City Council (2005) *Towards the new Enlightenment: A Cultural Policy for
the City of Edinburgh*, at: http://www.edinburgh.gov.uk/CEC/Corporate_Services/
Strategic_Support_Services/Cultural_Policy/Cultsum.html.

Evans, G. and Shaw, P. (2004) *Contribution of Culture to Regeneration in the UK: A
Review of Evidence*, London: Department for Culture, Media and Sport.

Everitt, A. (1997) *Joining In: An Investigation into Participatory Music*, London: Calouste
Gulbenkian Foundation.

Field, J. (2005) *Social Capital and Lifelong Learning*, Bristol: Policy Press.

Florida, R. (2002) *The Rise of the Creative Class*, New York: Basic Books.

Goddard, J. (2005) *The Response of Higher Education Institutions to Regional Needs*,
Paris: OECD.

Hamilton, C. and Sneddon, N. (2004) *Scoping Study on Cultural Engagement and Knowledge
Transfer in Scottish Universities*, Glasgow: Centre for Cultural Policy Research.

HEFCE (2002) *Evaluating the Regional Contribution of HEIs*, at: http://www.hefce.
ac.uk/pubs.

Jermyn, H. (2001) *The Arts and Social Exclusion: A Review Prepared for the Arts Council
of England*, London: Arts Council of England.

Jermyn, H. (2004) *The Art of Inclusion, Research Report 35*, London: Arts Council
England.

Landry, C., Bianchini, F., Maguire, M. and Worpole, K. (1993) *The Social Impact of the
Arts: A Discussion Document*, Stroud: Comedia.

Lingayah, S., MacGillivray, A. and Raynard, P. (1996) *Creative Accounting: Beyond the
Bottom Line, The Social Impact of the Arts*, working paper 2, Stroud: Comedia.

Lundvall, B.-Å. (ed.) (1992) *National Systems of Innovation: Towards a Theory of
Innovation and Interactive Learning*, London: Pinter.

Matarasso, F. (1997) *Use or Ornament? The Social Impact of Participation in the Arts*,
Stroud: Comedia.

Moser, P. and McKay, G. (eds) (2005) *Community Music: A Handbook*, Lyme Regis:
Russell House.

ODPM (2001) *Local Strategic Partnerships*, at: http://www.neighbourhood.gov.uk/.

ODPM (2006a) *A Framework for City-regions, Working Paper 1: Mapping City-regions'*,
at: http://www.odpm.gov.uk/pub/596/AFrameworkforCityRegionsWorkingPaper1PDF
3314Kb_id1163596.pdf.

ODPM (2006b) *State of the English Cities*, at: http://www.odpm.gov.uk/index.asp?
id=1127498.

Reeves, M. (2002) *Measuring the Economic and Social Impact of the Arts: A Review*,
London: Arts Council England.

Riaz, J. (2004) *Literature Review of Evidence Base for Culture, the Arts and Sports Policy*,
at: http://www.scotland.gov.uk/library5/education/lrcas-00.asp.

Scottish Funding Council (2005) *Cultural Engagement: An Imperative for Scotland's Higher Education Institutions*, at: www.sfc.ac.uk/library/06854fc203db2fbd00000102 15e7b9d5/Annex_B.doc.

Taylor, R. (2001) Book review on Delanty, G. (2001) 'Challenging knowledge: the university in the knowledge society', *Widening Participation and Lifelong Learning*, 7(3), at: http://www.staffs.ac.uk/journal/Volume73/rev-2.htm.

Universities Scotland (2002) *A Space to Create: The Cultural Role of Higher Education in Scotland*, at: http://www.universities-scotland.ac.uk/Publications/A%20Space%20to %20Create.PDF.

Universities UK (2006) Universities: engaging with local communities, at: http://bookshop.universitiesuk.ac.uk/.

Williams, R. (1958) 'Culture is ordinary', in N. McKenzie (ed.) *Convictions*, London: MacGibbon and Kee.

Chapter 16

Sustainable development

The role of lifelong learning

*Corinne van Beilen, Max van der Kamp
and Jacques Zeelen*

Introduction

Sustainable development was first exposed to an international audience with the publication of *Our Common Future* by the Brundtland Commission in 1987. The process was first defined as: 'sustainable development is development that meets the needs of the present without compromising the ability of future generations to meet their needs' (World Commission on Environment and Development 1987: 12). There followed World Summits in 1992 and 2002. At the World Summit on Sustainable Development (WSSD) in 2002, education was described as an 'indispensable element', capable of turning sustainable development into a reality (UN General Assembly Resolution A/RES/57/254 2003). One manifestation of this reality has been the declaration of the *United Nations Decade of Education for Sustainable Development 2005–2014 (UNDESD)*.

Around the same time, an interdepartmental programme, 'Learning for Sustainable Development (LvDO) 2004–2007', was launched in the Netherlands. This programme is directed at 'establishing more effective learning processes for societal stakeholders, which aims for a more sustainable balance'. The Dutch initiative is closely linked with the UNESCO programme, DESD. There is a focus on ensuring that all three of the key elements of sustainable development are considered: ecological, economic and social, with formal, non-formal and informal education considered to be important instruments to achieve sustainability.

Besides sustainability, 'lifelong learning' has been a prominent feature on political agendas for over a decade now. The OECD published the document 'Lifelong Learning For All' (OECD 1996), the UNESCO report 'Learning the Treasure Within' (Delors 1996) paid attention to the theme as well, and the EU launched the 'Memorandum on Lifelong Learning' in 2000 (European Commission 2000), which identified lifelong learning as an essential element for Europe's future. Several countries were stimulated by these international organisations and formulated their own national policies and action plans. For example, in the Netherlands, the 'National Action Plan Lifelong Learning' was launched (Ministry for Education, Culture and Science 2001). The increased interest in lifelong learning policies is only partly reflected by participation figures of (adult) education (Van der Kamp 2002). These figures reveal there are still large groups that do not participate in lifelong learning, such as early school leavers, the less formally educated, long-term unemployed, immigrants, and groups of senior workers and citizens. Additionally, these figures show that more men partake in education than women. In order to prevent a widening gap between the 'learning rich' and the 'learning poor' in the knowledge society, special educational efforts are being directed at such 'groups at risk'. These groups often have bad experiences with initial education and have developed negative perceptions of education. Taking part in education also entails a risk: the risk of failing yet again, with negative consequences for one's self-image and giving a bad signal to key peer groups. Providing educational activities for these groups therefore becomes a paradox: the solution to the problem is at the same time the cause of the problem. However, reaching such 'groups at risk' is of great importance in order to achieve sustainable development or a policy of sustainable development would otherwise miss one of its important targets. A further challenge is thus identifying and disseminating new and successful lifelong learning approaches to sustainable development.

To obtain insight into the contribution of lifelong learning to sustainable development, the initiative described in this chapter was developed as a research project with a purpose of identifying and disseminating so-called good practices. This project was carried out within the framework of the DESD, while the programme LvDO provides a specific Dutch framework. It was carried out by a team from the University of Groningen, commissioned by the Dutch National UNESCO Committee. The empirical input was derived from the collection and analysis of sustainable development practices. The research was specifically aimed at practices directed at learning for sustainable development in an innovative manner. The focus was on practices in the Netherlands, though relevant practices abroad were incorporated into the study. Eleven cases have been selected, described, analysed and reported in Van Beilen (2005) and Tebbes (2005). With the help of these case studies and a review of the literature, the main question of this study was explored: 'What can lifelong learning contribute to sustainable development?' Given the limitations of the number of cases (collected within certain practical constraints of time and budget), answers can only be tentative. However, this research study deepens our understanding of the challenging relationship between lifelong learning and sustainable development.

Conceptual framework

The UNESCO Draft Implementation Scheme (2004) expresses fundamental concerns regarding the lack of sustainability in each of the three pillars: the ecological, economic and socio-cultural areas. Formal, non-formal and informal education are considered to be important instruments to support sustainability and should therefore be directed at the 'three pillars of sustainable development'. These are named in the document as follows:

- *Society*: an understanding of social institutions and their role in change and development, as well as the democratic and participatory systems which give opportunity for the expression of opinion, the selection of governments, the forging of consensus and the resolution of differences.
- *Environment*: awareness of the resources and fragility of the physical environment and the effects on it of human activity and decisions, with a commitment to factoring environmental concerns into social and economic policy development.
- *Economy*: a sensitivity to the limits and potential of economic growth and their impact on society and on the environment, with a commitment to assess personal and societal levels of consumption out of concern for the environment and for social justice' (UNESCO Draft Implementation Scheme 2004: 12).

The role of culture might be underestimated within this scheme. One can discuss whether culture has to be added as a fourth pillar. In some cases culture is intimately tied to the pillar 'society' (socio-cultural dimension); however, generally the role of culture is viewed in UNESCO documents as follows: 'The values, diversity, knowledge, languages and worldviews associated with culture predetermine the way issues of sustainable development are dealt with in a specific context; culture in this sense is a way of being, relating, behaving, believing, and acting and which is in constant process of change and exchange of other cultures' (ibid.: 4). Thus, culture is an intrinsic part of each pillar; indeed it might be viewed as the underlying dimension. Culture therefore has its own role, concerned with cultural heritage, indigenous knowledge and locally-tied values.

On the other hand, one can express the view that the notion of the three pillars should remain as it is. However, culture should be more than an underlying dimension; it should serve as a cross-cutting element – an 'inter-connector' or inter-link' between the three areas (Opschoor 2005). This discussion about culture and the lack of general consensus for prioritising any one of the pillars makes it clear that the route to and the balance of a sustainable world is not a given. It depends on diverse meanings, frames of mind and various priorities. A single definition can hardly grasp this concept. However, due to its complexity, ethical and philosophical debates, and the intangible consequences, 'sustainable development' is at risk of becoming a 'buzzword' – a concept that loses meaning. To give it meaning, organisations, societies, governments, social movements and individuals will need to choose and negotiate their own particular balance. Once that choice is made, the debate regarding the route to sustainability and the balance between the elements of sustainable development can be decided on in order to turn the abstract idea of sustainable development into a reality.

Issues of sustainable development are not solely determined by expert knowledge, or by scientific ecological problems that can be fixed through technological, economic or political solutions. Beck (1999) states that in the 'Risk Society' not exclusively experts can answer the question: how do we want to live? Solutions

should also be sought in a global dialogue between cultures: a dialogue that takes into account that local connections should be developed to become part of global culture (Touraine 2000). This dialogue should realise that even though risks and threats affect all social groups, some groups are more vulnerable to these threats than others, as they do not have the choice to escape or prevent it from occurring. It should be a dialogue that takes into account that our actions are increasingly determined by their future consequences and much less by those based on the past. However, our decisions should not ignore the important implications of cultural heritage, ethnic values and indigenous knowledge. A dialogue should realise the implications of the interaction between cultures taking place in an environment in which the individual is neither entirely determined by societal demands, nor is entirely free to determine his or her own future; an environment without fixed reference points. A global dialogue would address the challenge to look at the future in a well-informed and creative way, and is one which cries for an approach which considers one's own future but also the future of others.

Therefore, future scenarios must encompass all of the issues addressed above. Reich (cited in Beck 2000: 137–138) states: 'we have failed to understand that a nation's real technological assets are the capacities of its citizens to solve complex problems of the future. This should encompass more than lifelong learning and flexibility alone; it should cover things such as social competence, the ability to work in a team, conflict resolution, intercultural communication, and the capacity to handle uncertainties and paradoxes of modernity.' Education may not be the only option; there are more complicated issues: power struggles can limit the learning process and certainly affect its outcome. Sustainable development depends for a great deal on existing global power relations and political priorities. However, education and learning could provide the appropriate tools to develop competences in citizens which stimulate an increase of social capital and political participation, enabling people to choose their own lifestyle and make life decisions within the civil society.

What, then, are the possible implications for lifelong learning policies and practice? The overall challenge is to put the global dialogue between cultures in a lifelong and life-wide learning environment; an environment in which citizens are neither determined by societal demands, nor are entirely free to determine their own future. The tension between individuals and their context of learning, in this case the public debate, should be addressed by dialogue and identity construction.

On the policy level, this means:

- education concerned with sustainable development should take place in a local context as information needs to connect with people's own experiences,
- education concerned with sustainable development should take into account people's susceptibility to global threats and whether they have the choice to change their behaviour.

On the programme or practical level, the following elements seem relevant:

- Context – sustainable development:

  - The practice should take place in a learning environment; an environment in which the individual (or practice) neither is entirely determined by societal demands, nor is entirely free to determine his or her own future. Therefore the practice should contain lively interaction between the practice and its context.

- The vision and purpose underpinning the practice with regards to sustainable development should be directed at one or more of the three pillars: economic, social, ecological, without neglecting the cultural dimension.

- Target group:

  - Practices that learn for sustainability should be directed at a wide range of societal groups and ages; it is actually vital for all members of society to have the capacity to assess and address their sustainability concerns – thus a priority should be the educationally disadvantaged minority groups and the socially excluded.

- Strategies:

  - The pedagogic climate and didactics are characterised by interaction and seek to connect 'thought' and 'action'. A variety of formal, informal and non-formal approaches are used. More specifically, the practice incorporates the elements of social learning. Social learning is concerned with solving social problems, uses interaction and communication as tools, focuses on action and experience and is characteristically interdisciplinary in nature.

- Participants:

  - The practice should give learners control over their own learning process and create an emancipated, democratic and transparent world with critical, competent citizens who are encouraged to actively take part in decision making and problem solving.

- Organisation:

  - The practice is carried out by several active partners in order to create leverage and embed the practice in policies and a wider context.
  - Practices and partnerships have a long-term perspective, continued over a certain period of time, and are concerned with the future.

On the level of the learners the following outcomes seem important. In the Dutch programme 'Learning for Sustainable Development' (LvDO), a list of competences have been suggested. These competences can serve as a basis for further discussion on desired learning outcomes and addressed in a lifespan perspective. The learning process ensures that people have more knowledge about sustainable

development (knowledge), are able to take a position by making a negotiated choice (ability), develop a preference for one choice over another (will) and dare to apply this choice in a real-life context (dare).

Methodology

The selection of cases

In order to be included in the inventory of possible projects, practices needed to conform to the following guidelines:

- the initiative is directed at one or more aspects of sustainable development: social, economic, environmental,
- 'lifelong learning' is part of the approach and stimulates participants to learn for sustainability, including the educationally disadvantaged,
- the project is carried out by several partners,
- the educative approach is characterised by interaction and attempts to connect 'thought' and 'action'.

Based on these criteria, 11 practices were finally selected. To ensure that those selected are good examples of Dutch practices, a few methods were used:

1 Consult organisations that have an overview of the present situation.
2 Visit LvDO and other meetings to collect information.
3 Use personal networks and ideas from the research project team members.
4 Search directly for specific practices (mostly using the internet) to ensure a diversity of practices.

Listing the possible projects, it became clear that there is a wide range of practices in the Netherlands in the area of lifelong learning and sustainable development. Our selection should not be considered as fully representative for the situation in the Netherlands. Moreover, we do not claim to have chosen the 'best' practices. However, we do believe the range of practices meet the set criteria, and are relevant for the context in which this research project is set. The selection of 'good practices' has been listed in the next section. The multiple case study methodology according to Yin (1994) was followed, and in each of the cases a variety of qualitative methods was used such as interviews with different stakeholders, participant observation, questionnaires and review of relevant documents.

Results: eleven 'good practices' of sustainable development

A closer look at three cases

For an extended description of the 11 cases and a description of the specific data collected in each case, we refer to Van Beilen (2005) and Tebbes (2005). Here we have restricted ourselves to a short presentation of three cases: SOM (new development plan for Duinpark IJmuiden by means of a participation trajectory); CVVG (participation and rights of the elderly by empowerment of client councils); Cubic Miles (schools in the Netherlands and Estonia researching a 'cubic mile'). These three cases are selected on behalf of the scope of this book, which is focused on lifelong learning and sustainable development within a regional context. See Table 16.1.

SOM: new development for Duinpark IJmuiden

Project Duinpark IJmuiden, carried out by the Velsen Council, in co-operation with Stichting Onderwijs en Milieu-projecten (SOM) in Nijmegen, is a partici-patory planning process for adults, children and adolescents in order to realise a new development plan for the dune park in IJmuiden's district Zeewijk. Over four evenings, the residents of the areas surrounding the park generate ideas, advice on the new development's plans and finally judge and evaluate the assimilation of these by the architect. The trajectory takes approximately eight months. The participation trajectory has been designed in close co-operation between several partners, such as Velsen Council and SOM. SOM has played a facilitating role with regards to the successful execution of interventions. Afterwards, a formal intervention will take place in which Velsen Council will notify the residents of the official development.

Strong and weak points

Many participants have shown an interest to remain involved with the construction, maintenance and upkeep of the park. People are positive about the participatory planning process, in particular with the working methods and professional organisation. They feel that their opinion has been listened to and taken seriously.

However, there is uncertainty about the extent to which the participants will feel positive about the project when some of them are inevitably disappointed with the final design. For example, the different perspectives between the youth and the older population have not been resolved. The young people are in favour of a place to 'hang-out' in the park, which is not embraced by some of the elderly – demonstrating some intergenerational cultural differences. From an urban plan-ning perspective, the participatory planning process seems to be a good approach;

it can improve the social cohesion in a neighbourhood and foster new developments. However, the question is: to what extent? It is obvious that there is a multiple stakeholder perspective and that diversity within certain limits has to be accepted.

CVVG: participation of the elderly

The project, carried out by the Client-Councils Retirement and Nursing Homes Groningen (CVVG), a co-operation between the National Organisation Client-Councils-region Groningen and the Regional Meeting Groningen Client-Councils, aims to promote further empowerment of client-councils through standardising and professionalising their support staff/volunteers and keeping them well informed. It further aims to emancipate the elderly through a cultural change approach: to keep improving life, (health)care and welfare of the residents of retirement and nursing homes, now and for the future. The project runs from 2002 to 2007. The project is a co-operation between several local and national partners, representing the care and insurance sectors, and national and local governance. The activities include quarterly theme and study meetings for client-councils, which are generally care-related, though increasingly focus on advising and legislation. Themes are supplied by client-councils and through national indication; meetings consist of presentation of information and sharing of experiences.

Strong and weak points

Participants are positive and generally find that they learn most from the other council's experiences, difficulties and solutions. Information about new legislation and increasing professionalism (e.g. on advising) makes them feel more independent, aware and powerful: 'The client-council stands up against management now,' says a participant (81), 'when it functions we have a lot of rights.' On the other hand, evaluation shows this attitude change is not yet turned into action in all cases. Fear of repercussions remains a reason not to voice criticism. The project is vulnerable as a result of governance issues and budget cuts in healthcare. Good collaboration between partners is stressed as a main ingredient for success, but due to lack of continuance of key people and client-councils this remains a fragile balance. In more general terms, the elderly have to overcome specific problems such as agism and being patronised. Looking at the three pillars of sustainable development, their economic basis is most vulnerable.

Cubic miles: schools in the Netherlands and Estonia researching a 'cubic mile'

This international collaboration project is focused on the exchange of experiences and views of learners in both countries, concerning the quality of the natural and

Table 16.1 An overview of sustainable development practices surveyed

	Description	Innovative aspect	Participants	Type of education	Sustainability themes	Country
1 **SOM**	Regeneration of underdeveloped areas	High level of participation	Very heterogeneous group	Formal and informal	Social: participation Environmental: spatial planning	Netherlands
2 **Stanthorpe Shire Council**	Sustainable development in communities	Use of ICT and creative industries	All ages, low-educated to highly-educated	Formal, non-formal, informal	Economic: ICT, economic development	Australia
3 **CVVG**	To advance empowerment client-councils	Participation and rights of the elderly	Elderly (80+)	Informal, non-formal	Social: health, intergenerational participation	Netherlands
4 **Karavaan**	Sustainable tourism	To train leaders/guides	Adults, usually highly-educated	Non-formal	Economical/social/ environmental: Sustainable consumption	Belgium
5 **Teleac**	Documentary liveability, demographic issues	Broadcasting as distance learning	Adults/all backgrounds	Informal	Social: health (HIV/AIDS), quality of life Environmental/ economic: demographics, climate change, development	Netherlands

6	**Ecomare**	Excursions to the water and nature in Dutch society	Learning with senses	All ages, immigrants, special focus on women	Informal, non-formal	Environmental: natural protection Social: cultural heritage, intercultural	Netherlands
7	**Commult**	Training for elderly employees	The use of recognition of prior learning	Adults (55+)	Non-formal	Economical: corporate responsibility and accountability	Netherlands
8	**NIV Scholen voor Duurzaamheid**	Involving young people actively in the issue of sustainability	Learning and applying the learning	14–18	Formal: high school	Social: intergenerational	Netherlands
9	**Natuur-museum Groningen** Cubic Miles	Schools in Groningen and Estonia researching a 'cubic mile'	Sustainable international co-operation	12–18, at least high school level	Formal: High school	Economic: poverty reduction Environmental: sustainable development projects	Netherlands and Estonia
10	**Van Hall Instituut** DHO	Follow-on training course for sustainable soil	Combination of work and study (co-operative education)	20+, also international students	Formal: higher vocational education	Environmental/ economic: natural protection, management of natural resources	Netherlands
11	**Wadden-vereniging**	Protection of the Waddenarea	Environmental awareness	All ages/all backgrounds	Informal and non-formal	Environmental: natural protection	Netherlands

social environment surrounding their schools. The Museum of Natural History in the city of Groningen, the Netherlands, initiated contact of two schools from Groningen and two schools from different towns in Estonia. The learners play a prominent role in researching the school environment. The four important elements are: (a) the development of a global view; (b) relevant research questions within the cubic mile; (c) artistic view (art images of the cubic mile); and (d) cubic dreams (plans for the future). Learners from both countries communicate their findings via a website, and eventually present the outcomes in the virtual museum, as well as in the Museum of Natural History. Besides the overall objective of exchange of experiences, more specific objectives are to stimulate reflection on and respect for the immediate environment, the enhancement of an intercultural approach, the fostering of interdisciplinary teaching and the promotion of active learning.

Strong and weak points

The learners are very positive about the project. The interdisciplinary approach beyond the normal school subjects is seen as very stimulating. Moreover, learners welcome their active role in the research and exchange activities. Working with the issue of sustainability was not seen as an explicit, always visible, activity as such. Learners were not always aware of it but concurrently many elements in their activities happened to be related with the ideas regarding sustainability. However, lack of accessibility of the website and the lack of support by subject teachers were mentioned as points for improvement. In particular in Estonia, pupils had limited time for the project as it was not embedded into the curriculum as it was in Groningen. Their reason to participate was therefore different from Groningen pupils: talented students were selected and were personally motivated to participate for a variety of reasons. Pupils from both researched schools mentioned that they had expected to have more contact with pupils from the other school. From an intercultural perspective, both schools had learned a lot about the other country; however, interpersonal exchange was limited and differences in expectation and motivation were not recognised.

Discussion

Most of the case studies take place within policies, legislation and regulations that are not directly related to promoting sustainable development and lifelong learning. The cases have developed their own approaches which fit in with these policies, most often because of financial reasons, such as needs for funds. Therefore it is not clear how these practices fit in with national policies of sustainable development and lifelong learning. In general, the Dutch national policies for lifelong learning and sustainable development have not had an impact at a practical level and the connections between the individual policies have not been made. The examples of case studies in the schools system indicate that there has been very little integration with the regular curriculum. They have often an incidental, even marginal, character, whereas they should be part of the explicit educational policy.

The cases incorporate one or more of the three 'pillars' of sustainable development, but the cultural dimension becomes visible in all cases: the diversity of the different stakeholders in the case of the IJmuiden community, the intergenerational and age-related issues of the client councils, and the cultural differences between the Netherlands and Estonia. Most cases pay attention to the here and now, look at the future for guidelines, take (inter)cultural and intergenerational issues into account, and take participation as their focal point. On the other hand, most cases are focused on the local context and pay limited attention to the global perspective, the impact of one's own action on others in the world and the role of related intercultural issues. A choice for a regional context such as in concepts like 'the learning region' and the concept of 'place management' might be powerful, but linking the local and the global remains an important challenge in the field of sustainable development.

Innovative aspects are the creative, interactive and participatory working methods and the attempt to put social learning into practice. Besides the participatory methods, the different combinations of formal, informal and non-formal education can be considered as a strong strategy to reach a variety of target groups. From a lifelong learning perspective, this resulted in the involvement of heterogeneous groups – people of different ages, different social backgrounds, different mental abilities, from various disciplines, with a variety of educational experience – simultaneously, in order to create mutual understanding and co-operation. This makes clear that issues of sustainable development touch all phases of the lifespan. They do not only concern the transition of knowledge, but demand cultural changes by participatory ways of (social) learning.

In most cases, the collaboration with other partners is necessary and recognised, but still locally based, though rather ad hoc than forming a core element of the strategy. In most cases possibilities to network and build up relationships with, for instance, social movements seems not to be one of the priorities. The long-term effectiveness of sustainable development could be enhanced by enduring networks of different levels of government and non-government service providers. Sustainable development must be based on sustainable cross-sectoral co-operation.

In conclusion, we can say that there is still a lot to be done to strengthen practices of sustainable development, to enhance the productive spin off in all elements of sustainability, and to embed them in more coherent and financially substantial policies which do connect the mutual and value-added focus on sustainable development and lifelong learning.

References

Beck, U. (1999) *World Risk Society*, Oxford: Blackwell.
Beck, U. (2000) *What is Globalization?*, Oxford: Blackwell.

228 Corinne van Beilen, Max van der Kamp and Jacques Zeelen

Delors, J. (1996) *Learning: The Treasure Within*, report to UNESCO of the International Commission on Education for the Twenty-first Century, Paris: UNESCO.

European Commission (2000) *A Memorandum on Lifelong Learning*, Brussels: European Union.

Ministry for Education, Culture and Science (2001) *A Lifetime of Learning*, Den Haag: MinOCW.

Opschoor, H. (2005) UNESCO, unpublished document.

Organisation for Economic Co-operation and Development (1996) *Lifelong Learning for All*, Paris: OECD.

Tebbes, S. (2005) 'Education for Sustainable Development', Masters thesis Rijksuniversiteit, Groningen: RUG.

Touraine, A. (2000) *Can We Live Together? Equality and Difference*, Oxford: Polity Press.

UN Conference on Environment and Development (1992) *Agenda 21: Chapter 36*, at: http://www.un.org/esa/susdev/documents/agenda21/english/agenda21chapter36.htm.

UNESCO (1997) *Educating for a Sustainable Future*, Paris: UNESCO.

UNESCO (2004) *Draft International Implementation Scheme*, Paris: UNESCO.

Van Beilen, C. (2005) 'On course. The contribution of lifelong learning to education for sustainable development', Masters thesis, University of Groningen.

Van der Kamp, M. (2002) 'Een leven lang leren en het streven naar duurzaamheid', in B. Wijffels, H. Blanken, M. van Stalborgh and R. van Raaij (eds) *De kroon op het werk*, Programma Leren voor Duurzaamheid.

World Commission on Environment and Development (WECD) (1987) *Our Common Future*. Oxford: Oxford University Press.

Yin, R.K. (1994) *Case Study Research: Design and Methods*, 2nd edition, London: Sage.

Chapter 17

Conclusion

Bruce Wilson, Kate Sankey and Mike Osborne

Our book is very much a reflection of its times. Tremendous changes are occurring in all parts of the world, apparently driven by the consistent spread of 'globalisation'. There are apparent similarities in the character of these changes, yet in no two places are they quite the same. While differences in scale can facilitate greater flexibilities in how regions and communities might respond, the confidence of the one in fashioning their own futures can be no greater than the other. Both transnational corporations and government policies have important implications for communities, yet the locus of power and the accountability for different kinds of response is dispersed. Both regional and national governments are part of this, as internationally negotiated environmental agreements, macro-economic policies, taxation and income redistribution, communications and border security all shape local and regional circumstances, even though outcomes can vary considerably.

A further dimension linking the global and the local is made explicit by Timms, who reminds us of the role of information and communications technologies in this process, although some of the assertions of Wellman's (2001) 'glocalisation' are fast becoming redundant as wireless technology and evermore pervasive devices become available to greater numbers of people. The adage of 'think global, act local' may, to borrow from Jarl Bengsston,[1] become 'think global, act local and act global' as social actions formally separated in time and space (Giddens' (1990) 'distanciation') relate more closely with each other. The danger of course, again borrowing from Giddens, is that these social actions become separated from local context as individuals and groups become disembodied from the local.

In this context, social researchers and theorists grapple with ideas and concepts to make sense of these trends, and with the challenge of learning how to describe and explain adequately the substance and meanings of these developments. Our contributors are all engaged in this work, mostly in the intellectual territory framed by notions of social capital, learning and place. At heart, they are concerned with providing better understanding of how social relationships and networks come to have significant economic and political force, facilitating learning over time in the context of a defined sense of place, whether region or community. The chapters indicate that there continue to be substantial variations in conceptual meaning, and substantial differences over how best to undertake research and to validate claims to be made about the value of the concepts and the programme and practices which they might inspire. The range of concepts itself might be seen as problematic. For example, the concept of 'social capital' may be seen as quite restricted as it concentrates on issues of social cohesiveness (and the associated ideas of 'community' and general well-being) rather than the structural dimensions of social and economic life, which drive not only the approach to economic development, but also the underlying processes which produce inequality. Other broad concepts, such as regeneration and sustainability, are hard to define precisely, particularly when they have become debased through excessive and inappropriate use. For example, regeneration is considered by some to mean investment of resources into an existing run-down inner city area but can be used by others to mean the expansion of the city into the surrounding green space, whilst leaving the inner city untouched.

Yet the contributors demonstrate also that there is an urgency about this work. The profound consequences for communities and families of international economic and political forces mean that governments must act, notwithstanding the intellectual tensions that continue to arise. While policy initiatives have often focused on ameliorating the effects of globalisation, this book demonstrates that policies for supporting action from communities themselves are becoming increasingly important, especially from the perspective of regional governments. This raises important questions about the insights generated already by researchers, and how they can be applied to policy and programme development. Without question, the historical reliance on national policies is now somewhat tenuous in its ramifications. Many governments have tended to view society as a single entity, where national policies for education, health, the environment and social development can be promulgated for the whole nation. Increasingly, regional governments have come to see the need for more local solutions, both to engage local energies more effectively and to acknowledge and respond to the diversity of settings and needs.

Linked with these developments, our contributors show that many people have come increasingly to identify with their local community, and to see their local relationships as an important foundation for economic, social, environmental and cultural action. While not a new phenomenon, community-based initiatives and connections have become a critical site for the expression of people's needs and aspirations, and for the practical development of economic, education, cultural and environmental projects. Conversely, 'community engagement' has been of increasing interest to governments, as a means of both refining and implementing social policy initiatives as well as delivering services.

The interaction of these trends has meant that governments have shown growing interest in interventions targeted at communities and regions. For example, social inclusion and sustainable development are emerging policy imperatives alongside competitive economic development. In some cases, the interventions have relied on the development or renewal of physical infrastructure, such as hospitals. This is much more straightforward, however, than interventions focused on locally-based social infrastructure and relationships. It is with the latter, in particular, that both greater conceptual clarity and research substance can be particularly helpful: what kinds of interventions work most effectively in achieving which goals?

These types of questions not only have considerable resonance for reasons of economics and efficiency, but are also crucially important to the social fabric of the lives of those subject to intervention. For example, one of the most public of all interventions in the UK pertinent to lifelong learning is that which seeks to widen participation to those from traditionally non-participant groups, in particular those from the lowest socio-economic classes. Yet despite a plethora of interventions, at a variety of scales (many targeted at a regional level) and considerable investment for over three decades, the evidence base for effectiveness is still sparse (see Gorard et al. 2006).

Partnerships

One clear emerging insight from this collection is the importance of public, private and community partnerships in facilitating the effective development of policy and the implementation of programmes. In all cases, partnerships have been an important mechanism for intervention, involving various mixes of public sector, private/commercial interests, and community-based, non-profit organisations. However, a range of important questions remain. What are the implications of different kinds of partnership for the effectiveness of various interventions? Are different kinds of interventions more appropriate for influencing some social or economic objectives rather than others? What lessons can be learned about the effectiveness of initiatives which have economic, social and environmental objectives?

Why a priority on partnership formation? At one simple level, it is a resource issue. In a climate where there are simply insufficient resources to address needs, partnerships can serve to facilitate more effective use of the resources which are available, both funding and expertise, and to use those resources to leverage others.

However, various chapters indicate clearly that the use of partnerships can add significantly to the quality of relationships and to the social outcomes for people in a locality. This is especially evident where those partnerships involve organisations which have a broader view of social processes and recognise the interdependence of economic, social and environmental factors. The benefits are reflected both in an enhanced sense of belonging in the locality, but also in tangible outcomes.

Again, conceptual clarity can be very important. For example, concepts associated with learning economies and societies are not new; however, the acknowledgement of a link between lifelong learning and social/physical infrastructure is a relatively new phenomenon. In the development of national and regional policies for investment, governments are giving greater consideration to an integrated approach, with the public provision of education facilities, transport, housing, communications, healthcare and the role of an enlightened private sector

232 Bruce Wilson, Kate Sankey and Mike Osborne

which may invest significantly more than the public sector if the investment climate created by governments is encouraging. It is important to discover what forms of partnership, linkage and co-investment work best in which circumstances, and are most effective at engaging with and enhancing constructive social outcomes.

This is not to suggest that all partnerships are necessarily effective. Nor should it imply that they are always congenial. There is a much broader body of research which indicates that even in partnerships which are seen, over time, to deliver significant benefits, there are times where divisive issues can threaten the continued commitment of various partners, and undermine the quality of the operational relationships. This raises questions about the conditions under which partnership formation can be seen to be desirable.

From the research undertaken to date by the PASCAL partners, it would seem that the following conditions are important not only in developing partnerships, but in sustaining them:

- *Clarity of outcomes*. In most circumstances, potential partners will have diverse objectives which they are seeking to achieve. This in itself is not surprising, nor unreasonable. Especially when public agencies are seeking private sector partners, whether as providers, investors or collaborators, the scope for divergence is constantly present – similarly, perhaps, where a small community organisation is becoming involved in co-operation with a much larger organisation. In these cases, explicit understanding of the shared outcomes which are sought from the initiative is fundamental, both to inspire the partners, and to provide a stable ground from which tensions can be addressed.

- *Agreed and maintained governance arrangements*. Governance does not necessarily require a dominant superstructure to provide stability to a project. However, it is important that there is a clear and shared understanding about the ways in which decisions will be made about different aspects of the initiative, and where accountability lies for maintaining the agreed processes. Again, there is now a broad body of evidence which illustrates that quite distinct approaches to handling governance issues have been applied in different contexts, frequently relying on different kinds of networks. These have encompassed:

  - not-for-profit companies,
  - largely informal gatherings or mechanisms, granted significant legitimacy by the partners, at least for a period of time, underpinned by local government,
  - development of statutory boards.

- *Effective approach to conflict resolution*. Conflict is an inevitable dimension of human initiatives, and affects the trajectories of many partnerships. Conflicts arise for many different reasons; the issue is not so much the reason but the underlying implications for the partnership, and how they are handled.

While linked to governance, it is apparent that conflict will test many governance arrangements, and that particular care can be required to ensure that
serious differences can offer an opportunity for learning. Effective processes
reflect not only proper attention to clarification of perspectives, issues and of
evidence, but rely also on an underlying acknowledgement of goodwill on all
sides, an expectation that the respect and reciprocity necessary for partnership
can be sustained despite the conflict.

- *Clarity about the specific character of the contribution which particular
  partners are making.* This implies careful planning to ascertain the principal
  resources required for the initiative, and explicit negotiation to clarify the
  allocation of accountabilities, or at least to determine the processes through
  which these will be resolved.

Many initiatives designed to deliver on social priorities include an explicit commitment to fostering learning, both as a part of the initiative in itself, and as a
means of sharing competence and building self-reliance. The role of formal
'knowledge centres', such as universities and research centres, in supporting this
learning can be important. However, at this stage, as Doyle's chapter indicates,
universities struggle with how best to maximise access to acknowledged expertise,
and to provide ongoing support to facilitate learning within the project. A common
difficulty is the number of stakeholders with whom a university must develop and
sustain a relationship. This can be demanding, especially where resources are
limited, and where the university environment, in itself, encourages an inwardly-
focused framework of operations.

An important implication of the research in this area is that initiatives to achieve
important social priorities should be framed to incorporate universities or other
knowledge centres. This is partly because their expertise is an important public
resource, and also because their involvement can help to build an ongoing commitment to learning. Joint initiatives of this kind can create qualitatively more
effective operations. These can in turn be more attractive to funding agencies as
they are more likely to deliver both benefits for general knowledge generation
as well as assisting with the practical application of lessons learned from that
research.

Questions about research

We concluded the Introduction by acknowledging that a persistent challenge
for social researchers is to be able to demonstrate that the claims that they wish
to make about particular policy or theoretical questions and issues are sufficiently evidenced and as such are legitimate and so warrant serious attention. Our
contributors have provided considerable evidence about this challenge.

In the first place, there is clearly some continuing uncertainty about how best
to reconcile the linkages between qualitative and quantitative approaches to
methodology. Some contributors, such as Kilpatrick and Abbott, address this

directly, with their effort to provide for both qualitative and quantitative indicators of social capital. However, even these examples are work in progress, and less than comprehensive in addressing the concepts of social capital, learning or place. Of course, this is an issue which permeates the social sciences. It arises in every situation which involves language, and the particularities of perceptions of social action which are inevitably partial. Notwithstanding the questions which can be asked about the legitimacy and the transferability of the insights which are offered by researchers, the contributions in this book illustrate that where care is taken to specify clearly the concepts which are being used to make sense of social phenomena, and some degree of reflexivity applies to the collection, analysis and reporting of research data, there is a strong basis for interpreting the knowledge claims which are being made, and for testing their validity in other circumstances.

Again, some contributors are concerned explicitly with the challenges in linking research evidence and policy formation. Indeed, this is a central concern for the whole PASCAL network. Researchers in various fields are conscious of the difficulties in engaging with policy-making processes, and adapting the timelines and requirements of sound methodological practice to meet the exigencies of the politics and policy making. The Hess and Adams chapter offers important insights into the advantages of ensuring a close linking of the concepts that are relevant in policy making, with the conceptual framework which focuses research activity. In their case, a focus on place and on community engagement is particularly helpful.

Similar issues arise in linking research evidence and programmatic action. However, it is perhaps an issue which is less pertinent for regional governments and policy makers, and more so for civil stakeholders, mobilising community members in support of a particular course of action. Frequently, of course, these initiatives or campaigns are aimed, in part at least, at local or regional governments. However, questions arise about the relationship between the lived experience of community stakeholders, and the ways in which they recognise and make sense of research. Clearly, the literature refers to a range of examples, in which the relationship of stakeholders with researchers can vary widely, from clients of research findings to active participants, and in some cases, as resisters of 'foreign' knowledge. The contributors to this volume do not make significant contribution to understanding these relationships, but it needs to be acknowledged as an area where ongoing research will be valuable.

It is a particular irony of this field of investigation that much of the research is focused on events and topics that have a particularly regional or local resonance. Partly because of the methodological issues mentioned previously, secondary comparison of regionally-based investigations is not easy. This does not help with addressing questions about the transferability of ideas and concepts from one region to another. A number of European and OECD projects have been established with the primary intent of enhancing comparative research and sharing the benefits of experiences in quite different locations. There is considerable evidence about the value of these kinds of initiatives, but there are relatively few initiatives which have the comprehensive research and policy agenda which characterises this collection of chapters.

Transferability of practice may be limited by particular cultural and political context and we may only be able to make what Bassey (1999: 51) describes as 'fuzzy generalisations' of what might be workable in another situation. Nevertheless, there may be important lessons that can be drawn from other societies, and it is clearly the case that across different nations common social concerns exist. The chapters by Ilieva and Zuwarimwe provide insights into the influence that the changing culture and political contexts have had on social and economic developments.

The implications for learning have been commented on by one of the editors of this book; Osborne (2003: 24) has argued that:

> the relationship between societal exclusion and educational participation is a concern of many societies in Europe. Moreover, in different countries, a variety of strategies have been developed to provide 'solutions' to these issues, and whether this might relate to structural modifications of educational systems, particular teaching and learning approaches or specific forms of intervention, there is little doubt that there exists enough commonality to propose ways in which one nation might usefully learn from another.

With the advent of more rapid and efficient systems of communication, it is inevitable that transfer will occur. Furthermore, there will be a hunger for external solutions, especially in regions which consider themselves under-developed by comparison to the West. However, Zuwarimwe points to traditional organisational models rich in social capital in Zimbabwe which demonstrate effective economic development and organisational learning. Scott (2002: 146–147), in the context of higher education (HE) generally, has spoken of the 'Lure of the West' in discussion of the reconstruction of the sector following the Communist era in this part of Europe. Ilieva provides a concrete example of this tendancy in describing the dangers and difficulties of replacing the communist system in Bulgaria wholesale with an external system based on Western-dominated educational values. Such tendencies are observable within a number of the domains covered by this book, and the tendency to harmonise and reject the past may be damaging in certain circumstances.

Conclusion

This volume represents a timely contribution to the research literature in linking conceptual and methodological examples which address social capital, learning regions and place-based approaches. It demonstrates the vitality of much of the work developing in this area, and offers strong evidence about its relevance to policy formation for regional and local governments. However, it is apparent also that a range of issues continue to permeate the field. These can be seen as constituting an ongoing research agenda. There is no question that the researchers who have contributed to this volume represent an international group of colleagues who will continue, with the support of the PASCAL network, to address these issues in the years to come.

Note

1 Unpublished keynote Address at 3rd PASCAL conference, October 2005, Stirling.

References

Bassey, M. (1999) *Case Study Research in Educational Settings*, Buckingham: Open University Press.

Giddens, A. (1990) *The Consequences of Modernity*, Cambridge: Polity Press.

Gorard, S., Smith, E., May, H., Thomas, L., Adnett, N. and Slack, K. (2006) *Review of Widening Participation Research: Addressing the Barriers to Participation in Higher Education*, July, HEFCE, RD 13/06, at: http://www.hefce.ac.uk/pubs/rdreports/2006/rd13_06/.

Osborne, M. (2003) 'University continuing education – international understandings', in M. Osborne and E. Thomas (eds) *Lifelong Learning in a Changing Continent*, Leicester: NIACE.

Scott, P. (2002) 'Reflections on the reform of higher education in Central and Eastern Europe', *Higher Education in Europe*, XXVII(1–2), 137–152.

Wellman, B. (2001) 'Physical place and cyberplace: the rise of networked individualism', in L. Keeble and B. D. Loader (eds) *Community Informatics: Shaping Computer-mediated Social Relations*, London: Routledge.

Index

Social Capital, Lifelong Learning
and the Management of Place

Social Capital, Lifelong Learning and the Management of Place aims to bring together inter-related research literature from three fields: social capital, place management and lifelong learning regions. It presents research on the development and implementation of policies and practices that improve the quality of living and working circumstances at local and regional levels, recognising the importance of social capital and the necessity of partnership for the successful implementation of policy. The book focuses on regional initiatives, particularly those which explicitly embrace lifelong learning, as a framework for developing a systematic planning framework that may encompass administrative, cultural, geographical, physical and/or political perspectives.

The book focuses on the substantive areas of these inter-related fields:

- Social capital
- Place management
- Lifelong learning regions

International in scope and at the cutting edge of research into this growing field that links lifelong learning to place, *Social Capital, Lifelong Learning and the Management of Place* will appeal both to academics undertaking research in this burgeoning field and to those involved in lifelong learning at local, national and international level. The collection includes contributions from a number of well-known academics in these fields including Ian Falk, Sue Kilpatrick, Max Van der Kamp and Erik Wallin.

Michael Osborne is Professor of Lifelong Learning and Co-Director of the PASCAL Observatory at the University of Stirling, UK.

Kate Sankey is PASCAL Associate at the Institute of Education, University of Stirling, UK.

Bruce Wilson is Co-Director of the PASCAL Observatory at the School of Global Studies, Social Science and Planning, RMIT, Australia.